To Hillcroft College
June 10th 2010

Lilian McGuckin 1959/60.

Sarajevo Under Siege

THE ETHNOGRAPHY OF POLITICAL VIOLENCE

Cynthia Keppley Mahmood, Series Editor

A complete list of books in the series is available from the publisher.

Sarajevo Under Siege
Anthropology in Wartime

Ivana Maček

PENN

University of Pennsylvania Press
Philadelphia

Published by
University of Pennsylvania Press
Philadelphia, Pennsylvania 19104-4112

Printed in the United States of America on acid-free paper

10   9   8   7   6   5   4   3   2   1

Library of Congress Cataloging-in-Publication Data
Maček, Ivana
     Sarajevo under siege : anthropology in wartime / Ivana Maček
       p. cm. — (The ethnography of political violence)
     Includes bibliographical references and index.
     ISBN 978-0-8122-4126-6 (alk. paper)
       1. Sarajevo (Bosnia and Hercegovina)—History—Siege, 1992–1996. 2. Political violence—Bosnia and Hercegovina—Sarajevo. I. Title.
DR1313.32.S27M33 2009
949.703—dc22   2008043969

Contents

Preface vii

Part I. Life Under Siege 1

1 Civilian, Soldier, Deserter 3

2 Death and Creativity in Wartime 34

3 Struggling for Subsistence 62

4 Tests of Trust 86

Part II. Ethnonationalist Reinventions 121

5 Political and Economic Transformation 123

6 Language and Symbols 136

7 Mobilizing Religion 148

8 Reorienting Social Relationships 167

9 Reconceptualizing War 191

Epilogue 218

Notes 225

Glossary 235

References 239

Index 247

Acknowledgments 253

Preface

In the summer of 1991, war broke out in the former Yugoslav Republic of Slovenia. On my television set in Uppsala, I watched tanks belonging to the former Yugoslav People's Army (Jugoslavenska narodna armija [JNA]) tear up the lawns in the parks of the Slovenian capital, Ljubljana. I realized that something entirely beyond my comprehension was happening. I knew about wars in the past and in other parts of the world, but I had been taught that the Second World War was the last war there would ever be in Europe. Now, a new war was here. I did not know what it meant or what forms it would take, but I was sure that my understanding of the world would never be the same again.

The next shock came at the end of the summer: the war started in Croatia. I listened to a Swedish radio reporter saying that the air raid alert had just been heard in Zagreb, my hometown. He sounded very agitated, reporting from his hotel room near the railway station. The streets were empty as far as he could see, peeking through his window despite the warning to keep away from the windows. Journalists were cautioned not to use cameras, as snipers could easily mistake them for weapons. On television, I saw young armed men in black and camouflage clothing, mixing military and civilian garb, with black bands around their heads. Someone called Crni Marko ("Black Marko") was giving an interview to the Swedish television network. With an air of self-satisfaction, he identified himself as a unit leader in the new Croatian army and explained that they were fighting for the long-awaited sovereignty of Croatia and freedom from Serbian hegemony. At the end, with a wide grin, he sent greetings to all the lovely Swedish girls. It was strange to see these big Rambo-like boys standing there as representatives of my own people and country.

I was even more deeply disturbed when I heard that one of my best friends had volunteered for the Croatian army. This young man had a genuine pacifist temperament. The year he did his obligatory military service he developed a nervous ulcer, not only because of the meaninglessness of his duties but also because he was an individualist who disliked any form of authoritarianism. He spoke four European languages, loved to travel, and relished mountain climbing, spelunking, and skiing in loose clothes which would flutter in the wind, giving him a sense of freedom. He had introduced me to Bob Dylan and Jimi Hendrix, Friedrich Nietzsche and Erich Fromm. I simply could not put these things together with what I had heard. I could not believe that he had turned into a Crni Marko.

Like many young people in the former Yugoslavia, I had believed that conditions of life and work were better in the West than at home. Before the war, however, few had the opportunity to leave. I came to Sweden in 1990 as a student in the language cooperation program between Zagreb University and the Swedish Institute. My grant was for the spring term, and after that I decided to use my private resources in order to study cultural anthropology at Uppsala University. I enjoyed my studies and the new friends I made.

Once the war began, it became easier to enter Western countries, but coming out of necessity, as a refugee, was much more difficult than making this choice of one's own free will. For my part, the start of war in my hometown meant that within a month I felt compelled to go to Zagreb and see for myself what was going on. Was anything left of the world I knew, and did I have anything in common with the people who once were close to me? Together with Karine Mannerfelt, a Swedish friend and journalist, I took the train to Zagreb in October 1991. We encountered the first signs of war in the Munich railway station. Sitting at a table near ours in the café was a Yugoslav family: an elderly couple dressed like villagers, a younger couple in modern clothes, and some children. In the evening when the train to Zagreb arrived, we realized that the elderly couple was going back to Zagreb while the younger generations were staying in Munich. The only others getting on the train were a group of young men who looked like a college sports team, except that we understood that they were volunteers, perhaps second-generation Croats living in Germany and elsewhere, traveling to join the Croatian troops in the war against the Serbs. When we arrived in Zagreb the next morning, the railway station was empty. I spotted a man in military-style civilian clothes with a big camera bag over his shoulder getting off the train. This was war: emptiness and foreign correspondents.

As I write this account sixteen years later, I realize that as outsiders we all receive the same first impression of war, usually through the media. We see a society collapse into a state of war, which empties out meanings and causes a vacuum of norms. War correspondents, shooting cameras instead of weapons, equipped with lenses of different calibers, their combat jackets stuffed with film instead of bullets, usually provide us with this information. The problem with Western media reports on events in the former Yugoslavia was that they rarely filled this vacuum with anything except politically em-powered actors on the highest international institutional levels. News reports most often showed images of destroyed villages and homes, people on the run, and many other varieties of human misery, while the studio anchor would read the latest announcements about peace negotiations that were planned, a ceasefire that was broken, and the statements made by diplomats and heads of state. This strange juxtaposition left the viewer with a sense of incomprehensibility mixed with terror and empathy for the people hit by the war. After a year or two of such information, a sense of powerlessness, some-times combined with rage, took over, as information combined with passiv-ity led to indifference.

To my enormous relief, when I met the people I was looking for in Za-greb, I found that our relationships remained essentially intact. They dis-missed out of hand my vaguely patriotic impulse to leave Sweden and be with my family and friends when times were hard. When I asked my best friend whether I should return, she said simply that it would do no good to anyone if I were in Zagreb. I could only go down into cellars when the air raid sirens sounded. It was much better that I was in Sweden, doing what I wanted to do with my life. A meeting with a colleague, who had outspoken pro-Croatian national feelings before the war, proved to me that people's ideas were chang-ing, but that this process was by no means a one-way road to nationalism. "You know," she said, "I always thought that the immense emigration of Croats in this century was due to the Serbs pushing us out, but now I have re-alized that the Croats were leaving because other Croats would not let them live." A year after this she moved to London with her husband and daughter.

As I was in Zagreb with a journalist, for a few days we went to the most obvious site of war: the front line. It was only about 30 kilometers south of Zagreb. The units watching the line were mostly composed of local residents, some of whom had been drafted, and others who had volunteered. After showing us the no-man's-land and the positions of Serbian snipers on the other side, they invited us for pancakes in one of the deserted houses that functioned as their base. Inside the country kitchen, seated at one long table, eating and chatting with all these men of various ages and one girl, the atmo-sphere suddenly felt familiar—like being at scout camp, or coming to a mountain hut after a long day's strenuous climbing in the Alps. I understood that, had I not been living in Sweden, I would be one of these people guard-ing the city's last line of defense. It scared me, and for a moment I felt privi-leged to be just a visitor from abroad. Later on, after the war had started in Bosnia and Herzegovina, I realized that during that day the war had entered me. It was no longer happening somewhere else to somebody else. It was my war, and I was in it.

During the late spring of 1992, when war broke out in full in Bosnia and Herzegovina, I wrote about the situation in the former Yugoslavia and national identities, but as an anthropologist I studied Africa and such intriguing phenomena as witchcraft. That summer, refugees from Bosnia and Herzegovina started arriving in Sweden in large numbers, and since I needed a summer job I began interpreting for the Swedish authorities. For three months, I worked full time at a refugee center, with the feeling of utter injustice constantly hovering over me. How could it be that these people, who had always been the least nationalistic of all Yugoslavs, had to suffer because of nationalist ideologies their leaders were promoting? Slovenes had always been Slovene patriots, Croats had a history of nationalistic movements, and Serbs took particular pride in their defense of the nation against both German fascists and Turks, but Bosnians? They were the most anti-nationalistic people of all. How could they be nationalists, when they lived good lives in a milieu composed of at least four major nationalities? They married and raised children in that mixed milieu; they made friends and had neighbors across ethnocultural lines. I was certain that there would be bloodshed if a war defined as a confrontation between different national groups ever started in Bosnia and Herzegovina, and because of that I thought it was impossible. But just that sort of war began, and unfortunately my worst fears materialized. For the whole summer I wanted to do something about it. I wanted to write about Bosnians and explain that they were not nationalists as the media had portrayed them, that Yugoslavia was not a boiling pot whose lid had suddenly been lifted, allowing people whose mutual hatreds had been suppressed to show their true nature. I had time only after my summer job was over, and I wrote. I realized that all my energies went into following, understanding, and explaining to others what was going on in the former Yugoslavia. I searched for a way to fuse my intellectual work and my personal engagement.

I decided to write a project proposal for a grant to do research on the processes through which national identities were being formed in Bosnia. I chose Bosnia, rather than my native Croatia, not only because it seemed most unjust that Bosnians were being hit hardest by a nationalistic war but also because I could not stand the idea of working with the aggressive Croatian nationalism of the early 1990s. This decision was painful, because it meant leaving the exciting world of African anthropology. But I had become entirely occupied by the challenge of understanding the situation of people in my former homeland. I say former homeland because by 1992 Yugoslavia had become my former homeland in a double sense: I had left it for Sweden, and while I was gone it had ceased to exist. I was born and raised in the former Yugoslavia, and when contemporary Croatia was formed I was already in Sweden. Croatia today is a strange state construction for me; it makes me feel more like a foreigner than its citizen, although the country and people still feel like home. Focusing on Bosnia, the least nationalistic of the former Yugoslav republics, seemed not only less personally fraught but also potentially more politically revealing.

This book is a result of my endeavors to make some sense out of the war in the former Yugoslavia, to put my world together again, so to speak, to make it somewhat more comprehensible, predictable, and safe again. In this sense, the story of the Sarajevan siege that I tell here has a wider meaning for anyone with experience of massive political violence or the drive to understand it. Students and researchers may find in these pages meaningful theoretical tools for framing war and a method for fieldwork during wartime. Diplomats and humanitarian workers may find it useful as a guide to the local knowledge that is crucially important for any constructive work in circumstances of war. People caught in the midst of war or recovering from its ravages may find that it eases the damage to know that others, in different times and different places, have shared their experiences.

The main difficulty with telling a story of such a massive destruction is that the social fabric, cultural habits, political ideas, moral beliefs, and even language are destroyed along with the physical environment. So much destruction creates a void in which nothing seems to remain. Nothingness has no form, so how can it be presented? We communicate through words and storytelling; we need language and forms to articulate our experiences and knowledge and make them available to others. In writing this book about the social consequences of war, I have utilized the same strategies that Sarajevans used to cope with its destructiveness. I found forms in Sarajevans' everyday lives in a city under siege: in the artifacts, practices, ideas, and phrases they came up with while living amid utter devastation. The description of these creative processes and their results in all aspects of life, including the complicated story of national feelings and politics, gives form to the destruction of war, much as a photographic negative or a shadow image can make a form emerge before our eyes. My hope is that, although this is my story, it will be recognizable to Sarajevans who were there during the war.

In this book, I have not attempted to explain why or how the war occurred, the key questions that interest many political and social scientists. I focus instead on constructing an account of what happened to people on the ground, because this is the basic knowledge that we generally lack. What happened cannot be comprehended through an analysis of Milošević's negotiations with Lord Owen, or by counting the dead and the bombs that hit Sarajevo. The war cannot be encompassed even by such powerful abstractions as "genocide" or "crimes against humanity." What happened was incomprehensible to both locals and outsiders. The Sarajevans whom I got to know shared their lives, experiences, and perspectives with me as best they could. Through the discipline of anthropological analysis and reflection, I share the knowledge built on this lived experience with readers.

I have employed two models to understand what happened during the siege of Sarajevo. One is based on Sarajevans' concern with whether they were still "normal." This question judged wartime existence by peacetime standards. It was almost always directed to those of us who came from the outside, for Sarajevans knew full well how profoundly their daily lives had been transformed by war. The other model is based on the seemingly contradictory moral stances that Sarajevans—like others in similar situations—adopted when it comes to destruction and the killing of human beings. In the existentially lethal and ethically sensitive circumstances that cannot be evaded in wartime, most of us respond by espousing a variety of positions, sometimes sequentially but often simultaneously, trying desperately to reconcile and justify our beliefs and practices despite grave instability and serious doubt. None of these positions proves entirely satisfying or tenable, but all of them are grounded in efforts not only to survive but to retain our common humanity.

PART I

Life Under Siege

Chapter 1
Civilian, Soldier, Deserter

How can people who have never experienced war understand what it is like to live in a city under siege in a state that has disintegrated into warring national armies? The terror aroused by the constant threat to life is intensified by the disruption of everyday existence that living in a war zone entails. Most of us have experienced a similar kind of shock on a smaller scale. Our first confrontation with the death of a person close to us, a disastrous accident with casualties whose faces we recognize, or a natural catastrophe in the place we call home—experiences of devastating loss seem incomprehensible and make us feel powerless. The world as we knew it has been destroyed. With no satisfactory way of dealing with this unprecedented existential situation, we question our previous faith in the orderliness of the world and the social norms that had governed our lives up to that point. This feeling of disorientation is not necessarily harmful in itself; indeed, it might even be necessary for the process of mourning that we must undergo to reorient ourselves to a new reality. War is like other experiences of devastating loss, but with two crucial differences: the losses are caused by fellow human beings, and we can never reorient ourselves completely to the new existential reality. Time after time, as the violence of war inflicts new losses, we are overwhelmed by the incomprehensibility of the situation and our powerlessness within it. As Michael Taussig puts it, we find ourselves swinging wildly between "terror as usual" and shock (1992:17–18). When the agents of death and chaos are not impersonal forces but other people, former compatriots, and even neighbors, who suddenly bring destruction down upon us, the situation is even more profoundly unsettling. The faith in humanity on which society itself is founded is constantly undermined, and every action we take to try to save ourselves seems trivial or pointless.

In this light, some of the most shocking experiences of loss and disorientation in our peacetime lives in Europe and America resemble wartime experiences. Deaths caused by criminal gang violence in the inner cities and by terrorist attacks in New York City, London, and Madrid—as well as the "peacekeeping operations" that the United States, NATO, and the United Nations conduct in African countries and the ongoing wars in Afghanistan and Iraq—are all caused by people, yet they are incomprehensible and out of control. In these circumstances, we react in ways that are similar to those of people caught up in war. This resemblance makes the experiences of people in Sarajevo during the siege of much more profound interest to us than we would have expected.

Both the immediate experiences that being caught up in war entails and the moral dilemmas that arise when struggling to survive in a city under siege make untenable the notion that wars are rational, controlled, sometimes even honorable, ordered and limited by the laws of war, with legitimate aims and clearly distinct opposing sides—a notion that still dominates the practice of international politics.[1] Almost without exception, whether conflict rages across international borders or attempts to impose new boundaries between peoples, war is gruesomely devoid of logic. Perhaps that is why fiction and film seem to capture wartime realities more powerfully than journalistic accounts and expert analyses. The moral unacceptability of "the laws of war" becomes appallingly clear when we examine the terminology designed to disguise the more ghastly rules of war: "collateral damage," "low-intensity conflict," and "ethnic cleansing" are among the euphemisms that obscure killing, starvation, and displacement. War legitimizes mass murder and destruction of property, which no other legal system allows on such a scale within such a short period of time.[2]

By trying to find the causes and logic of war—often in hope of understanding it and being able to control the damage it inflicts, if not stop or prevent it in future—we unavoidably fall into reifying the divisions into distinct warring sides, with their aims and justifications for mass violence. Such was the case with many expert analyses of war in Bosnia and Herzegovina, but also with many Sarajevans in their attempts to orient themselves in chaotic life circumstances and to justify their often morally ambiguous practices. In order to avoid the pitfalls of oversimplifying war and ignoring its incomprehensible, unjustifiable, and unacceptable nature, I chose to let individuals' lived experiences of violence stand at the center of research and from that point to trace the effects of war on society and culture.[3] This account explores Sarajevans' subjective responses to the death and destruction that engulfed their city and their repeated, though often futile, efforts to make sense of the disturbing and irrational situations in which they found themselves.

After struggling to orient myself in the midst of chaotic and contradictory experiences, I realized that these feelings and ideas could be sorted into three different modes of perceiving war. At first, people are so struck by the outbreak of a war they had thought impossible that the social norms they had thought secure collapse. I call this initial disbelief and the vacuum of meanings that follows the "civilian" mode of perceiving war. Then people attempt to order and explain the events and actors, adopting what I call the "soldier" mode. Aligning themselves with one or another of the warring sides, they seek protection and solidarity, giving some meaning to the risks they must face. The soldier mode offers a moral rationale for conflict, making the destruction and killing seem necessary and even acceptable. Finally, people realize through their own experiences of war that these explanations do not hold and shift to a third standpoint that I call the "deserter" mode.[4] Abandoning the neat divisions between citizens and armies, friends and foes that mark the civilian and soldier modes, people give up allegiances to any opposing side and take responsibility for their own actions. This stance does not constitute treason or betrayal but expresses profound skepticism about the high ideals that justify vicious acts and an effort to recover some small measure of humanity in a world gone berserk.

These modes of feeling and thinking are not necessarily sequential or mutually exclusive; often people hold them simultaneously or shift back and forth between them as their situation changes. Everyone caught up in a war, or dealing with war as a journalist, diplomat, or researcher, employs all three of these perspectives. The inconsistencies in perceptions of war that are characteristic of those who are subjected to it involuntarily arise not only from war's chaotic character but also from the best efforts to come to terms with it.

Imitation of Normal Life

As I focused on the experience of violence, I listened closely to what preoccupied my informants and how they spoke about everyday concerns. I noticed that people in Sarajevo often used the concept of normality to describe some situation, person, or way of life. The concept carried a moral charge, a positive sense of what was good, right, or desirable: a "normal life" was a description of how people wanted to live; a "normal person" thought and did things that were regarded as acceptable. The term pertained not only to the way of life people felt they had lost but also to a moral framework that might guide their actions. Normality not only communicated the social norms held by the person using it but also indicated her or his ideological position. The preoccupation with normality reflected Sarajevans' utmost fear and their

Figure 1. In 1995 graffiti appeared saying: "Nobody here is normal" ("*Ovdje niko nije normalan*"). Sarajevo, spring 1996. Photo by author.

utmost shame: that in coping with the inhumane conditions of war, they had also become dehumanized and that they might be surviving only by means they would previously have rejected as immoral. Had they become psychologically, socially, and culturally unfit to live among decent people?

Social norms are always in flux. Each person continuously defines and redefines his or her norms of conduct and perceptions of society in accordance with his or her daily experiences. In the context of war, the wholesale destruction of people's homes, the intensity of chaotic feelings, and the constant demand to respond to unprecedented conditions make the pace and scope of change so dramatic that it is more easily noticed than in peacetime. I found it useful to follow the process of change in perceptions of normality in order to understand and explain people's experiences of war in Sarajevo.

Schematically, change can be described as a process that occurs again and again:

- A *norm* exists.
- *Violence* disrupts normality; the norm does not hold anymore.

- *Chaos* reigns—a vacuum of meaning, disorientation, and normlessness.
- *New truths* compete to fill this vacuum: political ideologies, media interpretations, social contacts, rumors, and individuals' own experiences.
- A *new norm* emerges, but it too is disrupted as the cycle continues.

Massive political violence disrupts the way we know the world works in peacetime and makes it worthless for orienting ourselves in a war zone. We feel plunged into a state of chaos, yet we are forced to take action in response to constant emergencies. What we previously found meaningful has been shattered, vanished, or become impossible, even inconceivable. As we struggle to make some sense of our situation, we seek desperately to fill this vacuum with new meanings. At this point, differing interpretations of the conflict compete for our allegiance. These contesting truths are promulgated by politicomilitary organizations and power elites; they are manufactured or propagated by the media, whether politically controlled or independent; they arise and circulate within our social circles, often in the form of rumors; and they come from our own desperate efforts to make sense of our disparate personal experiences. Amid a dizzying variety of interpretations, we settle on whatever seems to us the most useful guide to action and a notion of the world we can live with. On this basis, we join with like-minded and similarly situated others to develop a new norm, however provisional. But the cycle is repeated as new experiences fracture whatever tentative certainty and fragile consensus has been attained. The process continues on all levels of our lives, from the most existential through the material to the ideological.

Two examples illuminate this process. The first highlights how perceptions of normality changed on the most basic material level. A young woman, a doctor of medicine who became a friend, told me a story from the first months of war, when most Sarajevans were still reasoning within their peacetime standards. She and a friend of hers were going to a party one Saturday evening. As parties were very rare at that time, they fixed themselves up the best they could. Her friend even put on nylon stockings, which were already a scarce commodity. As they walked, the shelling started, and the explosions were very near. My acquaintance threw herself into the nearest ditch and shouted at her friend, who was still standing in the street, to do the same. The bewildered girl shouted that she could not because her nylon stockings would get torn. "To hell with your nylon stockings," replied my acquaintance, "It is your head that will get blown off if you don't get down immediately."

The second example illustrates the changes in the relations between neighbors who belonged to different ethnoreligious and national groups and in the moral values attached to these relations. It was told to me by my host, a middle-aged man and an avowed anti-nationalist from a Muslim family background. At the height of the war, now and then he helped an old lady in the neighborhood by fetching water for her. It started one day when he saw her at her window and offered his help. After that she would sometimes wait for him with her canisters. One day a man in the street, presumably a neighbor who knew the old lady, commented, "Oh, you Serbs always stick together." My host froze and told him his name, which was Muslim. "I think the man was ashamed," he commented when he told me the story. As my host saw the situation, he was doing his neighborly duty. The man misinterpreted this solidarity in ethnoreligious terms, because the meanings of neighborliness and national identity were being renegotiated in the new atmosphere of rumors and media reporting of betrayal, or at least the lack of neighborly protection across national lines.

In peacetime, most people perceive normality as a stable, taken-for-granted state. Indeed, an essentialist conviction that this is how things really are seems central to our feeling of security, and discovering that nothing can be trusted anymore is almost as unsettling as the immediate dangers of living in a war zone. Political actors can exploit people's need for security to promote their own versions of reality, and consequently those with more power have more to say about what normality is. However, even in wartime people do not automatically accept new explanations, ideas, and norms. It is more accurate to say that the redefinition of normality takes place in a political space where the power to define the truth is highly contested.

Characteristically, during the siege of Sarajevo, as in other situations of war, occupation, and captivity, powerful feelings of shame followed each breach and fall of a cherished social norm, while feelings of pride were associated with every solution to a predicament or resolution of a dilemma that created a new meaning in daily life. Yet even resourcefulness and resilience did not break the cycle. There were ways of escaping it, either by disconnecting psychologically or by fleeing. The local term for the emotional numbness and irrationality that followed an excess of pain was *prolupati*.[5] People I saw who simply stood in open places during the shelling as if nothing was going on, or an elderly man with a distant look who was not interested in joining the rest of his family in their summer house in a peaceful part of coastal Croatia, might have escaped the exhausting circle of constantly reestablishing some sort of normality, but the price was the loss of all meaning. They lost contact with their feelings, including the fear necessary for physical sur-

vival and the need for closeness necessary for emotional survival. They were
the zombies of the war. Refugees who escaped from the physical perils of war
found very quickly that escape did not free them from a need to come to
terms with the politics of national belonging, the violence they had witnessed
and evaded, and their decision to leave while others remained, with all that
that meant materially, socially, and morally.

Each and every turning in this spiral of shattered and re-created norms
was marked by a movement between some semblance of normality and the
eruption of chaos. People who could easily give me a sophisticated political
analysis one day would the very next day express bewilderment and ask me
to explain to them why all this was happening. Something that had made
sense could suddenly become meaningless; what had momentarily seemed
normal could crumble into nothingness. Taussig has described this oscillation as a "doubleness of social being, in which one moves in bursts between
somehow accepting the situation as normal, only to be thrown into a panic
or shocked into disorientation by an event, a rumour, a sight, something said,
or not said—something that even while it requires the normal in order to
make its impact, destroys it" (1992:18).

What people meant by "normality" swung back and forth between two
points of reference, peacetime and wartime. When Sarajevans spoke of normal life, they meant the prewar way of life and social norms that had been
lost amid the violent circumstances of the siege. They saw the way of living
that they had been forced to adopt during the siege as abnormal, yet it became strangely normal during wartime. Taussig calls this incomplete shift of
mental stance the "normality of the abnormal" (1992:17–18). Sarajevans
coined the expression "imitation of life" to mark this coping strategy. They
patched together a semblance of existence, living from day to day on terms
they could neither finally accept nor directly alter. This stance enabled Sarajevans to conduct themselves according to wartime norms while remembering their prewar norms and enshrining them as the ideal of how life should
be. It did not, however, resolve the ethical dilemmas that arose amid their
daily struggles: What is an acceptable everyday normality? What is a decent
human life? Sarajevans were caught in a constant pendulum swing between
the two sets of norms. Should they resist the impulse to run before the
sniper? Should they cling to the cosmopolitanism that, like their city, lay in
ruins, or should they judge others on the basis of national belonging?

Almost every detail of everyday life was subject to constant evaluation
and revaluation. The most intensely charged and deeply disputed domain

was that of ethnonational identification. Sarajevans had to reconcile their own lived experiences as members of ethnocultural groups in a multicultural city with the mutually exclusive, even hostile constructions of ethnonational identity that political leaders formulated and the war increasingly forced upon them. Whatever position they chose, it was both existentially unstable and morally charged.

Finding a Method for an Anthropology of War

Most authors who have tried to understand individuals' lived experience of violence and transform it into words that others can comprehend encounter serious difficulties. The experience of traumatic violence is profoundly personal; it penetrates to the very core of our being. How do we translate existential fear and bodily pain into terms that those who have not shared this psychological and somatic violation of the self can understand? For all who lived through it, the siege of Sarajevo was a "limit situation,"[6] plunging them into life circumstances that were on the border of what is humanly possible to understand, conceptualize, and describe in words. Listening to the silences and noticing the gaps in people's stories that often betray an inassimilable experience is only the beginning; we must also observe and convey the full range of people's responses to appalling events. Even when people undergo common experiences, each person comes to terms with them—or fails to come to terms with them—in her or his own way. This existential loneliness in the process of making meaning in war exacerbates the erosion of trust between people, but at the same time it strengthens the need to find others with whom to feel a sense of belonging.

Wars are politically sensitive situations where lives are at stake and truth is hotly contested. When words are an integral part of a culture that has been so thoroughly jeopardized by political violence, it is important to be aware of whose words we use to describe these experiences. At the same time that trauma generates silence, language is manipulated and corrupted by the political culture of armed conflict. As producers of knowledge about war, anthropologists are in a sensitive position because our representations of war, though less powerful than those of the politicians, create a sort of truth about it that circulates internationally. That is why I found it essential to depict the situation from a multiplicity of different perspectives. I chose people belonging to various groups—defined by national identity, ethnoreligious background, place of residence, age, gender, and family position—and from different networks I established in Sarajevo. I also present as accurately as possible the contexts in which people constructed their interpretations of the situation and acted upon them.

Tape-recording Sarajevans' own words and integrating them into the text allows people whose voices and viewpoints could not be heard amid the competing truths about the war to be presented in their own language for describing their encounter with limit situations during the siege and to share their reflections on the nationalist politics that gave rise to and sustained such massive violence. I conducted over a hundred hours of interviews with approximately fifty different people. About ten of them I considered war friends, who generously shared scarce resources with me, taught me how to cope with conditions in the city, and recounted their experiences and perspectives on the war. Each interview was rich and covered most of the subjects I sought to explore: how people responded to existential dangers and managed amid material deprivation; changes that occurred within families and in relationships with friends and neighbors; shifts in the level of religiosity and the strength of national identifications. While the situations I describe and the responses I analyze here were common among informants, I illustrate these experiences and reflections with those voices that convey them most accurately and eloquently. I also quote informants whose positions and perspectives differed from those of the majority, since I am interested in sociocultural variations in people's responses to the war.

I draw on my own experiences and reflections as well as on Sarajevans' accounts in order to comprehend and communicate this shockingly concrete, yet subtle and elusive knowledge of war. Living in the besieged city alongside Sarajevans, I too had to employ all of my faculties—my intuition and cognition, my senses and emotions—in order to manage from day to day, as well as record what they and I were undergoing. In some instances, I found my own experiences helpful in understanding what Sarajevans were telling me.[7] For example, I recount my own responses to being shot at—sudden depression as my sense of purpose evaporated, and then a process of reaffirming my reasons for being in Sarajevo—because, even though my informants told me similar stories, my own experience was the one I could describe the best. I do not, however, include anything personal that does not bear directly on the central questions that animated my fieldwork—just as I include nothing about my informants' private lives that has no bearing on their wartime experiences.

"Giving myself over to the phenomenon," rather than constructing what Taussig calls "an account from the outside and above" (1992:10), seemed to be the only way of gaining relevant knowledge and representing it to others. The novelist Kurt Vonnegut once characterized anthropology as "poetry which *pretends* to be scientific" (1974:176). Having a poet's approach to fieldwork, as well as to writing, can yield valuable insights and suggest innovative forms of presentation for an anthropology of war. A disciplined subjectivity becomes not a flaw or obstacle but a crucial element for creating meaningful knowledge.

Doing fieldwork in war conditions may be hazardous to the project as well as the participant-observer because he or she might experience events that he or she has no way of dealing with and become so distressed as to be unable to continue the work. However, most people—ordinary citizens, not just anthropologists—have psychological defenses that enable them to function in distressing situations. The problem for researchers such as myself is that key psychological defense mechanisms make us hear, observe, and remember only those phenomena we are capable of dealing with and consign the rest to silence and seeming oblivion (Nordstrom 1997:21–22). When she was immersed in fieldwork on witchcraft in the Bocage, Jeanne Favret-Saada noticed how difficult she found it to remember parts of conversations that touched on what she "did not want to hear," even when transcribing her tapes afterward (1980:176–77, n. 1).

I encountered similar difficulties in recalling and processing conversations during my research. Two years after completing my fieldwork, I discovered many instances in which Sarajevans told me about their own breakdowns, or breakdowns that people close to them had experienced, during the war. I was astonished because by that time I had already read and analyzed the material several times. I recalled almost everything else these informants said, but not that they spoke about psychological breakdowns. I remembered one brief meeting with an elderly man in March 1995 who had obviously lost the will to live. I knew that one of my war friends had a physical breakdown, but I did not connect it with her story of how she suddenly became terribly afraid of getting hurt. I did not remember another war friend telling me that a friend of hers was taking sedatives in order to function; she worried because the sedatives were addictive, and no one knew how long the war was going to last. I had not recalled a young man telling me about his mother's breakdown. Only after the war had ended, when I myself had experienced some psychological effects of immersion in the war, was I able to hear and take in these stories, and a completely new dimension of war emerged in front of me. No amount of observation can enable us to see and reflect upon phenomena we are unprepared for and unable to assimilate. Yet what we have ignored or pushed aside tends to reemerge when we are ready to deal with it. The field notes, tape-recorded interviews, and printed material I collected in Sarajevo were invaluable as I returned to analyze them again and again with new insights and questions.

A Stranger and a Friend

My fieldwork was shaped by the peculiar social position I occupied in Sarajevo. I was an outsider and an insider at one and the same time; to adopt Hortense Powdermaker's expression, I was both "a stranger and a friend" (1966). I was not Sarajevan, and I did not know what life there was like before the siege. Yet I shared with Sarajevans a common Yugoslav sociocultural and political experience, with a common language and everything else that it implied. And I came to learn about the war by sharing it with them.

Still, most of the time I was treated like a guest. Ever hospitable, Sarajevans were willing to help me and take care of me when I needed it, which as a newcomer I often did. My presence was an interruption in their usual wartime existence—a very welcome one, I was assured—and I was never treated completely like one of them. However much I tried not to be special but to fall into their usual routines, life was never quite the same when I was around. I did not fully realize this until an incident in March 1995. I had said my goodbyes in the morning and left for the airport, but flights were canceled because of shooting, so I came back at lunchtime. My hosts welcomed me back, but they were slightly embarrassed by the very simple meal they had to offer me. I joked with one of their nephews that, as soon as I left, the food went back to the normal monotonous war diet, but inside I felt very naive. During that stay in Sarajevo I had the impression that I shared my hosts' usual wartime fare.

The former Socialist Federative Republic of Yugoslavia had six constituent peoples[8] (*narodi*)—Slovenes, Croats, Serbs, Muslims, Montenegrins, and Macedonians (and, from 1974, Yugoslavs)—as well as several national minorities (*narodnosti*). The three constituent peoples of the Republic of Bosnia and Herzegovina were Muslims, Serbs, and Croats. In 1995 the earlier label "Muslim" was replaced by "Bosniac" (Bošnjak) in the new constitution of Bosnia and Herzegovina. This substitution caused a lot of international confusion, and local discontent by Serbs and Croats, as "Bosniac" sounds very much like "Bosnian" (Bosanac), which implies all the people of Bosnia, and often of Herzegovina, too.[9] I chose to use the term Muslim rather than

Bosniac because this is the term that my informants used. In Sarajevo, the two largest national groups before the war were Muslims and Serbs, while the Croats were less than 10 percent of the population.

At first I wanted to assume that my identity as a Croat would not matter to my fieldwork. After all, I was not a nationalist and did not come from a religiously observant family. Only after my work in Sarajevo was completed did I come to recognize how profoundly my views on ethnonationalism had been shaped by my grandparents. My maternal grandmother was a Croatian Serb, an atheist, and a communist sympathiser, and her views influenced my life and ideology. Her husband, my grandfather, was Croat but he, like her, was anti-nationalist and a communist sympathizer. He did his time in Jasenovac, a concentration camp,[10] because of his illegal support of communists and Jews during World War II. He died when I was a child, so I have only early memories of him, but my grandmother passed on these ideas to me. During the war, however, I seldom told others about my Serbian roots, because I feared that all my anti-nationalistic arguments would have been dismissed as a simple reflection of the fact that I was of "mixed blood," as was presumed by the ideology that was predominant during the war. I wanted to present myself as a "real" Croat and say that it did not matter all that much! My father's family was entirely Croatian in background and especially the women were practicing Catholics in a low-key manner that was common during the socialist period.

My national identity influenced my fieldwork primarily, however, because it affected how others saw me. Amid the war that convulsed the former Yugoslavia, national identity became a life-and-death matter, and the ideas that people held about their own group and the others became highly salient in shaping interactions in Sarajevo. When the horrors of war were interpreted in nationalist idioms, most people looked at one another through national lenses. And they looked at me in the same way. I often expressed my support for the notion that nationality was not really important, and I made it clear that I had no allegiance to Croatian nationalist ideologies. Nonetheless, people related to me as a Croat from Croatia. It took a long time before I understood that, no matter how I felt and defined myself, I was still classified within the Sarajevan categories of "us" and "others." Being a Croat placed me in different positions in regard to the various people I met and interviewed. Though I often thought this positioning was unnecessary and even unfortunate, it gave me firsthand experience of what nationality meant in Sarajevo during the war.

I was lucky because the couple who became my hosts was "mixed"; he came from a Muslim family, and she from a Serbian one. Characteristically, they had strong anti-nationalistic sentiments, a view that I shared. This commonality in difference created a secure and relaxed home atmosphere and rapidly generated mutual sympathies among us. We often joked about our ascribed national identities. For example, if in a debate I supported his wife's position or she supported mine, my host would always declare: "udruži se krst sa križem" (the cross [*krst*] got united with the cross [*križ*]) against the Muslims, the first representing the Serbian variant and the second the Croatian variant for the Christian cross. Another running joke between us was my ignorance when it came to religious expressions, which were often synonymous with national ones. One day, during my first stay in 1994, my host asked me what the Catholic greeting was when someone entered a house. Muslims say "Merhaba" or "Selam alejkum," and he wondered what Catholics said. I had no ready answer. I knew the greeting had a central figure such as Mary, Jesus, or God, and the first expression that came to my mind was "Pomoz Bog" (God help). But that was the Orthodox and Serbian greeting; the Catholic and Croatian one was "Hvaljen Isus" (Praised be Jesus). As soon as I said it, I realized that it must be wrong, but it was too late. They were already teasing me for not being a real Croat. Some years afterward my host told me that from that moment on he was sure that I was no nationalist.

My lack of nationalist views and religious observance made it somewhat easier for a Croatian from a family background that was presumed to be Catholic to get along in Sarajevo. At the same time, I initially did not see the national lenses through which the majority of Sarajevans redefined their relations with one another during the siege. Even when I noticed the distrust between national groups that grew as each blamed the war on the others, I found it difficult to grasp that people were relating to me in the same way.

I was first struck by this fact in March 1995 when I accompanied a Swedish friend who was a journalist to a set of interviews about Sarajevan religious communities to serve as her interpreter. In the Muslim community's building we were met by two serious men in suits. They were very polite and treated us properly in every way. Our bags were searched, as was routinely done, and we were shown into a room where one of the men invited us to sit down and asked us to explain who we were and what the interview would be used for. We gave our names and my friend explained that it was for her program on Swedish radio. During the interview, this man answered her questions but said not one word more than was absolutely necessary. The other man sat at a large table that was slightly removed from the interview scene, and I realized that he was there only to observe and take notes. After this stiff, unsatisfying encounter, we went to the Catholic community. There we were met in a somewhat more relaxed fashion. The man we were to interview received us on his own and took us to a very beautiful neoclassical room dating from the Austro-Hungarian period. He asked how he could help us, and my friend presented us and her task in the same manner. The man livened up at the sound of my Croatian name, which he remarked was "beautiful," and then happily told me of his years in Zagreb. The interview passed in an atmosphere of goodwill. Although he was reserved, he described some of the problems the Catholic community was having with the situation and expressed some criticism of the city's domination by the Muslim community. Walking in the street afterward, I felt more trust in this man than in the Muslim representatives, which surprised me. It felt like a genuine "here is where I belong after all" experience. So I began to understand how difficult it was not to put on national lenses during the war.

Our visit to the representative of the Orthodox community was rather sad. The clergyman, who was the only official representative of the Orthodox Church in Sarajevo, was a tiny man who appeared both scared and forgotten. He said almost nothing and never uttered a whole sentence, except when he told us that the government was very correct toward him and always saw to it that he was invited to official ceremonies, along with the Catholic and Muslim religious representatives. Being a very visible Serb in Sarajevo during the siege made him a vulnerable and isolated figure. Most other Sarajevans with Serbian family backgrounds kept a low profile, since the city was still besieged by the Serbian armed forces on the surrounding hills and in parts of the city. Indeed, I too kept quiet about my Serbian grandmother.

While new acquaintances made simple presumptions about my identity, people whom I got to know over time tried to explain to themselves who I was and to figure out what national or ideological category I fit into. The fact that I was obviously Croatian and self-consciously not a nationalist was not enough; they had to sort out my position in relation to themselves, not simply regard me as a stranger and outsider. On my first visit to Sarajevo I got acquainted with a Catholic Croat family who helped me a lot and invited me to be with them for Sundays and Catholic holidays. I was happy to come, since it gave me the opportunity to meet people, to learn about their customs, share, and enjoy them. Only in 1996 did I realize that they were inviting me because they thought I should not be alone, without a family, on a holiday. They were treating me as one of them, while I was regarding them as different. In my eyes, they were very religious, going to mass, taking the holy sacrament, praying at home, and blessing the food. They noticed that I knew little about Catholicism, especially Croatian customs. One of the younger women in the family once told me that it must be because Croats were an absolute majority in Croatia that people like me were not so religious. At that moment, it struck me as a strange comment, especially since religion was making a tremendous comeback in Croatia, but later on I realized that she was right. Our identities are always shaped by our sociocultural context, and it matters whether you belong to a minority or to a majority group. The main purpose of her comment, however, was to explain to herself why I was not as religious as she was, since both of us were Croats. She was looking for a way to think of me as belonging to "us" rather than "them," despite such important differences between us. As a Croat from Croatia, I could be nonreligious but nevertheless all right.

Another encounter with a Sarajevan Croat ended with my summary dismissal. He was a sociology professor who had done some work on war, so a mutual acquaintance suggested that we meet. The man treated me as if I were his student and told me in no uncertain terms that I could not do research on religious questions in Sarajevo. I never understood why, and I felt bad after this conversation. Later, when I transcribed the interview, I saw something I did not remember. In telling me of his time as a student in Zagreb, he emphasized how arrogant the Croatian Croats were toward him, a Bosnian Croat, and how the Croatians always thought that they understood Bosnia, although they did not. His comment condemning my interest in religions in Sarajevo came in this context. Again I was identified as a Croatian Croat, but this time characterized as an ignorant and arrogant person, thinking that the explanation of the war in Bosnia could be found in religious questions.

Those Muslims I became closest to, because of mutual sympathies and proof that we were willing to help each other, often said, "Look at you, you are like one of us," although it was obvious to all of us that I was neither Muslim nor Sarajevan. This exclamation came usually when I did something in a way that they were used to. For instance, I preferred to drink coffee out of a *fildžan* (a small coffee cup without a handle) rather than out of a *šoljica* (demitasse, a small coffee cup with a handle). Traditionally, a *fildžan* is a Muslim coffee cup, and a *šoljica* a Christian one. To ask a non-Muslim guest what she would prefer had always been a matter of politeness, an adaptation to the frequent social interaction among members of different ethnoreligious communities. In the former Yugoslavia, the rest of Europe was perceived as a sociocultural ideal. Since the Italians and the French drank coffee out of demitasse cups, secularized people tended to see the *fildžan* as backward or slightly exotic. During the war, some anti-Muslim citizens regarded using a *fildžan* as a primitive custom, and in some homes I was told with a chilly tone that they did not have any *fildžani*. In Muslim houses, by choosing the Muslim coffee cup I demonstrated to my new acquaintances that I was open to them and accepting of their customs. Of course, I had absolutely no idea beforehand that this mattered; it was just a natural part of my anthropological attitude and curiosity to learn new customs, as I tried to explain. But, whatever my intentions were, by adopting simple everyday ways, I was also signaling national sympathies.

Once I was perceived as being "like one of us," I was presented that way to others. To most Sarajevans, my name was obviously Croatian; it was Slavic, non-Muslim, and not the Serbian variant, Jovana. My accent, too, often needed an explanation when a Muslim introduced me to another Muslim: "Ivana comes from Zagreb, but she is like one of us," or "She is Croatian, but she is all right." This was the usual way of relating to someone whom one liked but who belonged to a different ethnoreligious or national group.

Being one of "us" did not always necessarily signify a national category. Some alternative collective identities were forged during the war; the solidarity between all Sarajevans who stayed in the city was among the strongest. Toward the end of the war, when Sarajevans were becoming annoyed by all the foreigners coming to their city after the siege was over, a Muslim friend introduced me to a colleague who was to help me with my research by saying, "Ivana is doing research about war in Sarajevo, and she has been here with us from the beginning, through all the worst." When we left, I pointed out to her that I actually had not been in Sarajevo through the very worst, but she cut me off and explained that she had to say so because at that point people were so sensitive and the man would not have helped me otherwise.

During my fieldwork I met a lot of people with whom I never established closer relations, although I conducted interviews with them. This pattern was characteristic of my interactions with Muslim "internally displaced persons"[11] from Eastern Bosnia. We found no common interests, probably because they were not in the focus of my research, and neither they nor I cultivated a relationship. I interviewed several Serbs and would have liked to get to know them better. But the Serbs were really the losers in Sarajevo; they were scared to stick out, so I did not insist on more meetings. I had a feeling that frequent visits from a stranger would have called attention to them in the neighborhood and aroused suspicious gossip.

Had I been of Serbian or Muslim origin, I would have been able to gather different material, but it would still have been incomplete and affected by my origin. As my host pointed out to me when I said that Croats seemed to be so negative toward Muslims while it was not the case the other way around: "You should only hear what your Muslims say about Croats in front of me!" Of course, I could imagine, because I knew what Croats were saying about Muslims and what Muslims were saying about Serbs, so it was unlikely that it would be any different the other way around.

The Ethics of Research on Suffering

I started my fieldwork during the Croatian war, spending two weeks in Zagreb and its surroundings in October 1991, and then one month in March 1993 traveling to Croatian and Herzegovinian front lines in Nova Gradiška, Dubrovnik, Ravno, Mostar, and Zadar. In the autumn of 1993 I spent three months in Zagreb preparing my way to Bosnia and interviewing Sarajevans who were in Zagreb at that time. Fieldwork in Sarajevo, which is central to this analysis, was conducted during five different periods: two weeks in September 1994; one month in March 1995; two weeks in September 1995; three months in the spring of 1996; and two weeks in September 1996. All in all, I spent six months in Sarajevo, and an additional six months in Croatia and Herzegovina.

My stays in Sarajevo were so short, especially in 1994 and 1995, because of the circumstances of the war and the limited duration of UN identity cards. When I once complained about not being able to spend a whole year in the field, as was conventional among anthropologists, my host told me that living in Sarajevo would make it impossible to do research. I could write a very good war diary, or even a novel, he said, but I could not do social-scientific research. I believe that he was right, because several times during my fieldwork I experienced the urge to abandon my research and do something more immediately useful. The rather abstract humanitarian project of documenting and analyzing people's responses to political violence did not seem meaningful under the circumstances. I felt compelled to get a job that helped people directly, perhaps with a humanitarian agency or where I could use my skills in a more practical way. Many of my Sarajevan friends whose studies had been interrupted did useful work, which seemed to help them keep their balance. But then, I realized that, had I been a Sarajevan caught up in the war involuntarily, I would surely have done everything I could to leave the city, as many people of my generation and background actually did.

The constant awareness of life-threatening danger and the pressure of time demanded more emotional energy than long-term research in peacetime. As a native speaker sharing a similar prewar culture, I noticed small details on the streets, overheard conversations in cafés, and noticed the nuances in people's expressions. Everything I saw or heard was material, and I was desperately trying to catch as much of it as I could. Working as well as living in Sarajevo under siege was so intense and exhausting that the only way I could relax a bit was to remember that I did not have to write detailed notes on my tape-recorded interviews while I was there.

After each of these periods in the field, I wrote and published articles in newspapers and scholarly journals. It was difficult to find my way through all these experiences, interviews, and written materials and figure out what was most important to say about the war in Sarajevo. Had I not done the analysis along the way, I dare say that the task of writing about the war would have been overwhelming. Working out the analysis gradually, between periods in Sarajevo, provided me with a fairly clear structure by the time I finished the fieldwork in 1996.

Still, the periods I spent out of the field were burdened not only with the usual adjustment to different living conditions and social circles but also with fear that something terrible might happen to the people I cared about in Sarajevo and a clear awareness of how utterly powerless I was to help them. When I had a respite from the traumatic situation for the time being and was safe in Sweden, I was beset by a diffuse post-traumatic depression and stress. Only after the war was over and the situation in Sarajevo was more secure did this sense of constant apprehension lift.

When I first sought to enter Bosnia, in the autumn of 1993, the situation was very bad. The fighting between the Army of Bosnia and Herzegovina (Armija Bosne i Hercegovine) [ABiH] and the Croat Defense Council (Hrvatsko vijeće obrane) [HVO] made traveling as a private person from Zagreb to Sarajevo almost impossible. The country was full of checkpoints held by all sorts of military formations. Only Bosnians fleeing from the war were desperate enough to run the risks. The only viable option for entering the country was to travel with a UN accreditation. The UN was the only neutral military force in the region, with relatively good logistics, and it enabled a limited number of accredited civilians to move into and out of Bosnia. Most of the accreditations were held by non-governmental organizations (NGOs) recognized by the UN, humanitarian workers, and journalists. Although passengers had to sign a form saying that the UN had no obligation to them and that they were traveling at their own risk, this option was still the safest. I became well acquainted with people in NGOs recognized by the UN, but they used their accreditations to enable Bosnian staff members to travel out of the war zone to strengthen contacts and have a brief respite from the war. The rationale for the UN's decision to restrict the number of people it helped to move into and out of Bosnia was to limit civilian casualties. The effect, however, was further isolation of the country, which suited the leaders of the warring sides and increased the suffering of the population.

Human rights and peace activists in Zagreb were cautious about traveling to Bosnia for ethical reasons as well. Many felt that they should do so only if they could ameliorate the situation in some concrete way. Foreign journalists who found a civil war in Europe intriguing and wanted to make fast and flashy accounts of it frequently called on activists in Zagreb for assistance. One journalist from Australia demanded to talk on the phone with an English-speaking woman who had been raped during the war in Bosnia. This sort of voyeuristic sensationalism and exploitation of victims caused revulsion among activists. The episode made me think about my motivations for doing fieldwork during the war. I felt compelled to find out about the war in the former Yugoslavia not because my life was boring and I was looking for stimulation but because my whole world was falling apart and I had to understand it in order to put it together again, even if only partially. I did not know whether conducting an ethnographic study of the siege of Sarajevo would be useful in any way, but I remained convinced that giving voice to the civilians whose experiences were left out of war accounts justified my working there.

During the years of my intermittent visits to Sarajevo, I questioned this reason many times. In the spring of 1995, when the situation in Sarajevo was deteriorating after a long period of relative quiet, I felt totally powerless. I tried to do something more practical for the people I had become attached to, who were once again at the mercy of destructive forces beyond their reach. I thought that since I could travel in and out of the city, I could do something they could not do for themselves. I was wrong. True, I could record their story and eventually share it with the world, but at the time that did not seem to matter. Nothing they or I did could make any real difference. After I left Sarajevo in late March, I just had to sit and wait for reports of Sarajevo being shelled. Overwhelmed by frustration, I fought an inner battle not to give up, not to let my work drown in a flood of meaninglessness and depression. I clung to the idea that documenting the war from an anthropological perspective must be worth while, and that proved to be my lifeline. As I thought of the people I left in Sarajevo, I knew that my being there off and on did not

Figure 2. My hosts' daughter made a collage with my face on a funny figure bearing a sack of gifts flying over Sarajevo. She used the panoramic photograph that I took in 1994, when her parents took me to see this celebrated view.

make much difference, but it was a change from the monotony of their wartime existence. My visits broke through their isolation from the rest of the world, which was killing their spirits more surely than shells and bullets. Through me they could hear about their relatives and friends abroad, receive a letter, and get a tiny present containing something that they had not seen since the beginning of the siege. Perhaps I could be a part of their lifeline.

It was through family connections between Bosnian refugees and Sarajevans living through the siege that I found a home in the war. At the beginning of 1994, although I knew that I wanted to conduct fieldwork in Bosnia, I had still not found a place to do it. I decided to discuss doing fieldwork in Sarajevo with a native of the city, a female acquaintance about my age and from a similar social background who left Sarajevo during the first summer of the war but whose parents were still there. She showed me some of their letters describing the situation. When I asked what she thought about my doing fieldwork in Sarajevo, she not only endorsed the idea but suggested that I stay with her parents, who had an apartment in the center of the city. Some years later we laughed about this conversation when it became clear that we had both seen a chance to make use of each other. I gained an initial contact in Sarajevo, a place to stay, and local residents to show me around. What I did not know then was that her parents would become my war family, offering me a home that meant much more to me than the information they provided. She, in her turn, saw a way of sending letters, money, and food to her parents, which was her main preoccupation during those years in exile. Over time, this initial mutual interest has grown into a strong bond. Relationships forged in wartime on the basis of shared concerns and mutual trust are difficult to explain in civilian terms of friendship or family, but strong ties, formed quite quickly under trying circumstances, are characteristic of the social and emotional relationships that emerged in Sarajevo under siege.

Sarajevo

Ivo Andrić (2005 [1946]) opens his marvelous short story "Letter from the Year 1920" by describing a young man who has just returned to his native Sarajevo from abroad. Lying awake at night, the young man listens to bells ringing out of sync from a Catholic cathedral, an Orthodox church, and a tower clock on Bey's Mosque (Begova Džamija), and he dwells on the absence of a chime from the synagogue, which has no clock. It wakes intense contradictory feelings of both love and hatred for his hometown, and he agonizes over his decision to return. The story could have easily been written today. To outsiders, as well as on local television, Sarajevans pointed out proudly that from a single spot you could see the buildings of the city's four dominant religions: the central mosque (Begova Džamija), the Catholic cathedral, the Orthodox cathedral, and the synagogue. During my first stay in Sarajevo, one of my new acquaintances took me to Bembaša hill in order to see this view. For Sarajevans, this scene was the physical embodiment of the blend of religious traditions that found their place in the unique concoction of culture, customs, beliefs, social skills, and dispositions that they experienced as characteristically Sarajevan

The capital of Bosnia and Herzegovina and an urban conglomeration with every important feature of a city, Sarajevo still felt like a town because of its social mixing and informality. It lies in a valley of the river Miljacka. Following the valley from its amphitheatric east to the plain in the west, the

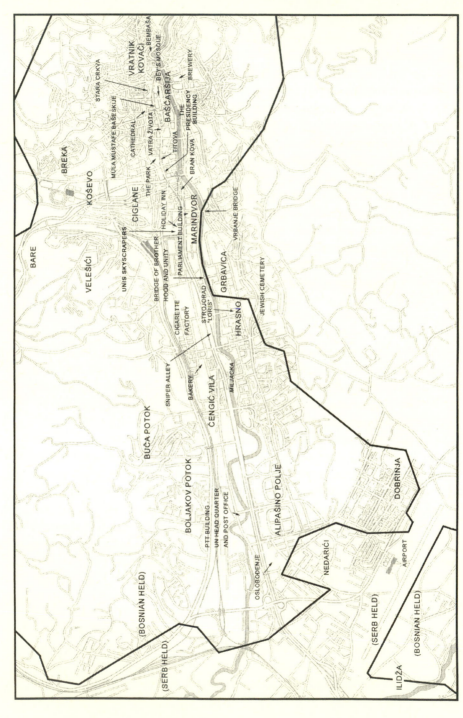

Map 1. Sarajevo under siege.

history of the city unfolds. Sarajevo was formed as a town around 1461, during Turkish times, and by 1660 it had become the largest city in the Balkans. All towns in the Ottoman Empire were structured by division into quarters, *mahale* (pl.), or distinct districts. Each *mahala* (sing.) belonged to a different religious congregation, with its characteristic place of worship. The larger religious groups had a larger number of *mahale*. Sarajevan *mahale* occupy the eastern, amphitheatric part of the city; the view shows a striking concentration of minarets and church towers. After the Hapsburg Empire annexed Bosnia in 1878, Austro-Hungarian architects began building to the west of the older Ottoman center. This phase of its growth makes downtown Sarajevo resemble any Central European city center from the end of the nineteenth century and the beginning of the twentieth. After World War II, expansion to the west continued. Yugoslav socialist architecture characterizes such buildings as the Parliament, the Holiday Inn, the UNIS twin skyscrapers (before the war popularly called "Momo" and "Uzeir" after Serb and Muslim characters in a humorous television series), the PTT (Post, Telegram, and Telephone) building, and the TV building. The modern suburbs of Grbavica, Hrasno, Čengić Vila, Alipašino polje, Neđarići, and Dobrinja grew here from 1960s on, as in other Yugoslavian and European cities. Different sorts of developments occurred on the slopes around the valley. In Velešići, Buča Potok, and Boljakov Potok, for example, villagers from Eastern Bosnia and Sandžak in Serbia moved in during the 1980s, giving the outskirts of the city a more rural look. In the west, where the valley merges with the plain, is the international airport—my point of entry into Sarajevo.

I had never been to Sarajevo before, and I had met only a few Sarajevans. I was familiar with the images of Bosnians that circulated in the former Yugoslavia. I had learned about Bosnian history and read Bosnian literature by such renowned novelists as Ivo Andrić and Meša Selimović. I loved to sing Bosnian melancholic songs despite their patriarchal tone. I enormously enjoyed the popular prewar satirical program *Top lista nadrealista* (Top of the Surrealists) by a group of young Sarajevan men.[12] I laughed at, and retold, jokes about Suljo, Mujo, and Fata, the stereotypical Muslim characters who figure in much of Bosnians' self-deprecating humor.[13]

History and fiction taught me about the appalling brutality of the Ottoman occupiers toward the population. Boys were kidnapped to be trained as Ottoman soldiers, *janjičari*, a practice called *danak u krvi*, a tribute in blood. The history of Western Europe from the Middle Ages through the Inquisition and the European conquest of the rest of the world was no less bloody. Yet from the liberation of Sarajevo from the fascists by the partisans in 1945 until the dissolution of Yugoslavia, history was a horrific story firmly located in the past, bygone and never to return. When Franjo Tudjman, during his term as president of Croatia, said, "We live in historical times," he was widely mocked not only for his pomposity but for his ignorance: while he was thinking of the heroic nature of Croatian nation-building, people were thinking of the misery that the nationalistic war had brought upon them. They would have been glad not to live in "historical times"!

The distinctive characteristic of Bosnians in general and Sarajevans in particular seems to have been—and still is—the shockingly lucid humor that flourished in the 1980s and continued throughout the war. No one who has seen it can forget a prewar sketch by the "Surrealists" in which Björn Borg comes as a refugee to Sarajevo because Sweden is at war with the penguins. Although no one recognizes him, people feel compassionate toward someone so far from home and try to help him the best they can. They find him a job in a coffee shop run by a Kosovo Albanian. His height, long blond hair, and incomprehensible speech make him look very stupid and out of place among the darker, shorter, and more alert Bosnians. At one point the kids in the street are playing tennis, and it turns out that Björn Borg is good at it. Everyone is happy for him and encourages him to keep it up! We all laughed at the absurdity of this upside-down situation, and no one could even dream that only a few years later forty thousand Bosnians would be seeking exile in Björn Borg's native Sweden. In another prewar sketch, two stupid-looking street cleaners throw rubbish over a wall onto each other—a wall that was built in Sarajevo in order to separate the two warring sides and maintain the peace! At that moment, the Berlin Wall was falling and Europe was uniting. All these unimaginable reversals were true in the dream logic of nightmares—and soon became true in the "historical times" into which Sarajevans were unwillingly plunged.

The "Arrival Story"

Although war-torn Sarajevo was hardly a conventional anthropological field site, I could not help noticing certain resemblances—at least on the surface—to the fieldwork situation described in many a classical monograph (Pratt 1986). There was the "primitive other" whom we in the West did not understand, although in the case of Bosnia the "others" looked like us, were literate, and even spoke our languages. The colonial bureaucracy was present in the form of the UN. Life conditions were "primitive": water was scarce and dirty, food was strange and difficult to get. Visitors were well advised to take their own provisions. There was no electricity. The utilities and comforts expected in a "civilized" place were lacking. The difference from the classical anthropological "bush" was that in Bosnia these conditions were situated within the remains of civilization, not outside of them. Bosnia had been part of Europe, but it seemed so no longer. Many westerners may have come to regard Bosnia as outside of Europe because they did not want to acknowledge that forces within their own societies and nation-states could lead to such a situation and were discomforted by the idea that they might be responsible for the city's plight. Finally, there was the anthropologist as hero, entering the danger zone inhabited by "wild people" who were at war—a Hermes, to borrow Crapanzano's metaphor (1986), a messenger between two worlds, the powerful, peaceful West and war-torn Sarajevo.

The road to Sarajevo, which started at the Croatian coast and then ran through territories under HVO and ABiH control, at the end passed through territory under the control of the Bosnian Serbs' Army (Vojska Republike Srpske [VRS], Army of the Republika Srpska). In order for outsiders to reach Sarajevo by road, all three parties in the military conflict had to maintain a ceasefire. Whether formally negotiated or the result of stalemate and exhaustion, these intermissions in the fighting were unpredictable and highly unstable. The longest period that the UN-supervised routes called the "blue ways" were open was two or three months during the summer of 1994. Most often it was the Bosnian Serbs' side that blocked land transports to Sarajevo. The ABiH and HVO were in conflict from late 1992 until early 1994, and during that time even the Bosnian Croats' side blockaded the city. The Bosnian government's side facilitated the passage of people and goods by using the tunnel under the airport, which was constructed because, even when the airport itself was under UN control, the UN denied passage to people seeking to enter and leave the city. Before the tunnel was dug, Sarajevans had to run across the runway hiding from the UN searchlights and the hail of bullets from Serbian snipers to reach the road into and out of Sarajevo. This tunnel was eight hundred meters long and it took thirty-five minutes to go through it, in a stooped position, with water up to one's knees here and there. Only the energetic and determined could manage it, and even then they could not bring much baggage with them.

The airport was Sarajevo's lifeline, but its capacity was very limited. In the autumn of 1994, there were military and diplomatic UN flights from Zagreb, humanitarian flights sponsored by the United Nations High Commission for Refugees (UNHCR) that carried goods and personnel from Zagreb and Split, and flights that brought goods and journalists from Ancona, Italy. There were various types of UN identity cards, depending on the grounds for one's accreditation. "Local personnel" included everyone who had a passport from one of the former Yugoslav republics. These cards conferred the same privileges as those held by "international personnel," except that when sufficient space on a flight was not available the "international" card holder was given priority.[14] No form of UN accreditation was granted to social researchers. The UN had an obligation to provide information, but letting journalists stay in war zones seemed to satisfy the foreign demand for information. The statement "Anthropologists Against Ethnic Violence" published in *Anthropology Today* in December 1993 and signed by some of the most prominent scholars in the discipline contends that the problem of access for researchers should be taken seriously and carried forward to the highest political levels: "It is the responsibility of anthropologists to expose the seductive simplicities which invoke primordial loyalties to ethnic origins. We can do this equally well by providing local knowledge as by formulating scientific statements. In any case, we must not shirk the responsibility of disputing the claims of demagogues and warning of the dangers of ethnic violence" (1993:28).

As a holder of a "local" passport, I decided that it would be safer for me to fly directly to Sarajevo and avoid various "national" checkpoints in Bosnia. In addition to contacting NGOs working in Bosnia, I tried to become accredited with the UNHCR as a researcher. The UNHCR informed me that it made contacts only with organizations, not private persons. This struck me as a peculiar statement, since it implied that I was doing research for personal reasons or private purposes. But my work was financed by the Swedish Council for Planning and Coordination of Research (Forskningsrådsnämnden [FRN]), a public body to which I also reported my results. I had no choice but to obtain a journalist UN identity card, which I managed to do in Zagreb.

With the card in hand and in the company of Staffan Löfving, my Swedish friend and fellow anthropologist with a background in journalism, I set out for Split. But no flights were taking journalists to Sarajevo. We spent a day at the airport waiting for information along with a motley collection of characters, both local and international, who were also trying to reach Sarajevo, including journalists, humanitarian workers, and UN soldiers. Christian Palme, a correspondent for the largest Swedish daily newspaper, *Dagens Nyheter*, told us that there was no point in waiting in Split to get on a flight as a journalist; Ancona was a better bet. So we took a night ferry to Ancona.

It felt strange to travel through a foreign nation to reach a city in your own country, even though it had formally dissolved. It took an hour to get off the ferry, with the Italian police and customs officers asking everybody where we were going. They focused especially on people whose origins were in the former Yugoslavia, whom they suspected of seeking to enter Italy illegally. I felt really stupid saying that I was going "to Sarajevo," trying to look as serious as possible and to make it sound like the most natural thing. Why else would people travel from Split to Ancona?

When we finally arrived at the airport in Ancona, it was practically empty. The airport in Sarajevo was closed because two UN aircraft had been fired on the day before when the pope was supposed to visit Sarajevo. The Serbian side would not guarantee his security, so the pope canceled his visit and most of the journalists went home. The day passed without shooting, and the next morning the UN decided to reopen the air bridge. Everything went surprisingly smoothly. Six people flew to Sarajevo in half-empty planes; I went on a German aircraft along with a journalist and a chess player from Sarajevo.

The UN provided transport from the airport into the city, directly to the UN Headquarters (HQ) in the PTT building in Alipašino polje. I remember seeing Sarajevans walking peacefully in the damaged suburbs, crosscut with protection walls made of rusty, splintered, and bullet-riddled cars. I was fascinated by people moving freely across the open spaces of this townscape that so obviously embodied the constant threat to life. Within a few days I was one of them, not really capable of grasping how this process of adaptation occurred, perhaps because it happened so quickly.

Multiple Key Informants

Leaving the security provided by the UN behind, I contacted the three families I was to visit and delivered the parcels I had brought for them from their relatives abroad. Our circle of acquaintances grew quickly and provided a rich source of informants. While in Split, we had borrowed flak jackets from an Irish priest who ran a Catholic NGO in Sarajevo. When we visited him in his office to return the jackets, he introduced us to a young Sarajevan man who worked with him and was happy to meet us later for a coffee. To this meeting he brought a young woman along, a friend of his. They were both Catholics, but while she was religious, he was not. With both of them I formed a friendship whose development seemed accelerated by wartime circumstances. In anthropological terms, they became key informants, explaining to me things I did not know or understand and obtaining information and contacts that I needed. At the same time, they invited me to their homes, took care of me as friends do, and spent their free time with me whenever it suited us. These war friendships might appear coincidental, but they were always based on mutual affinity. Most often they came about because of some common interest, experience, or ideals, but also because we seemed to share a sense of being outsiders.

Another chain of friendships came through Staffan, whose mother knew a refugee family from Sarajevo who was living in Sweden. Members of the family asked him to contact their good friend in Sarajevo and ask her to obtain copies of official documents for them. She received us in a warm and friendly manner, taking us to her offices and introducing us to her colleagues and neighbors. Gradually we also became war friends. She eventually told me that she had divorced her husband, a Bosnian Serb who was now living in Belgrade, and that their two teenage children had gone to Holland. Through her I met a woman in a neighboring family who had lived in Sweden as a child. We also became friends, and her husband was one of the few ex-soldiers I felt comfortable asking about his experiences as a soldier at the front lines.

All of the people who figure as informants in this analysis were ordinary residents of Sarajevo. I decided to focus on ordinary citizens because their experiences and knowledge of the war were not represented in either the media accounts or experts' analyses of the conflict. The problem of describing a "limit situation," of finding words for the incomprehensible and inexplicable situations that Sarajevans encountered in daily life, followed our work from the start. Almost everyone I asked for an interview answered that she or he did not have much to tell about the war. There was nothing to say. They had not experienced anything special. Many suggested that I should talk to refugees from Eastern Bosnia who had fled their homes under dramatic circumstances, those who had been in concentration camps, those who had left their aged, infirm parents behind or lost a child, those who had been raped and traumatized. This idea about research on war proves how deeply embedded the conventional notion of war is in all of us, Sarajevans as well as Western Europeans: civilians figure only as innocent and helpless victims of military forces, not as residents of a city under siege. I explained to everyone that I was not competent to conduct interviews with deeply traumatized persons; it would have made me no better than the journalists who exploited suffering in order to sell a story. They understood this explanation, and after I had reassured prospective informants that they did have a lot to tell about the war and that I would help them by asking specific questions, most agreed to meet me for an informal interview that I could tape-record—but only to be quoted anonymously in works I authored.

We usually started with the most obvious, seemingly simple things, such as how they provided themselves with food and heat. They described fantastically inventive solutions to wartime shortages. As our conversation continued and they mentioned those with whom they shared these daily struggles, I asked about family and old friends, about neighbors and new social contacts. In explaining their own choices, as well as trying to understand other people's decisions, they necessarily touched upon subjects of national belonging, political ideologies, and religious beliefs. In this way, we jointly undertook the task of finding a language with which to describe the war.

Analyzing Cultural Change in Sarajevo

The structure of this book follows the processes through which normality was dissolved and reconstructed in various domains of Sarajevan life: material, psychological, social, ideological, and moral. Each chapter focuses on ways in which people coped with specific forces that were disrupting their lives and points to the contradictions that occurred in this process.

Part I scrutinizes life in Sarajevo under siege. The next chapter describes how Sarajevans dealt with imminent threats to their physical existence. Was it safer to run before the snipers, or to act as if they were not there? Was fear an enemy or a friend? Sarajevans' coping strategies included psychological techniques that people utilize to imagine that they are in control of their surroundings when real control is out of their hands. At the same time, Sarajevans knew that calmly and realistically assessing the dangers was as crucial to survival as fooling your mind into feeling safe in life-threatening situations. Humor emerged as a way of keeping everything in perspective, no matter how absurd it seemed.

People's most important concerns, after not getting shot, were not being cold and not going hungry. Fortunately, these were matters they could do something about; indeed, during the siege these tasks took enormous amounts of time and energy. Chapter 3 explores the concept of "imitation of life," which Sarajevans used to describe their struggles to preserve the prewar norms and standards of material life under abnormal conditions, often through activities that were considered degrading. Risking your life to fetch the water required to keep up your personal hygiene as if in peacetime is an example of the desire at once to forget and to remain aware of the near total alteration of life, which generates humiliation and pride simultaneously. When thieving becomes a necessary means of survival and even religious bodies and international humanitarian agencies participate in the diversion and misappropriation of essential supplies, troubling moral questions unavoidably arise.

Social bonds that are the basic guarantees of security even in peacetime become more vital when other institutions, such as those provided by the state, break down or disappear, yet wartime conditions also strain more intimate ties of family and neighborhood. When half of the prewar population left the city, many long-standing bonds were broken, often painfully. The theme of Chapter 4 is the striking combination of pragmatism and intuition through which people reevaluated their old relationships and quickly established new ones.

Part II explores the transformation of identities and relationships by ethnonationalist movements. Chapters 5, 6, and 7 describe the massive political project of substituting ethnoreligious national identities for the former Yugoslav ideology of "brotherhood and unity." Nationalistic leaders on all sides promoted animosity between Muslims, Serbs, and Croats and marginalized those who refused to identify with a single nationality. Although many Sarajevans resisted the pressure to make ethnoreligious identity the basis for the state, the war itself enforced the primacy of national identities. Political elites did not simply mobilize people on the basis of preexisting differences or exploit old antagonisms opportunistically in their pursuit of power; the war itself acted as a major force in making ethnonational identities count. In this sense, political violence was more the cause than the result of ethnoreligious conflict.

While Chapters 6 and 7 explore the mobilization of religion by ethnonationalistic ideology and its increased importance in everyday life in Sarajevo, Chapter 5 deals with the less well known, but equally important, political and economic transformation carried out by the new nationalistic elites. Under the veil of different ethnoreligious traditions, now claimed as the basis of nationalistic projects, the prewar social welfare system was dismantled and replaced by capitalism of a highly exploitative kind. In this transformation, too, international, nationalistic, and neoliberal organizations and interests proved to be important, and the moral questions that arose in this context concern us all, not only the people of Sarajevo.

How did Sarajevans respond to these socioeconomic and ideological changes? Chapter 8 traces the ways they reorganized their everyday interactions under these politically charged circumstances. During the war, when people met, they almost invariably began by identifying one another's national identities. Even if they had known one another before, each assessed whether the other had changed as ethnoreligious identity became more salient. Behind the issue of national identity, though, lay more important questions: Was this person still worthy of trust? Could he or she be considered morally decent? Or had he or she crossed an ethical line beyond which further relation was morally impossible?

Finally, Chapter 9 moves to the front lines and then beyond them in the telling of the story of a middle-aged Sarajevan man who was at various points a civilian, a soldier, and a deserter. His is a fairly typical story, as this war conducted largely by nonstate armed forces against civilians by besieging the city blurred the distinctions that characterized conventional wars in the past. Here is a world in which the shock of war, the antagonistic logics of nationalism, and the moral imperative of taking responsibility for one's own actions in an unpredictable world coexist. When we grasp the civilian, soldier, and deserter perspectives on war, and let the necessity of their contradictions enter our own world, we come to comprehend the war as Sarajevans experienced it. The Epilogue looks back at Sarajevo on the twelfth anniversary of the Dayton Peace Accords, asking, as its residents and exiles do, what has become of Sarajevanness today.

Chapter 2
Death and Creativity in Wartime

Culture is after that permanence and durability which life, by itself, so sorely misses.
—*Zygmunt Bauman, 1992*

The fundamental difference between peacetime and wartime is that in war death and destruction are massive and unremitting. War acquires an all-encompassing quality that makes peace inconceivable. During our lives, we go through periods of confusion in which our understanding of the world does not help us to organize our experiences in a meaningful way. In peacetime we describe this unstable state as a life crisis. We wonder whether life has meaning when its predestination is death. Culture is central to the ways people create meaning in the face of death. In Western culture many have found death meaningful because it marks the limit of our existence and in that way makes it possible to grasp.[1] A life without limits is formless, an endless continuum or even a vacuum. Death enables us to define ourselves, and our mortality is an essential dimension of our identity. We deal with life crises and with death though our capacity to create new meanings in our profoundly altered situation.

When our civilian expectations of life are shattered by war, we search for ways to organize our shocking encounters with violence. However, even the most convincing explanations of "whose fault it is" and "which side is mine" are seldom long-lived in a war zone, as none of the warring sides provide protection and justice. When social institutions dissolve and meanings disappear, we use the full array of our cultural resources and inventiveness in order to make sense of our wartime existence.

Wartime conditions do not facilitate creativity, as Carolyn Nordstrom has pointed out (1997:15). Our capacity for making meaning often proves useless when we are confronted with the sudden terror of violent death and destruction. Mass murder is incomprehensible. While in peacetime we grad-ually reassess our situation in order to come to terms with death and loss, in wartime we must balance between acknowledging and ignoring the life-threatening circumstances in which we exist. Being too aware of the very real dangers we face inhibits our capacities not only to make sense of our situa-tion and respond to it creatively but even to cope with it from one moment to the next. When meanings evaporate as soon as we have imagined them, when whatever map of the new world we construct is shattered as soon as we construct it, we find ourselves in a "limit situation."

The experience of chaos that was characteristic of Sarajevans' struggle to recreate normality during the siege, as well as their constant oscillation be-tween knowing and not-knowing, was a typical limit situation, resembling the Holocaust and other instances of massive political violence. In limit sit-uations the scale of destruction makes life conditions unrecognizable and in-comprehensible: people feel powerless in the face of hostile forces; their survival or death is random; and the conditions of life are no longer morally recognizable as humane. Chaos and paranoia are the order of the day. In this situation, paranoia is not irrational but is founded on the experience that nothing can be trusted. In this "gray zone" (another term coined by Primo Levi [1989]), nothing is fixed and known; any action and view is potentially acceptable. Norms and normativity itself are eradicated. The debates that arose after the Holocaust about whether God still existed and whether poetry still was possible express this void of meaning.

This type of destruction surpasses anything that can easily be docu-mented or communicated. While material destruction and mass killing can be caught on film or summarized in statistics, the destruction of cultural meanings is hard to express, as the very creation of meaning becomes diffi-cult. The visible destruction caused by war has much deeper effects on us than meet the eye. It reminds us daily of our mortality, and by destroying our cultural artifacts it reminds us that there is no way in which we can achieve permanence. At the same time, the omnipresence of destruction that makes death a constant companion of people living in a war zone drives them to respond with startling creativity. They need not only to re-create culture through reshaping knowledge and forms of expression but also to deal with profound existential issues when death becomes possible, not in an unknown future some decades away, but any moment—as people are killed randomly, here and now, just a minute or a meter away from where one is standing.

The process of coming to terms with such fundamental existential

Figure 3. Vilsonovo šetaliste (Wilson's Promenade) in central Sarajevo, seen from Grbavica. March 1996. Photo by author.

changes centers on taking control over your life in spite of mounting evidence of your powerlessness.

During the first days of war people lived in a state of shock. Frightened, they hid in cellars without understanding what was going on. The awareness that the war would not be over in a few days came only gradually. An extraordinary situation had to be normalized under completely new circumstances. The first forays from shelters were short, in order to provide food, but over time became longer and freer. We started to stroll around the town searching for food or fuel. People went on with their lives and started increasingly to see themselves as the only reliable source of energy. Life began renewing itself, the culture livened up, and the hunt for survival started to take on meaning, but this was a completely different meaning from what the world is familiar with. One started to live a peculiar and dreadful life, which in its preposterousness seemed consummate. One lived with death as much as one lived with arts. No cultural activities stopped, but neither did the dying.

We lived a Spartan life and were more hungry than full. Almost all our strength went to the struggle for physical survival. Immeasurable time and energy were needed to provide water, food, wood. Under such circumstances the needs of an exhausted body lessen, and the soul seeks its peace wandering through the past. In a completely new way thought got nourishment and imagination wings. . . . As if a new inner need emerges, in a situation in which life is threatened and has lost its value, to establish an

Figure 4. A residential area on the front line between Serb-held Grbavica and the government-controlled part of Sarajevo. March 1996. Photo by author.

island of quiet understanding during a concert, theater performance, exhibition, or in the intercourse with thoughts and feelings of the characters in a book. . . .

An actor and theater manager in Sarajevo [said]: "It seemed as if we by performing in the moist cellar moved the walls and the entrance to that dark room. We scared away the fear from children's faces; they forgot what was happening out there." (F. Trtak 1996:28–30, my translation)

The same impulse that moved Sarajevans under siege to create art animated their daily struggles against death-dealing circumstances.

Comprehending this sort of destruction requires a description of the war "from within," as Michael Taussig (1992) has put it, rather than from the comparatively safe world outside. Photographs do not speak for themselves. Stig Dagerman, the Swedish writer and the first reporter to be sent to post-war Germany, wrote in a letter to a colleague and friend, dated November 8, 1946, about the state of mind and soul that comes from observing mass destruction:

In Hamburg one can get off the train at Landwehr and walk for an hour in any direction without seeing anything but inner walls and floors hanging like flags in their holds and frozen radiators clinging tightly as blowflies to their walls. It is nearly in the middle of the town and one does not see a human being for approximately an hour. I walked for three quarters of an hour toward the east, then I walked back. When I came home to the hotel I switched on the lamp over the mirror, thinking: If I do not look different there is something wrong, sir. Perhaps I should have gone west first.

Yes, in the beginning the mirrors were the worst, but afterward it takes no talent to understand that one can cope with seeing everything without going blind. It is not even gruesome to be here any more. It only makes one tired and one sleeps well at nights. (Dagerman 1996:115, my translation)

Everyone staying for some time in a war zone has similar experiences. The overwhelming destruction numbs one's sensitivity, the sight of death becomes an everyday fact, and exhaustion takes over after the initial rush of adrenaline in one's body. Most of the people I met in Sarajevo had experienced this shift. One woman said: "Before the war I thought how war is so awful, and if I was in the war I could not sleep for days, or something. But you are so tired from the grenades that you . . . [laughingly] you just fall down and sleep. That's . . . that was surprising, really." I was amazed at how quickly I got used to the devastation, first of the Croatian frontiers and later of Sarajevo. While I was there, I never took a step back and looked at the town through the lens of peacetime standards. I suppose that, like many a Sarajevan, my senses of mortality were sufficiently engaged with avoiding sniper fire and occasional shelling. My creative forces were concentrated on the task of documenting life during the war. I lost this state of mind and emotion only a few times, when I experienced what other people in Sarajevo experienced throughout the war: the awareness of having no power whatsoever over your own life, the feeling of meaninglessness that resulted, and the omnipresent emptiness. Although we are aware of our mortality, we seem to have a limit as to how much of this knowledge we can take in at a time. This human quality was expressed many times by

Figure 5. Although all of Sarajevo was subject to shelling and sniper fire, some parts of town were directly exposed to shooting from the mountains. Signs were posted in these places saying, "watch out, sniper" (*pazi snajper*) or "dangerous zone" (*opasna zona*). Sarajevo, spring 1996. Photo by author.

Sarajevans as a somewhat shameful amazement over their "getting used to it." They often wondered whether they would look and act normal to people outside Sarajevo, because they were aware that in the outside world the material destruction and deaths caused strong emotional, social, and political reactions. They themselves no longer felt this way, as a young woman described:

In the very beginning, every person killed was reported in all of the mass media. As time passed—it may sound a bit cruel, but it really is so—we started getting used to all those victims, and people began to turn into mere numbers. It was reported only: so and so many killed, so and so many hurt. . . . And then we came to a stage when they would for example report: ten hurt, and you would say: well, it isn't so many. Two or three killed—oh, then it is not so many today. You know. But that is terrible.

This numbness registered the war's excessive violence.

A play with this theme was put on in Sarajevo; it was based on the life and work of Mula Mustafa Bašeskija, a Sarajevan chronicler who lived in the eighteenth century (Lukić 1991). His "Chronicle" included a time of plague in Sarajevo. At the beginning of the plague people who died were named and their lives were briefly described: who they were, what they did, and their characters. Toward the end of the play, the narrator only reported that by that time thousands of people had died. The play ended with a long list of names of the recently deceased. The connection through two hundred years of the experience of the plague with the experience of the siege was simultaneously terrifying and tranquilizing. From the perspective of shared human experience, personal mortality lost its significance. Art was the form through which this awareness could be expressed. When the authorities renamed a part of Titova Road for Mula Mustafa Bašeskije, the notion of sharing the war experience beyond the limits of their own time and their own mortality effectively became incorporated into the body of the town.

It was only when the immediate danger to their own lives had diminished that Sarajevans were able to see the destruction and let it affect their feelings. In 1996, after the Dayton Peace Accords, a new graffito appeared saying "kad se saberem—oduzmem se" (when I pull myself together—I fall apart). A young woman's account of the effects of the first relatively long ceasefire in 1994 is characteristic: "For me it was much more difficult when the situation got better. . . . I felt terrible! The shooting ceased, but the town was very ugly looking. I mean, until then I didn't pay very much attention. All is so destroyed . . . Only the skeletons of the stores, so much garbage in the town. A lot of concrete, cement, glass, everything." In 1996, the situation was even more appalling, since along with the material destruction the destruction of the social, cultural, and moral fabric of the city became visible. The Dayton Peace Accords, cheered in 1995 because they stopped the shooting, were now understood for what they really were: an official and international formalization of the division of the country and people into three political and territorial entities, based on the different ethnoreligious backgrounds of people in Bosnia and Herzegovina. Until that moment, many

Sarajevans had hoped that those divisions would end with the war. This story of Sarajevo shows that this division was destructive in a way that residents found impossible to comprehend; it felt like more than Sarajevans could take—so they "fell apart."

To Know, Yet Not to Know

Entering Sarajevo for the first time, I was aware of the dangers awaiting me as I moved about in the town. I was fairly cautious and took every opportunity to learn the places where sniper fire and shelling were most likely. The most dangerous places in the center, I learned, were the crossroads around the Holiday Inn, as well as Hrasno and "Sniper Alley," parts of town bordering Grbavica, which was under Serbian control. This undertaking was of limited usefulness, since the danger was omnipresent and hovering over us. Looking toward the surrounding mountains, everyone could clearly see where the military positions were. It was almost a rule that wherever there were no trees, the territory was under the government's control; the trees had been cut by Sarajevans during the previous winters. In the forests you could see a blue UN flag here and there, which meant that on one side was the ABiH and on the other the Serbian Bosnian forces. The town was practically surrounded by Serbian positions. You could assume that almost every spot in the town from which you could see the mountains was a place where a sniper could see you.

As far as the shelling was concerned, the most dangerous places were around the Presidency Building in the center of the town, the public water pipes where long queues formed during the water shortages, and any other place where people gathered, such as marketplaces and bread lines. During the periods I spent in the town, there was not much shelling. Only once, in September 1994, as the ceasefire was coming to an end, did I experience random shooting and shelling of the town during the daytime. In March 1995, too, the city center was shelled at night. As people were used to much worse periods, I never spent long hours in a cellar. During lighter or intermittent shelling people hurried home, listened to the explosions in order to judge whether it was incoming or outgoing fire, estimated how far away the explosions were, and decided whether it would be necessary to leave the apartment for the cellar.

I became aware of the constant calculus of danger one evening during my first stay in Sarajevo, sitting on Kovači and chatting with a young Sarajevan woman I had met some days earlier, with whom I developed a friendship during the war years. We were waiting for Staffan, my Swedish colleague, to finish taking photographs of the newly extended cemetery. It was a pleasant September evening, sunny and quiet, and so was our mood. Suddenly she said agitatedly: "Now what is he doing? Does he think that he's on holiday on Hawaii?!" I was surprised, and suddenly became aware of the mountains and forests surrounding us. We could have hardly been more exposed. I felt nervous, but there was really nothing to do. I asked her whether I should fetch my colleague, but we saw him coming so we just got up and continued our walk.

This episode taught me that even when people did not show it, they were always subliminally aware of their exposure, and some half-conscious meter in them constantly measured the necessity of an errand against the odds of being shot at. Sitting on Kovači was a necessary exposure, since we were there to see the town and document local life. But the meter in my new friend at one point indicated to her that we had been there for too long.

How did she know when it started to be too dangerous? The answer is: she did not. And this was one of the basic arts you had to learn in Sarajevo during the war. You had to be aware of the dangers and at the same time ignore them because there was not much that could be done about them. During my second stay in Sarajevo I heard a joke that captured the incomprehensibility and irrationality of Sarajevans' situation, in which Sarajevans found some sort of shared logic that guided their lives: An American team of psychologists came to study Sarajevans. They went around the town asking people, "What is 3 times 3?" The first person answered "Tuesday." The second person answered "365." The third person said "9." "Well, how did you come to that answer?" the psychologists asked the third person. "Well, it is simple," the research subject responded: "Tuesday minus 365 is 9!"

As an example of stupid behavior, I was told about an ignorant foreign humanitarian worker who tied her shoes in the middle of the Holiday Inn crossroads. While the privileged foreigner was condemned for being unaware of the dangers, the ignorance of Sarajevans at the beginning of the war was described rather as childlike. A young woman explained:

For instance, when there was shooting, I could peep through the window. My dad told me: "Hide yourself, you see that there is shooting!" And I hid behind the blinds, and I was supposedly safe there because I didn't see the street any more. Or in the bus, or in the tram. . . . If at Marindvor you could hear a sniper, people might raise up their hand, so as not to see the side from where it was shooting. . . . Someone could put up newspapers, women their bags, they covered the children. . . . Or, if there was shelling you could hear it whizzing. You knew that it would fall somewhere near or

Figure 6. Gathering in front of the Catholic cathedral in central Sarajevo. Sarajevans used to linger there after mass even though they were directly exposed to shooting from the surrounding mountains. Sarajevo, October 1995. Photo by author.

that it had already fallen, and then everyone ran and pulled their heads between their shoulders. As if you pull your head in a bit, and you've escaped the shell.

I remember my own reaction to my first air-raid alarm in Zagreb in September 1991. I was alone in my great-aunt's apartment on the fifth floor of a building near the center of the town. As I heard the sirens, I decided to go downstairs and see what the others would do. I took the staircase, having learned during earthquakes in my childhood not to take the elevator in such situations. I had also been told not to panic and rush, because many people had been trampled in the subways during the Blitz in London. I found people gathered on the ground floor. Some tried to convince children to go to the basement, but most of us went out to see what was going on. It was very quiet, unusual for a city with nearly a million inhabitants. We could only hear an occasional car speeding along the empty streets. We were looking at the skies in order to spot airplanes. The only problem was that the entrance of the building where we were standing faced north, and the military air base from which the planes were coming was to the south. But none of us seemed aware of that fact. We just stood there, watching in the wrong direction and exposing ourselves completely unnecessarily, with the feeling that we somehow were in control of the situation!

Afterward, when I thought about it, I remembered what a soldier told me in Nova Gradiška, a town on the front line toward Serb-controlled territories in Slavonia. "It is the first bomb that kills. Because that is the one people watch out for. If you don't get hit by the first one, the others, no matter how many they are, won't harm you because you'd be in a shelter by that time." The young woman who described naively hiding bullets and shells from view continued: "But when the first shells exploded in front of our building, and when the shrapnel from the neighboring apartment went through our apartment, well, then we started to take shelter. . . . Either in our hall, or by going out to the staircase, so that we wouldn't be near the doors or windows. And there were days when the shelling was going on all the time, and when all of us were in the cellar for the whole day."

People behaved irrationally at the beginning because they could not recognize real danger. They could make stupid choices because they were still reasoning within their peacetime standards. As their experience of the war grew, some Sarajevans were seized by fear that could become paralyzing. They called those who were too scared and who sat in their cellars all the time *podrumaši*, cellar people. Being so frightened was judged as a weakness and staying in the cellar was regarded as absurd, because in war there was no way to protect oneself. I was told several versions of a common story that was meant to prove this point. Some person, a young man hiding from the armed service, or a panicky older woman, spent all of the first two years until the ceasefire in the spring and summer of 1994 in the cellar, firmly refusing to go out. The relatives provided him or her with the necessities. When it was finally quiet, the person dared to go out for the first time and got killed by a random sniper bullet or one of the few shells. The moral of the story: if you were meant to get killed you would, no matter what you did. Trying to protect yourself entirely was futile, it made your life even more restricted, and any semblance of normal life vanished.

During the war it became acceptable to be afraid, even for men who traditionally were not supposed to show their fear. In such extremely dangerous circumstances it was impossible not to be afraid, so social norms adapted to the situation. Sharing fear and having it acknowledged enabled people to cope with it when necessary. As a young soldier told me, everyone was afraid, and what was important was not to be overcome by panic. At the front lines, if you felt afraid it was okay, because you knew that the guy on the other side of the front line was afraid, too. If you happened to meet face to face with an enemy soldier, you could count on both of you being afraid, and you could either shoot him or hide. But if you panicked, if you lost control of yourself, then he would certainly shoot you.

Casualties and fatalities were a fact of life. People got shot at, got hit, and got killed. In the *Sarajevo Survival Map* I read: "The State Museum . . . was on the front line. . . . The building was hit by more than 420 shells. . . . In front of the museum stood a UN transporter that was supposed to protect the citizens riding in the trams. A lot of people were killed and injured on that spot" (Kapić 1996). The first time I went there to meet an acquaintance for an interview, she told me that a woman had been killed there earlier the same day. The first time I experienced direct shooting was also there. The shots came from Grbavica, in front of UN soldiers in their tanks who did nothing to protect me. At first I bent over, ran, and swore. But soon I started to feel numb, heavy and empty, instantly depressed. Seized by the paralyzing realization that I had no control over my life, I lost all will to do anything. When I thought about it afterward I understood that what was happening inside me was a half-conscious realization that my life—all I ever did, my qualities and qualifications, the righteous purpose of my being in Sarajevo—was no longer worth anything. I remember a soldier on the Croatian front line showing me a bullet. "You see this bullet?" he asked. "That's how much your life is worth in war: 1 deutsche mark!" In Sarajevo, being confronted with my mortality in this direct way rendered all cultural phenomena, including money, meaningless. My life was not worth even a deutsche mark! After a day, when I managed to convince myself that my stay was worthwhile and worked out a way of exposing myself as little as possible, the depression disappeared. My world was reestablished through reaffirmation of my own values.

Most Sarajevans experienced this seemingly never-ending pendulum swing between strength and depression. Periods when they could dismiss the dangers of their situation were followed by periods when their sense of normality was fractured, and then they had to struggle to reaffirm their sense of purpose, even of self.

The circle of fright starts with the fear for one's life and ends with the fear of death. And so it goes on in a continuous circle—with a rational beginning and a rational end, or with an irrational end and an irrational beginning—and so on to infinity. Altogether it develops into a fright of the fear itself, which threatens to become an all-encompassing feeling. And so a new fear emerges, which is not cowardice, but a fear that one might lose one's fear and become a hero. And then the fear appears anew. (F. Trtak 1996:29, my translation)

People developed various techniques for dealing with snipers and shells, but there was really not much to do about it in practice. Strength lay in the belief that you could survive.

For instance, people did not look at the sniper positions all of the time. Indeed, some people never looked, on the theory that if you looked at them they would shoot you. Others cast a confident glance toward snipers when passing the dangerous places to show that they were not afraid. Some thought that it was wise to go firmly but not too fast, in order not to provoke the snipers by showing fear. Others thought that it was better to speed up a bit, or even run if necessary, in order to show the snipers that they were aware of them, which would satisfy the snipers and keep them from shooting. All these strategies were equally futile in terms of avoiding getting shot; they helped people deal with being in a situation that was beyond their control.

A young woman described her reactions to the constant threat of snipers while moving about in the town:

Every day I used to pass one part where a sniper was shooting all the time. I don't know if it was because of pride or some sort of obstinacy and stubbornness, but I didn't want to run. . . . It often happened that I looked toward the hills like I could see whether he was going to shoot or not. [laughter] As if, to see first, and then I could hurry a bit, then stop, and so on. . . . Only when I heard shots all the time would I stop, and then again that instinct would start working, so—run as fast as your legs can carry you!

To run or not to run became a question of pride and humiliation. Like many Sarajevans, at some point in the war my host felt humiliated because he was being forced by some "primitive maniac" (that is, a sniper) to run in his own town. So he stopped running. He went firmly, with his head held high, straight over the most dangerous crossroads, feeling good because in this way he restored his dignity and showed the "primitives" that they could not break him. And so he continued for some time, until one day, in the middle of a dangerous crossroad, he came to think of his daughter in exile. Suddenly he was struck by the thought of what pain it would cause her if he got killed—and he ran as fast as he could!

To realize that one's life or death was out of one's hands could cause depression, and people had to ignore this fact in order to get on with their lives as best as they could. To lose control over one's life to some unknown person's whim was an utterly humiliating experience. To reassert some sense of control, at least to choose whether they would live in fear or not, enabled people to regain some pride.

I remember how all of us in a Zagreb NGO in 1993 were amazed to meet a refugee who had come directly from Sarajevo to the headquarters. The man was wearing a perfectly white and ironed shirt with a perfectly new and proper tie: he was not exactly the picture of refugee we expected, since we were aware of the shortages and knew that he had come through the tunnel. A young woman in Sarajevo explained:

The war did not affect my way of dressing. . . . It could be 15 to 20 degrees below freezing outside and 8 below in the room, but I had to wash my hair each time before I went on duty, so that my hair was clean when I worked, so that I was fresh, so that my lab coat was always washed and ironed, so that I wouldn't go around untidy. It was probably a way of fighting back. During the time of the worst shelling and lack of water and gas and electricity, when the conditions were really miserable, I noticed that people were clean and ironed, and tidy. It was so during the whole of the war.

People struggled, not so much to maintain some prewar standard of decency, as for emotional and moral survival in the face of overwhelming degradation. Sarajevans were unable to prevent the decline of living standards, but they could still choose to look like citizens of a European city. In that way, they tried to take decisions about how to live their lives into their own hands.

The darkness of long winter nights was one of the most difficult disruptions Sarajevans had to cope with. A young woman's account from September 1994 describes how people were thrown back on themselves:

The worst thing is that it gets dark early. You see already now—it is dark at half past seven. Eight o'clock, and there is no electricity. Terrible. You don't know what to do with yourself. . . . And there is shooting . . . you can't go anywhere. . . . You can't read, you can't do anything. Like, you strain yourself to read by candle, you lose time, and then you go to sleep at seven, eight. . . .

As soon as I started thinking of what was happening to me, what I could have done, what I didn't, what I could and what I couldn't, I would fall into a crisis. And that leads nowhere. And then it is better not to think about these things, but just go on, as long as it goes.

With nowhere to go and nothing to do, alone with their thoughts and sounds of explosions outside, Sarajevans were imprisoned by darkness. Fighting off this sense of isolation and utter powerlessness demanded great inner strength. Memories of prewar life were a double-edged sword: they helped people escape from the wartime destruction, yet thoughts of the life they once had were painful. An old Jewish curse captured the pain of loss: "May God let you have, and then not have."

A cultural worker of Sarajevo evoked the words of Dante as well as the music and words of the Hebrew slaves in "Va, pensiero" from Verdi's *Nabucco*, where the destruction of the beloved land and the tormenting memories of the better past, including dear ones now far away, end with a plea to the Lord to "inspire a harmony that we may have the strength to endure":

The long winter night starts at 4 PM. It is cold in the room and there is only one flickering candle light. One cannot read and that which one writes is illegible the following day. The thoughts come to a standstill and continuously go back to the past, and one realizes that Dante was right when he wrote: "Nothing is so painful as to in misfortune remember the happy moments." You get overwhelmed by despair and escape to bed from the 'Choir of Hebrew Prisoners' in Verdi's *Nabucco*: "Go, thoughts, on golden wings. . . ." You cannot sing, cannot hum, but you feel a need to sing out loudly, so that everyone hears and joins in the song. When the eyes fill with tears the catharsis has come to its end. You get used to the idea that the following day shall be the same and you prepare yourself for the sources of happiness that are going to be found in small changes. And the melody of the Hebrew prisoners' choir resonates in you, for you. It does not take much to feel happiness the following day: a look from a neighbor and it is a triumph if the fetching of water goes a quarter of an hour faster than the day before. (F. Trtak 1996:29, my translation)

The most intimate thoughts, coming when imprisonment by darkness left people nothing but the freedom of mind and soul, could find expression in something larger than the vulnerable individual life: a connection across time and space, a sense of belonging to humankind, which is achieved through art.

Magical Thinking

People coped with life conditions beyond their ability to control or even comprehend through magical thinking and small private magic routines, another "childish" solution to an objectively unbearable situation. I was surprised to find myself engaging in magical rituals. The first time I was on my way to Sarajevo, my grandmother, who had never read horoscopes and certainly did not believe in them, said that my horoscope was good for the period I planned to remain there. Although we acknowledged our skepticism with a chuckle, we were both glad that the horoscope was propitious. Knowing there was nothing practical I could do to improve my security, I also looked for a protective amulet to take with me. I did not find one, but when I left Sarajevo I realized that the shoes I had worn were the same ones that I had worn during my visits to Croatian and Herzegovinian front lines in 1993. From then on, I wore my anti-sniper shoes every time I was in Sarajevo.

Many people in Sarajevo told me that in the middle of shooting and shelling they would resort to some prayer. As religious observance was not common in prewar Sarajevo, most did not know how to pray, and people of Muslim background often did not even know how to pronounce the words. But still, praying gave people a feeling of protection. A secularized woman from a Muslim background said:

Shells were falling, I was going out, I had to water the garden, because it was important for me that the cabbage plants grow, so that I could survive, and I went and I prayed to God. . . . In the Muslim way, I don't know any other way. . . . I know only "bilsmilah ilahim rahim," everyone can learn that, even a two-year-old child. And I prayed to God. Why? Only to chase away the fear, not because I believe, because of my own security. . . . I felt safer when I went out like that. There, I thought, some higher power will save me.

For a religious young woman from a Catholic family, the belief in a suprahuman power had a stronger and broader protective effect:

My family is religious, practicing believers. . . . It helped us through the war in a much more painless way than the others. I tell you, even if He was dead, there is something. There is God. . . . Look, people were losing hands, legs, heads. Whole families. I didn't lose anything. You know, I have to knock on wood. [laughter] I didn't lose anyone or anything. . . . We never went to bed hungry or thirsty, while people were dying of hunger. I never froze. . . . I was singing in the cathedral choir. Boy, ooooh it was madness, shooting from all directions! . . . You have probably seen where the organs are in the cathedral. There is a rosette through which they could spit from Trebević [the mountain facing the cathedral entrance], let alone fire a shell. And there were hundreds of young people in the choir. And no one got hurt. You know, I don't need better proof.

As former unbelievers, as well as religiously observant people, prayed to God in situations of danger, religious practices facilitated the entrance of the nationalist political project—the division of the former Yugoslavia into separate ethnoreligious states—into the most private dimensions of life. Religion was often invoked as a vague reminiscence from childhood, such as a grandmother praying, or ascribed as an identity by being an offspring of one of the three major religious traditions. Sarajevans noticed the irony of dividing into three groups through praying in three different ways to God, because they perceived God as one and the same.

Some Sarajevans of Muslim background took their newly discovered belief in destiny as a proof that their Muslim roots really mattered, since belief in destiny was perceived as one of the characteristics of Islam. But many more understood it as a philosophical recognition that their lives were entirely out of their hands. It was a way of rationalizing away the dangers in order to do the daily errands. A middle-aged woman told me: "I was not afraid at all, you know. . . . You never know whether you must rush or go slowly, whether you go toward your mortar shell or you run away from it. . . . You just go and think about that it is some sort of destiny, or something like that."

Others made logical arguments to themselves in order to dispel their awareness of danger. The probability of getting killed in Sarajevo was no larger than in any big city anywhere in the world: people were more likely to be injured in traffic accidents and violent crimes in New York City than to be injured by shells and snipers in Sarajevo, I was told. As in the story about cellar people (*podrumaši*), the moral was that dwelling on or even thinking about the dangers was useless. Or, as the young soldier told me, a way of keeping yourself together at the front was to realize that the soldiers on the other side were just as scared as you were.

I found that being with someone and talking about something else was a good way of forgetting that you were constantly within the sight and reach of shells and bullets. If you were walking alone, the best thing was to think about things you had done, people you had met, or what they had said.

It was impossible to keep these illusions continuously intact. Everyone went though cycles of not caring, followed by periods of fear and feeling exposed. When I asked one of my friends how she felt after a shell exploded in her garden only a few seconds after she went into the house, she said she felt miserable. After such an experience she usually called a friend to talk, made something special to eat or drink, or did "something nice—to forget it." Her technique was to reaffirm life in a way that brought back feelings of comfort and security.

Sarajevan Humor

Naming, or even caricaturing the myriad disruptions of normality was an effective way of resisting distressing conditions and of preserving prewar norms or creating new values amid the war. Joking was a significant form of resilience in Sarajevo. Not only could the most painful problems and traumas be expressed and shared through jokes, but their self-mocking perspective achieved a sense of control and distancing from everyday circumstances. These jokes were always directed at those with whom the speaker identified, the stereotyped "us," rather than at the stereotyped "other," as in many ethnic jokes or other instances of wartime humor.

In the former Yugoslavia Bosnians were known for poking fun at themselves, and this practice continued throughout the war. Jokes about two Bosnian characters, Mujo (Muhamed) and Suljo (Sulejman), sometimes accompanied by the female character Fata (Fatima), were plentiful and very popular. The characters were naive, yet shrewd. One of the first jokes that appeared during the war was about Mujo and Suljo fleeing Bosnia and seeking refuge in Slovenia, where Bosnians were mainly known as immigrant laborers and had a lower status than Slovenes. When Mujo and Suljo got to the river that marked the Slovenian border, they found it difficult to get across and made a little boat that could bear only one at a time. Mujo got in first, and when he landed on the Slovenian side Suljo called to him: "Come on Mujo, send the boat back so that I can also get over!" Mujo answered from the other side: "Get lost, you Bosnian. Who cares about you?!" The joke was based on Slovenian feelings of superiority, but the sting in it lay in Bosnians' critique of the unscrupulousness of their fellow Bosnians.

This quality of being able to laugh at oneself characterized the youth culture of Sarajevo before and during the war. If you were to be accepted as one of the group (*raja*), you had to show this capacity. Not knowing this, I was put to the test by some young people with whom I spent a lot of time during my stays in Sarajevo. The situation was totally ludicrous, and I was perplexed about it for some time. One night, when I was walking home with two friends after a nice evening together, the moon was shining brightly above one of the totally destroyed houses in the town center. I was taken by the atmosphere and, as all of us were accustomed to ruins, I declared romantically: "What lovely moonlight." The girl in my company, whom I had gotten to know fairly well by that time, looked puzzled for a moment, looked at the ruined house, and then started to laugh. "Lovely moonlight!" She could not stop laughing and repeating this stupid sentence. I was puzzled and tried to explain myself, but she and the fellow who was with us kept laughing, and eventually I started laughing too. Whenever I tried to change the subject, they started laughing and repeating what I had said. Eventually, when this continued for weeks, I got annoyed. Every time we met it was impossible to start talking because my friend would repeat my comment about the moonlight and start laughing, and whomever we met would be informed of the good joke. After I got back to Sweden, I told another Sarajevan friend about this incident, and she explained to me in a matter-of-fact, dry, un-Sarajevan way that this was the way young people showed that they liked each other and considered them to be their *raja*. But then she too started laughing, and as I stood there bewildered, she realized that I did not know that what I had said was a line from a joke about Mujo and Fata. When Fata complained that Mujo was only interested in sex, Mujo, trying to be a romantic lover, said, "Look, Fata, what lovely moonlight!" before he threw himself all over her as usual. As the joke was very popular in Sarajevo, if not the rest of Bosnia and Herzegovina, it never occurred to my Sarajevan friends that I could not know it. Suddenly my cultural incompetence was revealed, and my friend in Sweden could not resist concluding jokingly: "You see, we *are* different, and it is right that we no longer live in the same country," meaning Croats and Bosnian Muslims. She enjoyed making this comment, as both she and her parents were emotional Yugonostalgists. Because I was unaware of the joke, I could not laugh at myself for saying this line, as I otherwise probably would have done. I am not sure whether I passed the test, but I might have been forgiven since I was born in a dry and cold place like Zagreb and lived in an even worse one, Sweden. In any case, we remained friends.

Jokes were a typical way of commenting upon situations of destruction and humiliation. For example, the joke that runs, "What/how[2] does a smart Bosnian call a stupid one? From a phone abroad!" expressed one of the most acute dilemmas during the war: to leave or not to leave. By sharing the joke, people were letting one another know that they shared the same problem.

Many of the jokes were impossible to tell outside the town because of

Figure 7. "Maybe Airlines," check-in desk for UN flights from Sarajevo. Sarajevo, October 1995. Photo by author.

their macabre humor.[3] People who did not have the same sort of experience, who judged situations by peacetime standards, had no way to appreciate such jokes. Instead, they tended to find them disturbing and morbid, as was the case with the joke that went: "What is the difference between Sarajevo and Auschwitz? There is no gas in Sarajevo."

In their daily lives, people did all they could to take verbal revenge on those whom they saw as the cause of a particular disruption. The twenty-year-old biscuit that was sent as humanitarian aid from the United States was called a "Vietnam cookie," implying that the United States was getting rid of leftovers from the Vietnam War. The out-of-date powdered eggs were called "Truman's eggs," as they had been in the aftermath of the Second World War; in local language, the same word means both "eggs" and "testicles."

In jokes snipers were made into fools, as in the joke where Mujo killed Suljo with his sniper rifle. The astonished people asked, "Mujo! Why on earth did you kill your brother [in the Muslim faith], Suljo?" "Well, you never know these days," answered Mujo. "I saw Suljo and when I looked through the sniperscope I saw a big cross on his forehead. So I fired." The cross was in the rifle sight, but Mujo thought that it was on Suljo's forehead, which would mean that Suljo had become Christian and gone over to the enemy. Another joke that ridicules snipers was about an old man rocking in his rocking chair by the river where the snipers were continuously shooting. A passerby asked him what he was doing. "Teasing the sniper," answered the old man.

Even the UN soldiers stationed in Sarajevo adopted the same sense of humor: they called their air bridge to Sarajevo "Maybe Airlines," insinuating that anything could happen and nothing could be counted on. The last time I was at the Sarajevo airport a little advertisement was hanging at the check-in desk (see fig. 7). It was possible to hang up the advertisement after the resignation of Yasushi Akashi, the UN's highest civilian commander of the operation in the former Yugoslavia, who had prohibited the joke about the UN air bridge in 1993. In 1994 a UN officer complained to me that it was a bad sign if the highest authority for the whole operation did not have a sense of humor. To me, it seems that Akashi did not have the Sarajevan sense of humor, which implies that he did not have the same life-references that the civilian population and UN soldiers did. From this perspective, it is not surprising that the UN operation did not do much for the people of Sarajevo. Akashi acted in the "soldier" mode of relating to the war, rather than perceiving war as those with firsthand experience did. Sarajevans and UN soldiers serving in Sarajevo had more critical distance on the war, and their war-specific sense of humor often articulated the "deserter" mode of understanding.

Artistic Life

The determination to resist the omnipresence of war, the impulse to deny or forget it, the desire to feel some continuity with prewar life, the drive to express and share experiences, and the need to feel connected with others beyond the limits of the besieged town, the aspiration toward a sense of pan-human belonging—all resulted in an amazingly active artistic life in Sarajevo.

Under the circumstances in which the new was not death but continuing to live, when one was forced to accept the despair as a normal human condition, arts became the fount of the life-force. It gave back life to people, gave birth anew to optimism and strength, and gave meaning in a time when it looked as if life had lost all meaning. In surroundings where all was dead and threatened by death, this old human—and in these circumstances new—companion gave permanency and existence to a threatened and degraded life and showed the indestructibility and the beauty of the spiritual life. (F. Trtak 1996:31, my translation)

A coordinator of arts and entertainment in Sarajevo throughout his professional life, Fahrija Trtak gathered materials about the many cultural events taking place during the war and generously donated them to me.

Individual musicians, artists, writers, and other cultural workers performing alone or together, . . . anonymous individuals who organized soirées in their residence quarters, cellars, apartments, and backyards, . . . various types of amateur companies. . . . Many a foreign artist and cultural worker participated in the cultural life of Sarajevo. All of them came to help. They were there with completed programs, they directed plays, prepared and organized exhibitions, played music, filmed, started collaborations, planned aid and guest performances, and also taught. Over eighty performances by Sarajevan theatres were staged in fifty-nine European cities; painters and sculptors from Sarajevo exhibited in thirty-four countries; musicians performed in all important European centers. Films made in Sarajevo were shown in fifty-two international festivals [during the period from April 1992 until April 1995]. . . . The cultural activities had the scale and content resembling those of peacetime. . . . The cultural life of besieged Sarajevo refutes the Latin proverb *Inter armas musae silent*, "While weapons talk Muses become silent." In Sarajevo Muses did not become silent. (Trtak 1996:30, my translation)

In the situation of extreme existential danger, people needed the creative force that the arts provide. By performing internationally to the extent that they did, Sarajevan artists were able to call world attention to the plight of Sarajevo. At the same time it also gave them an opportunity to come out of the siege and reconnect to the normal world, which everybody longed for. Some probably used this opportunity to seek asylum and stay abroad.

In the town, Sarajevans performed and attended performances against all odds, and every performance was a victory of civilian life over the war. Lest the city's surprisingly vibrant cultural life convey the misimpression that Sarajevans engaged daily in the production and consumption of art, however, we must note that the significance of these artistic events lay mostly in the fact that they were happening at all and that it was possible once in a while to attend them. A secularized Muslim woman explained: "We used to

go to the concerts, to the theater. . . . I could not go very often because most
of them were at twelve or at one o'clock, when I was at school. . . . It was because of the electricity. They could not give a performance in the evening
without electricity, so they performed during the daylight."

Most people rarely went to the town center because it was so dangerous.
Instead, they made time pass in different ways. A young doctor of medicine
said: "I read anything that came into my hands, especially while on duty. We
worked every third or fourth day in order to minimize the need to go out. . . .
We stayed at work for twenty-four hours, but you didn't have to work all of
these twenty-four hours. . . . We exchanged books, just . . . to make the time
somehow pass." Reading books kept Sarajevans connected to the world outside, to humanity at large.

One of the most powerful symbolic events was the staging of the anti-
Vietnam War musical *Hair*. A middle-aged woman recalled: "I can remember *Hair* in the Chamber Theater. When I went, there was shelling, you know,
and you just had to run to get there. But the performance was . . . so nice. . . .
Most of the people were crying, really, during the performance, because . . .
it was a change, you know, a small one. It was a change in the way that it reminded us that this war was not the only one." I remember myself, seeing the
film some years later in Sweden, crying at the scene of Hercules airplanes
swallowing young men like gigantic metal monsters. My Swedish friends
were surprised, perhaps thinking that I, who had flown in and out of Sarajevo in a Hercules several times, would be skeptical of this well-known scene.
But I became overwhelmed with sorrow that we humans repeatedly produce
this inhuman, cold machinery that destroys innocent life under the pretext
of "righteous" causes. The Hercules, in that moment, symbolically connected
the suffering of the flower-power generation to the suffering of Sarajevans.
While my tears flowed because of the never-ending cycles of meaningless violence, Sarajevans cried because they felt, for once, understood by the world,
or at least that they had something in common with others. Running under
the shells was worth it on that day.

Many performances, concerts, and exhibitions featured anti-war mes-
sages. In the center of the town, figurative artists constructed their sculptures
and installations with material from demolished cars, houses, and any other
war-destroyed objects, which were plentiful. Using the remnants of demolished objects was common during the war, in part because this was the only
material available. The contrast between destruction and creativity bespoke
of a tremendous creative life force. In the spring of 1996, an exhibition was
held in the completely burned-out central post office building. The iron

Figure 8. A sculpture by Sarajevan sculptor Enes Sivac made of salvaged metal for a joint exhibition by Sarajevan artists in the destroyed central post office building. Sarajevo, March 1996. Photo by author; reproduced courtesy of Enes Sivac.

sculptures and large paintings that had been hung against the background of the remaining walls of the shattered building had a powerful artistic effect.

Sarajevan artists frequently evoked the Winter Olympic Games of 1984, which had put Sarajevo on the world map. No previous event in the former Yugoslavia had aroused so much professional and emotional engagement. Sarajevans were instructed to be open and welcoming to the international guests, which gave rise to many jokes about Bosnians treating the foreigners in an overly familiar way. "Hey, Japanese, you've lost your glove!" ("Japanka,

Figure 9. The painting *All I Need Is Love* by Sarajevan artist Amra Zulfikarpašić, part of the exhibition in the destroyed central post office building. Sarajevo, March 1996. Photo by author; reproduced courtesy of Amra Zulfikarpašić.

ispala ti je rukavica!"), shouts Mujo after an Asian-looking visitor. Mujo, who would otherwise have stolen the glove, followed the authorities' instructions to be honest and friendly. His provincialism shows in the way he addresses the stranger; he is not familiar with polite expressions such as "excuse me" or "madam," because everyone he had addressed during his whole life was a relative or a neighbor whose name he knew. His self-assured way of talking to the foreign woman in his own mother tongue shows his naiveté; more educated and self-conscious people would have been embarrassed at not know-

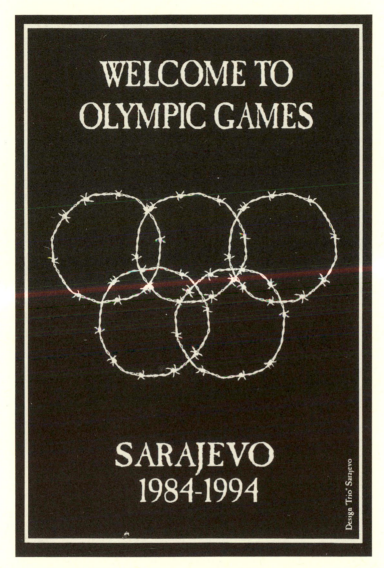

Figure 10. Postcard by the Sarajevan design group Trio on the tenth anniversary of the Olympic Games in Sarajevo. A note on the back reads: "This document has been printed in war circumstances. No paper, no inks, no electricity, no water. Just good-will." Purchased in March 1995; reproduced courtesy of Trio.

ing some international language. Mujo's communication is more direct, more childish, but also purer. As a stereotype of Bosnian self-perception, Mujo comes off as provincial and bad-mannered but open-hearted in his naive sincerity toward others. In the context of war and the UN involvement at the site of the Olympic Games, the message is morally loaded: we were open to you and met you in our innocence, although we might not have been familiar with your international rules of conduct. In peace you were happy to be here, but in war, when we needed you, you let us down.

International reputation, competence, "brotherhood and unity," peaceful competition between nations—the games symbolized all that was lost in the war.[4] Remembering the games was a way of connecting the besieged town with the rest of the world, with the peacetime and civilized mode of existence that was regarded as normal, reminding both local residents and the rest of the world that Sarajevo once was a part of it. Sarajevans hoped that reminding the world of the Olympic Games would make the world understand that there was nothing unusual or peculiar about Bosnians, and in this way break through outsiders' passivity and apparent incomprehension of, or indifference to, the humanitarian disaster taking place in the city. As Sarajevans became exiled from the world, they turned their longing and hope into hostile retreat. This reaction resembled individuals' responses to being left alone involuntarily: if you don't want me, I can do without you! In this way, the humiliation that rejection and ostracism entails is replaced with injured pride.

The reactions of Sarajevans to their abnormal life circumstances kept them mobilized in a fight for survival. At the same time, they spontaneously developed a wide range of useful psychological techniques for coping with situations that were objectively beyond their control, or humanly unbearable. Often the first thing we do when we cannot stand a situation is talk to someone else and share our predicament. If we cannot change the situation, with the help of others' empathic understanding we can come to accept it. When things are bad, maintaining a structured daily routine and taking physical care of ourselves helps us keep our emotional balance. Both Eastern disciplines such as yoga and Western psychotherapy aim to keep people centered and preserve their sense of balance despite the stresses upon them. This feeling is even more important when the situation is objectively out of people's hands, as it was in Sarajevo. The psychological competence that in peacetime grows gradually, often in connection with life crises, in war becomes a matter of survival. In wartime, people must mature rapidly, which is probably why those who have not experienced war often appear naive in comparison with a war survivor.[5] But even more crucially, while in peacetime psychological competence helps us to orient ourselves in the world, in war these techniques help us to maintain a bearable inner world despite unbearable outward circumstances. When people in Sarajevo listened to their inner impulses in situations where dangers were entirely unpredictable, they acted on the basis of their own self-awareness and avoided becoming lost in hopelessness. Sarajevans compensated for the impossibility of living comfortably in the world with fantasies and positive thinking, ignoring, denying, or rationalizing away the dangers. Magic routines and belief in some power beyond human comprehension helped some cling to hope in a hopeless situation. Sarajevans created distance from intolerable circumstances through naming them, talking about them, joking, and treating them ironically. For a moment, they could experience their predicament from a detached perspective. Through the arts, they created positive aesthetic experiences that countered the everyday fact of destruction.

Chapter 3
Struggling for Subsistence

If I have three children, I shall call them Electricity, Water, and Gas!
—A ten-year-old boy in Sarajevo

Sarajevans struggled to secure basic necessities during the war. The effort to provide everyday subsistence not only tested people's endurance and adaptive capacities but also called forth their ingenuity and black humor. Some Sarajevans described their wartime existence as an "imitation of life," highlighting their sense that the prewar routines they tried to maintain under the siege had been emptied of their previous meanings. Sarajevans experienced the material deficits imposed by the siege with a deep sense of shame and humiliation, feeling keenly their inability to sustain prewar norms of decency, independence, and hospitality. Nevertheless, continuing peacetime routines as much as possible proved to be a powerful tool, enabling people to retain their sense of dignity and strengthening their will to fight for survival. They took pride in the creative expedients they devised to cope with deprivation and attained some sense of agency despite their powerlessness. In sociocultural terms, the imitation of life served as a way of preserving customs and norms even when they could not be fully practiced and wartime existence resembled the desired way of living only in form. This strategy created sociocultural continuity between prewar and postwar life once circumstances allowed for the reestablishment of what was considered normal.

Under wartime conditions, preserving normal forms of life required people to engage in activities that were highly abnormal and they found personally humiliating as well as anxiety producing. A young woman told me in 1994:

Everyone is well dressed, cafés are open, music is playing. And everyone looks somehow normal. But in reality everyone is troubled by the same worries. . . . Men think about their next trip to the front lines, . . . what will happen when the winter comes, what will happen at home, how to provide . . . who shall provide. . . . Now, you're sitting in a café, enjoying . . . but when you come home you have to fetch water, you have to stand for hours, you have to drag those canisters. . . . But, like, we all make efforts to somehow look normal.

Making an effort to appear normal was important to Sarajevans, enabling them to feel less defeated by their circumstances than they might otherwise have done. The ways in which people confronted the uncertainties and profound changes in the terms of life during wartime are visible in their coping with most basic facets of material existence. To adults, getting water and finding a source of heat were unfamiliar and difficult chores. As children growing up in the state of siege recognized, electricity, water, and gas were so rare and precious that they were celebrated.

The breakdown of norms and shifts in values that seemed unavoidable in wartime remained troubling to many, however. What happened to social norms of reciprocity and solidarity, enacted in hospitality and mutual aid, when theft, smuggling, and plunder became commonplace? What happened when people who were proud of their independence were forced to depend upon humanitarian aid and what they considered charity? What happened to Sarajevans' secular culture when material survival often depended upon assuming a public religious affiliation?

When I first came to Sarajevo I was told a story about a man who found himself in a place of utter immorality. He gathered his civil courage and stood up, agitating for a better life. The authorities let him talk, but nobody listened to him. The years went by, and he daily repeated his message to people, but no one listened. One day a passerby asked him, "Why do you still repeat the same stuff when you see that no one listens?" The man answered, "In the beginning, I spoke because I thought I could change the people and the way they were living. Now, I repeat it so that I will not forget."

Preserving the memory and form of prewar life at a time when its contents had been totally destroyed and filled with war-conditioned meanings that were perceived as destructive enabled that form to be filled with the desired meaning once again when greater freedom of movement and thought became possible—or so Sarajevans hoped. The imitation of life that appeared in war-torn Sarajevo was central to the changes of normality, because it allowed for sociocultural continuity in circumstances that unraveled the social fabric as well as disrupting material existence.

Breaking Down Normality

The problem of securing basic necessities—food, water, and some source of energy—in order to sustain physical life pervaded everyday life in Sarajevo to a degree that most city dwellers in economically developed nations find impossible to imagine. Often I found myself waiting for water or electricity to come at some point in the day. When this happened, my field notes invariably began with something like "Today around twelve o'clock I heard water coming. . . ." The explanation of this preoccupation lies in the fact that not only were these things essential for physical survival but also they were scarce and available intermittently: They were not completely missing. Yet the irregularity of their supply had effects that seemed more powerful than their simple absence might have been, underlining the dependence of Sarajevans on forces that lay entirely beyond their control.

Authorities of all warring sides alternated between cutting off supplies and letting them reach the city as a way of achieving their military and political goals.[1] Whether or not military leaders were aware of the effects of this strategy on the population, it made the war in Bosnia into a war against civilians. In the beginning, people in Sarajevo were confused by the randomness of the supply situation. They did not understand why the Serbs sometimes let them have electricity, water, or gas. All the cables and pipelines went through Serbian territory, so they could have easily cut off supplies completely. Instead, the Serbs stopped and restarted supplies, seemingly arbitrarily and entirely unpredictably. As the war went on, many Sarajevans became disillusioned with their own government and blamed it as well. In September 1994 I was told that the current shortage was caused by the Bosnian government. The general opinion was that supplies were stopped in order to victimize the population of Sarajevo. By that time, Sarajevo had been established internationally as the symbol of Bosnian suffering. As the international community's will to do something radical in order to stop the war was again fading, the renewed suffering of Sarajevans was supposed to remind the world that the situation was untenable. The "slow strangling of Sarajevo" dramatized the need for action. In what Sarajevans regarded as a perverse twist on their plight, intensifying their deprivation would improve the position of the Bosnian government in the international political arena.

As a result of these military strategies, any fixed daily routine became impossible. During the periods when there was no water at all, whole days were spent queuing up at the cisterns and then transporting water home, often in freezing temperatures and under random shell fire. The physical hardships of transport and psychic exposure to nervous, depressed, or angry fellow townspeople engraved the experience of supplying water in people's bodies and memories as something to avoid by all means. The normal water supply system did operate occasionally, though never regularly or for long. Everybody waited eagerly for the sound of water dripping from the taps in order to catch every precious drop. This meager supply was worth waiting for—anything to avoid water queues.

The supply of electricity was equally random. People who were forced to spend long winter evenings in the light of a precious candle or under a weak light of a small bulb driven by a car battery; people whose homes were filled with modern electrical appliances that were out of use for more than two years; people who were tired of washing clothes by hand in tiny quantities of precious water; people ashamed of their dirty homes, which used to be vacuumed once a week—these people welcomed every second of electricity in order to reestablish the standard of living they considered decent for human beings. It helped to combat the recurrent fear that they were being reduced to a subhuman existence in which the struggle for food and shelter was everything.

The occasional appearance of water and electricity made people feel that they were able to live more normally. Normality was understood to be the standard of living they had been accustomed to before the war, which resembled standards of living in any Western city of the same size. But the randomness had disastrous effects on their ability to cope with the situation.

A young woman told me that her mother always had a bathroom light on in order to wake up in case electricity came during the night, as it often did in 1994, so that she could get up and vacuum. When the electricity came one night at three in the morning, her daughter woke up, too. She saw that her mother was too tired to do any work so she begged her to go to bed. The woman returned to bed, but she could not give up the idea and could not fall asleep for a long time. I witnessed similar situations in the family with whom I lived. One day water and electricity came at the same time and my hostess was overjoyed. Although she knew that both could disappear at any second, this was her happy moment and she hurried to start the washing machine. As expected, in less than half an hour the machine stopped working, and she ended up rinsing everything by hand.

After the ceasefire that was a consequence of NATO's bombing of Serbian positions in August 1995 and eventually led to the signing of the Dayton Peace Accords in November 1995, these conditions continued, but they no longer had any direct connection to the military situation. In October 1995 I saw a calendar in the kitchen of one of my friends in Sarajevo. It was filled with small notes. She explained that her father noted the days when the authorities said there would be water, electricity, or gas. The scheme was very complicated, but it was possible to work out on which days they would have both water and electricity so that they could plan to do the laundry that day. A month later, water, electricity, and gas were once again cut off, coming only occasionally and randomly.

The same pattern of inadequate and intermittent supplies applied to food and wood, but here the issue was different in character because the black market was involved. Smugglers and salesmen earned more money when the town was closed than when supply routes were open. The matter of profits figured in people's explanations of the fighting that escalated in September 1994, while I was there. After the explosion of shells at Markale marketplace in February 1994 killed sixty-eight people, media coverage resulted in pressure on all sides, including the United Nations, to agree on a ceasefire for heavy weapons. The ceasefire led to the opening of the "blue ways"— routes under the authority of the UN—during the summer months of 1994. The increase in supply meant lower food prices. "People are gaining weight because of this withdrawal of heavy weapons," my host commented jokingly only a few days before the shooting started anew, effectively closing the blue ways and the air bridge. Prices rose overnight. People felt that their life conditions were subject to the merciless logic of domestic marketing, as well as to the ebb and flow of international politics and goodwill.

As Sarajevans were forced into waiting for the barest essentials and subordinated to the whims of destiny or the authorities, the message that was slowly but surely engraving itself was that people could not understand the logic governing their lives and could not do anything to protect themselves or improve their living conditions. They had no power over their lives, and consequently their lives were worthless.

Humiliation and Shame

There is a subtle but distinct experience of shame involved in coping with the disruptions of normality that Sarajevans were forced to grow accustomed to. When talking about their situation people not only used the notion of "normal life" but also expressed the shame they felt because they could not invite me for a decent meal, because their homes were not as tidy as they wanted them to be, because they had lost their dignity by losing control over their lives and destinies, or because they no longer cared if somebody was killed that day as long as it was not somebody they knew.

During the first year of the war, almost the entire population of Sarajevo went from being fully employed professionals who could provide a decent standard of living for themselves and their families to being recipients of charity, dependent on the goodwill of organizations ranging from the UN and humanitarian NGOs to religious organizations such as Caritas and Merhamet, as well as Islamic relief coming mostly from Saudi Arabia and Kuwait. In the beginning, people with greater financial resources or larger food reserves were better off, but this situation lasted for only a few months. Soon, the majority of Sarajevans became poor and dependent on help from the outside. Those who managed to get work during the war, people in larger households, and those living nearer the city center had somewhat better conditions. But the provision of basic subsistence was difficult, and the differences soon became fairly insignificant. After some time new economic elites started to emerge, rooted in wartime criminality, organized thieving, the black market, and connections with political elites. This social stratification became one of the cornerstones for the new forms of stratification that existed after the war.

Given the general deprivation, the humanitarian aid that came through the United Nations High Commission for Refugees (UNHCR), which was perceived as a religiously and politically neutral party, was longed for and welcomed. But it soon became obvious that its quality was poor and quantities meager. The paucity of international humanitarian aid became one of the primary sources of Sarajevans' humiliation, disappointment with the West, and outrage. I estimated that each adult received approximately 5 kilograms of aid per month, a considerable part of which was taken up by heavy, rough soap for washing clothes, a fact that was pointed out to me with disbelief and bitterness. The basic food articles received through the UNHCR were flour, oil, sugar, rice, and canned goods. One type of canned fish was received with resentment: "Even our cat will not eat it!" people said with some amusement. Cans of beef, tuna, sardines, and *đuveć* (lamb and vegetable stew) were much appreciated. So were macaroni or other types of pasta and dairy products, such as powdered milk and feta cheese. The monotonousness of food aid was an additional source of humiliation. During my fieldwork in 1994, people were getting beans all the time and everyone was sick and tired of them, although at the beginning of the war beans were rare and commanded high prices. Before that, it was lentils. In 1995, most of the aid was canned fish with an odd taste and smell. Then in 1996 it was peas. Many Sarajevans told me that the humanitarian aid they were receiving was composed of old surpluses that Western industries were getting rid of in this way, the "Vietnam cookie" being a case in point. They were convinced that it had nothing to do with a genuine concern for the well-being of Sarajevans. How could it? Others pointed out that quality articles such as fruit compotes and chocolate were sent but never reached the population in the town; these items would be confiscated at the military checkpoints, and at best people could buy them on the black market for astronomical prices.

Shame gradually became the order of the day, which indicates that a change of what was considered to be normal had taken place. This process was reversible, but it never stopped.

My hosts in Sarajevo were a couple in their late fifties, both of whom had university degrees. All of their lives they had provided for themselves and made a decent living, which included much more than basic provisions. Even during the first months of the war they could buy their own food and fuel, when electricity and gas were cut off. They simply could not face the humiliation of receiving "mercy from foreigners," as they expressed their view of humanitarian aid. Queuing for hours in the cold and under the threat of shelling in order to be given food that would last only a few days was unthinkable. But after some months their reserves of deutsche marks were gone, and they were compelled to apply for help from foreigners as if they were welfare cases. It was a sign of their social degradation caused by the war. By the time I stayed with them in Sarajevo in September 1994, queuing for humanitarian aid was a part of everyday life. They explained its original humiliation to me, but they did not feel it any more.

At the same time, my hosts still refused to take charity in the form of bread paid for by foreign donors whom Sarajevans called "sheikhs," most of whom lived in wealthy countries in the Middle East. Bread was a staple food in the whole of the former Yugoslavia, and in 1994 the UNHCR managed to provide sufficient flour to the town bakery so that everyone could buy subsidized bread in the local stores for the local currency, the Bosnian coupon. In September 1994 one deutsche mark was equivalent to approximately 360,000 Bosnian coupons. The price of a loaf of bread was 60,000 coupons, and an average salary sufficed for a loaf of bread a day. On some days, "sheiks" were permitted by the Bosnian government to buy all the bread in a certain municipality in order to give it to the people free of charge. This act counted as a good deed, giving the donor a higher status both in this world and in the afterlife. As the bread was subsidized by the government and the UN, this charitable gift would cost the donor approximately thirty or forty deutsche marks. On such a day, no one could buy the bread. But my hosts refused to receive this charity and instead used their own precious flour and yeast and spent almost a whole day walking to the home of a relative who had a wood-fired oven in order to bake the bread themselves, much as they used to do before the bread became available in 1994. Making bread required the use of precious wood or coal and entailed an obligation to return the favor to the relative sometime in the future. But all of this they could still afford. They perceived receiving help in the name of Allah as much more degrading than losing social status. They felt that they could be poor and still live in a secular society, which they were used to living in before the war, while accepting charity in Allah's name would imply a moral obligation to accept a foreign, Islamic society with a whole set of different norms.

At the time, I asked myself how long it would take before they would be forced to accept this sort of charity as well. To my knowledge, they never did, but I knew of others who were forced to concede on this matter. For example, a war friend of mine, a medical doctor from a Catholic Sarajevan family whom I met in September 1994, commented that she was disturbed by the propagation of Islam in civil and official everyday life, most often carried out by "Arabs." During my visit in October 1995 Saudi Arabia began donating money to pay salaries to medical doctors in Sarajevo. Since the beginning of the war, physicians had been working for free, or for minimal salaries of ten deutsche marks in Bosnian coupons. The Saudis gave fifty deutsche marks per month to each medical doctor. Even though it meant going every month with her ID card to two Saudi Arabian representatives, a man and a woman who was wearing the veil in the very strict way, which clearly communicated her conservative Muslim identity, my friend was happy to receive the money and never made any comments about it. The money was not as much as she needed, but it was a welcome increase in the family budget, and at that point she was glad to receive it no matter how and from whom it came.

Feeling cold makes life as difficult as physical pain does. But the practices that were forced on Sarajevans in order to survive the cold added insult to injury. Both their own cutting down of the trees in the town and the UN policy of providing Sarajevans with thermal foils for their windows were experienced as humiliating. The urban population, with its characteristic emotional attachment to parks and alleys, experienced the cutting of all the trees and bushes all the way to the front lines with deep pain. Something essential was gone. The emptiness the trees left behind them symbolized the brutality of the war. It had no mercy for unprotected life. It seemed that civilization, even humanity itself, was killed anew with each fallen tree. The pragmatism of survival took precedence over sensitivity to natural beauty. Those who could not afford to buy wood gathered as much as they could on the outskirts. When that was insufficient or impossible to do, they burned their furniture, books, and clothes. A young woman described her family's situation: "Our apartment is in one corner of the skyscraper; underneath is a café that didn't work, which means that it was not heated. During the first winter we didn't have glass in any of the windows, only thermal foils. In the apartment above us they were heating lousily, so we made fire, and made fire. We tried to have fire from seven in the morning until seven in the evening and we would achieve a maximum of +9 degrees centigrade. We froze." At first the foils were hard to get, but eventually the whole of Sarajevo was covered by the opaque thermal foils covered with blue UNHCR letters and symbols. They made the apartments and town look even more like ruins.

When they grew uncomfortably cold at home, Sarajevans strolled around the center of town. I discovered this during my stay in 1996, when I sat at home writing for entire days. Soon I felt as though the cold and damp were creeping into my bones, and I realized that the only way to warm up was to go out for a while and walk. Although the foils protected the apartments from the worst cold in winter, it got very cold inside when the whole building was not heated. So I strode together with others in the center without any purpose except for getting warm, coincidentally meeting an acquaintance now and then.

Inventiveness and Pride

Suffering shortages of basic material necessities and experiencing the abnormal, corrosive conditions of wartime caused humiliation and shame, but coping creatively with hardships also generated considerable pride. For example, dishwashing machines, refrigerators, and deep-freezes that did not function because of the cut-off of electricity were used to store food reserves from the humanitarian aid rations, most of which could be stored at room temperature. The amazing resourcefulness and ingenuity that people showed in the management of water and vehicles for transporting it is another case in point.

It took practice to learn how to wash in minimal quantities of water, so that personal hygiene could be properly maintained and clothes and dishes kept clean by usual standards. I washed my hair in 1 or 2 liters. No more was

Figure 11. Washing and filling containers at the hose that was the only source of water for the entire neighborhood. In the background, lawns have been planted with vegetables. Sarajevo suburb of Hrasno, September 1994. Photo by author.

needed for a shower. The famous Sarajevan shower technique consisted of standing in a plastic vessel and taking a deciliter of water at a time by a small cup from another vessel and pouring it over the entire body. Then came the soaping. Finally, the rinsing was done with small amounts of well-directed water. The dirty water was saved for flushing the toilet. Hands could be washed in a deciliter.

When nothing was dripping from the taps, water could be found at various places, nearer or further away from home. The general rule was that the better the military situation and the lighter the siege, the nearer the water. So, on the days that we did not get any water on the second floor, the neighbor in the basement apartment might have had it. If that tap was dry, then perhaps some other house in the neighborhood, with a lower position, had water. When the situation worsened a bit in September 1994, we had to go half a kilometer to a public pipe and queue. When the shooting started, the only source of water was in the center of the town several kilometers away. That was when transporting water home from the public pipes became crucial. My host used a metal contraption with wheels that was designed for suitcases. He had two of these, he told me with great satisfaction, so he gave one to his friends; that was the best present they ever got. One day I met him in the town with canisters tied to his bicycle, which he was pushing. When he saw me, he smiled proudly and explained how he managed to repair the tire on his bicycle that morning, and how by pushing the bike he could load it with more water. His brother was with him, and he pulled his canisters on a skateboard. On the streets I saw all sorts of wheeled vehicles loaded with all many different kinds of vessels filled with water.

The car battery was another crucial expedient that became basic to every household. A battery could be bought, but many people simply took the batteries out of their own cars. The battery and a front seat were the only remains of my hosts' car after a shell had hit it at the beginning of the war. The battery could be used for television, but then it lasted only a week, and recharging was expensive. I think that in 1994 one recharging cost fifty deutsche marks, and it was done by taking the car battery to people who managed to make or obtain the recharging equipment. So my hosts used their car battery only for the radio and two lamps. In the living room hung a tiny blue neon bulb giving just enough light to play cards by, but not enough to read; in the kitchen was a small white bulb that I could write under. Both lamps had a metal shield in order to reflect as much light as possible. The lamp that was in the kitchen had a hook that made it easy to move into the bathroom. Other households improvised lighting devices from recycled or scavenged materials. A war friend showed me a kerosene lamp made of a glass mayonnaise jar, a slow-burning wick, and a metal part from a bullet to hold the wick. It could be filled with anything that burned, from cooking oil to kerosene.

Walking in the town, I saw many strange devices generating weak but usable electrical power. They were often placed just outside a ground-level window, but they produced terrible noises and unpleasant, harmful gases. Once I went to a toilet that was in the same room with such a machine, and tears started streaming from my eyes because of the fumes. Most of these generators must have been engines from destroyed vehicles. One of the more fascinating scenes I witnessed was a group of young men in front of the Youth Theater beside a very battered Fiat 550 (the smallest car that existed in the former Yugoslavia, nicknamed Fićo). The car had no wheels, and the engine compartment at the back was opened. The men were connecting an espresso machine to the engine. Together with Staffan, my Swedish colleague, I started photographing the scene. One of the men watching the enterprise smirked at us, correctly judging that we were strangers. He said proudly, "You

Figure 12. A "Sarajevo tin can" (*sarajevska konzerva*), a stove constructed out of a five-liter tin can from humanitarian aid. Sarajevo, September 1994. Photo by author.

people would die, starve to death, if something like this happened to you!" In a different situation I would have thought him an arrogant prick, but I could not help but agree. I could not imagine either myself or Staffan making coffee in this way. "Come for an espresso tomorrow!" he shouted after us when we were leaving. And we did. It was one of the few places where you could get espresso at that time.

The most famous invention of the war was the "Sarajevo tin can" (*sarajevska konzerva*), a stove that was constructed out of a five-liter tin can from humanitarian aid. A little window for putting in the wood and lighting the fire was cut out on the front side. On the back, somewhat higher, the tin obtained by cutting out the window was rolled and stuck into a round hole to

Figure 13. Improvised ovens used for cooking and heating. On the right is a *fijaker*. Baščaršija, Sarajevo, March 1995. Photo by author.

make a chimney. Pots and pans were placed on the open top of the can (sometimes on two metal rods, as my host did). The most useful oven invented during the war was the fiacre (*fijaker*). It got its name from its form. One end was lower, with a compartment where the fire was made. The upper surface of this part was used as a stove. The warm air from the lower compartment rose to a somewhat larger higher compartment, which served as an oven. A chimney pipe led the smoke out of the house. When the gas started coming, a burner could be placed in the lower compartment instead of making the fire there.

At the beginning of the war relatively few households had gas, but toward the end of 1993, and especially in 1994 and 1995, the gas network was extended. The installation cost money, but as the system of payment for the use of gas was not established (meters started to appear in 1996) and buying wood was much more expensive (in 1992, two hundred deutsche marks for a cubic meter, or twenty-five deutsche marks for a sack), most households installed gas. The streets were crisscrossed by ditches for new gas pipes that led from one house to another, which made driving a bumpy adventure. Although gas was an improvement over other sources of energy, these gas installations were done by amateurs, often using whatever material was available. Most were made of plastic pipes with leaky joints and installed on the floors, where they were exposed to all sorts of damage. Any leakage promptly filled the whole room with gas. In 1996 the gas installations were controlled and proper metal pipes were installed near the ceiling with automatic valves. Until then the valves for turning the gas flow on and off were operated manually. As the gas came irregularly, it could disappear for some time, the fire would go out, and if the people were not alert, when the gas came back on it could fill the whole apartment and blow it to pieces at the smallest spark. Sadly, this happened occasionally, and black holes from internal combustion were visible in quite a few apartment buildings. Not only were they so dark that they made one feel uncomfortable, but it seemed strange that the explosions blew out single apartments but not the buildings—as if some demonic hand had chosen to destroy just one family with all its belongings. Gas explosions were powerful and the damage was irreparable. These hazards were the dark side of free but unskilled labor and improvization. Paradoxically, the damage from mortar shells looked much cleaner: the interior colors of the apartments were the same as before the shells exploded. The shells came from outside and destroyed parts of buildings, but they always left remnants of the apartments' interiors intact.

Inventiveness and creativity in preparing food were not only necessary for quelling hunger but were also a good way of combating humiliation. Two important dishes were war versions of *pita* and soups or stews. *Pita* is not the flat, Middle Eastern bread popular in European and American supermarkets, but a traditional Bosnian dish made of a filling spread on very thinly stretched dough, which has to be turned by hand. After the filling is spread, the dough is rolled into a long tube and put in a spiral baking form. A woman who was not able to make a good *pita* was traditionally seen as an unfit housewife and, especially in Muslim families, girls used to start learning to make *pita* with their mothers at a very young age. The filling could be of cheese, spinach, or meat, hence the names *sirnica, zeljanica*, and *burek*.

Pita and stews were originally the common food of poor people, filling the stomach in the cheapest way; no expensive meats or fresh vegetables were required. This type of food could be made out of almost any ingredients. With water and flour people could concoct all sorts of meals, depending on what else was at their disposal: a bit of cheese; canned beef, fish, or vegetable; macaroni or rice; a bit of onion or even garlic; an egg; perhaps salt or some other spice. As vegetables and spices were constantly lacking, people turned to picking wild greens. Later, when the UNHCR started providing the seeds, people took up gardening. Leaves of *podbjel* (a small vine), dandelion, *radić* (a type of lettuce), and nettle made soups and fillings for *pita zeljanica*. People felt humiliated at having to pick bitter and dusty greens in order to avoid the snipers and heavy artillery that were placed on the outskirts of the town where the clean and rich meadows were located. But that was counterbalanced by their pride in managing to prepare a decent dinner out of meager ingredients. Similarly, the possibility of gardening evoked mixed feelings. Turning urban green spaces into utilitarian gardens was seen as humiliating. My hosts, who refused to plant a garden, had some vegetables in their flowerpots on the balcony. As a form of resistance, they kept flowers, a completely useless investment of care and water. But the flowers restored some sense of dignity and normal life. It was as though my hosts were saying, "We refuse to reduce ourselves to bare physical survival—our souls also need to survive!" And from nearby balconies, palms, lemon trees, and other exotic-looking plants indicated neighbors who felt the same way. Like the balcony pots, gardening outdoors seemed to have primarily positive psychological effects. It gave some hope for survival, a little security, and a sense that it was possible to do something, generating a feeling of agency that restored a bit of life as it should be. The actual quantity of vegetables grown might be small, but the joy and pride of picking, preparing, and savoring them was huge.

While the meager aid that came through the UNHCR was met mostly

Figure 14. Gardens between modern housing complexes in Hrasno. September 1994. Photo by author.

with contempt as a defense against the feelings of humiliation it caused, private food parcels and new banking routines were a part of wartime inventiveness that stretched beyond the besieged town. Family members or close friends who had fled the war or were living outside Sarajevo did everything possible to pass food parcels and money to their loved ones in the city. A myriad of humanitarian organizations and workers took whatever they could to people they had become acquainted with. The most reliable organization turned out to be Adra, which delivered parcels that came mainly from Belgrade, the Federal Republic of Yugoslavia, and Serb-held parts of Bosnia and Herzegovina.

For a long time, money was sent in letters that were delivered through private connections. Eventually some banks in Germany and Slovenia (and probably some other countries with large refugee populations from Bosnia and Herzegovina) established contacts with Sarajevo, so money could be sent the official way. However, these banks sometimes took more than 50 percent of the total amount for their services. These high "taxes" that eroded the line between private business and public authority seemed to be common during the war. They were perceived as unavoidable and had a quality of feudal extortion that was alive in people's memory of the pre-Yugoslav past when they were ruled by more or less merciless foreigners. The excessive charges and outright thieving specific to the war situation in Sarajevo[2] seemed to have compromised people and organizations abroad as well. Established institutions, such as some German banks, quickly adapted to the situation in Sarajevo and did not hesitate to take material advantage of people's desperation by charging astonishingly high fees for their services. These extortionate rates resemble war profiteering more than they do accepted banking practices in the West. The question is, by which moral standards should we judge these Western banks: by the thievery that is commonplace in wartime, or by the customary moral standards of peacetime Europe? And there is an even more discomfiting question: Why did we not judge? We Europeans became involved in increasing the suffering of populations already hard-hit by war through our banking businesses and our economic interests in exports.

Humor

Just as Sarajevans dealt with their constant vulnerability by using humor, so they described their appalling material conditions in ways that emphasized their amusing absurdity. Almost every account of a struggle or difficult experience was spiced with humorous comments and twists. Consider the description that a young man who lived with his mother in Čengić Vila gave me of the water shortage. When the water eventually disappeared from all of the pipes around their building, the neighbors discovered a reservoir on Hrasno brdo that was around one and a half kilometers away. It stood on a clearing near the front line, an easy target for shells and snipers. Luckily on that pipeline there were no massacres, and although now and then a shell would fall, the young man had never heard that people were hurt in large numbers, as happened in the town. For some time they could fetch the water at this pipeline during the entire day. Then a shell fell and killed one or two people. After that the water could be fetched only after 10 PM. People asked themselves how they could fetch water after 10 PM when that was after the curfew, but then a directive came that all who had canisters in their hands could move outdoors after 10 PM. "So, in all this misery, it was a bit funny, because you didn't have to have an identification card—it was enough to have canisters, and you were allowed to go out after the curfew," the young man concluded.

Humor was a way of meeting humiliation. Take as an example the description under the heading "Gifts" in the *Sarajevo Survival Guide* (Prstojević

1994:39): "Passionate love is being expressed here by a handful of wood, a bucket of coal, a complete edition of books which lack humor and poetry. Could you spare some Vladimir Illich Lenin? Last winter has proven that his books burn well!" Most of the experiences people had were a complicated mixture of humiliation, ingenuity, and good luck, but many descriptions ended with a humorous twist instead of an analysis or conclusion. A young man described how in the beginning he had the good fortune to buy cheaply thirty kilograms of oats when the bakery was selling out. His family made bread out of this grain as best they could, but it was hard and tasted bad. "But," he added in the end, "it turned out that oats have a lot of B vitamins, so our nails started to grow and our hair became nice!"

Mutual Aid and Theft

One paradox of war is that we humans induce suffering upon other humans, while at the same time we depend on one another for physical and emotional survival even more than in peace. Social norms of solidarity, mutual aid, hospitality, and reciprocity contend with the opposing forces of selfishness, corruption, theft, black marketeering, and plunder. In the competition for scarce resources, especially in a country that was for centuries under foreign rule—from Venice and the Ottoman Empire, to the Austro-Hungarian (Habsburg) Empire, and then Nazi occupation—and had a tradition of cheating the authorities and evading the laws, the line between mutual aid and individualism was very thin and the distinction between what was considered moral and immoral became blurred. A middle-aged man told me that he met an old friend on the street during the harsh shortages of 1993. The friend complained of having no money and no oil to take home to his wife to make a meal; he seemed completely distressed. So the man who told me the story went home, stole the next-to-last bottle of oil from his wife, who would never had allowed him to take it, and gave it to his friend. Later he learned that his friend procured several bottles of oil in this way, by lying and taking advantage of his friends. He was not really profiting, he was merely trying to make ends meet, but the man who told me the story regarded this act as a betrayal of their friendship.

While some relationships were broken because of diverging perceptions of morality, many new relationships were established through unselfish help and mutual interests. Often neighbors who had not even greeted each other before the war began to cooperate in making ends meet. In Čengić Vila, for example, two young neighboring men got together and made a carriage on which both families could put thirty canisters of water, because the father of one of them worked in a workshop where he could weld. People who lived in houses on the outskirts of town had more garden produce than apartment-dwellers in the center, and people with gardens often shared their greens with friends or relatives. Some houses had big, wood-fired ovens of an older type, in which it was possible to bake bread. A woman from Breka told me how they baked three-kilogram loaves for everyone who lived on the staircase in their apartment building. They could do it because a boy in one of the houses in the neighborhood fancied a girl who lived in their building, and he offered the use of his family's oven to her family. They also used to cook joint dinners at the beginning of the war. Four families could join: one had only minced meant, the other only macaroni, the third tomato sauce, and between them they made a tasty dinner, with a bit of soup, too.

In this way, mutual aid blended with socializing. In the midst of their strenuous, dangerous, and humiliating lives, Sarajevans were able to find positive elements in the sociability that survival strategies generated. A young man from Čengić Vila told me that fetching water with a carriage was a bit like going out to a café at night. All the neighbors would gather, and although they could hear shooting, at that moment no one thought that they could get hurt. It felt like they were on an excursion, he said, with the benefit of physical training too, because a person had to be physically fit in order to bring 100 liters of water from a hill.

The main type of social get-together in Sarajevo was drinking coffee, a custom that held the same importance before, during, and after the war. Drinking coffee had always been a social necessity, but its meaning changed somewhat during the war, as did the meanings of many other customs. A woman in Breka told me about the female gatherings (*sijelo*) where she and her neighbors told fortunes from the sediment in an upturned coffee cup as a way of relaxing from men and their endless discussions of news and politics. In the situation of siege, telling of fortunes became a more attractive way for these women to orient themselves in an unpredictable world than men's political discussions! When there were no coffee beans, people found all sorts of substitutes: barley, various kinds of wheat, and lentils, which made terrible coffee but left rich sediments to tell the future from.

The war brought people closer and distanced them. At the same time, it changed their perceptions of what was morally acceptable in the daily struggle for a decent way of living. Once on a visit in the center I saw a network of wires through a kitchen window. When I asked about it I was told that the thick cable was the "priority electricity" to which people in the neighborhood attached their thinner wires to take the current into their homes. "Priority electricity" was meant for essential public institutions such as hospitals, police stations, and government offices, and for some important people. Everyone knew which electrical cable was the "priority" one, but they had to be careful not to use too much energy because then the whole system would collapse. I have seen similar networks in Chiapas, Mexico, where poor Mayans make ends meet in this way. The unauthorized appropriation of supposedly common goods by the underprivileged is a survival strategy for millions of poor people around the globe. In more prosperous times, this strategy can be morally called into question, but in times of crisis it is accepted. Many of the new survival techniques in Sarajevo created tension between what used to be considered moral and what used to be considered immoral but which during the war became moral, at least for portions of the population.

A good example is the case of the ingenious engineer who produced eggs in his little private firm. He had an agreement with Koševo hospital, which had incubators and a constant supply of electricity since it had its own generator with highest priority. He placed his hens in incubators, and in return, the hospital received a portion of the eggs. It sounded like a smart solution, and I was careful to show how impressed I was, which I felt was expected of me. After all, one of my hosts' neighbors introduced us because she worked for this man. But the meeting left me feeling uneasy. The neighbor was a hardworking and upstanding person. But what about the man who could pull off such a deal with Koševo hospital? He was certainly clever, but he must have had connections with people in power and a sense of morality that did not question using the electricity and equipment from a public hospital for private ends, although he made sure it was in the hospital's interest, too. I thought that he was a smart merchant and a good engineer, but also that he was a war profiteer. He used the crisis to start a private business through which he freely exploited his workers, and he used his connections with politicians in control of public resources to divert these resources for private purposes under the cover of economic benefit. I had a disturbing gut feeling that I was smiling approvingly at capitalist corruption under wartime circumstances.

The black market and the tunnel were typical instances of institutional thieving during the war, when new economic elites emerged in clear connection to political elites. A case in point is the poor management of the wartime currency, Bosnian coupons, in which the state paid its employees' salaries. The very name "coupon" signals that this was not real money; coupons were worthless at the only real market—the black market. With coupons you could buy only bread and newspapers! They were treated as a ridiculous invention, a piece of paper you did not throw away because it could buy you bread, and because it at least pretended that there was a state, something to hope for, an "imitation of life," or rather an "imitation of a state"! Goods that were bought with foreign currency on the black market or in private stores were mostly imported by merchants, stolen from the storehouses of the UN and other organizations, or pillaged from destroyed houses, apartments, and shops. It was said that all shop owners who opened their doors during the war had robbed and destroyed the old shops, since that was the only way to get hold of goods. The government was collecting high taxes from what was sold in markets, shops, cafés, and restaurants. So it was in the government's interest that business went well.

Sometimes soldiers could get special privileges. For instance, the unit that carried goods through the tunnel for the government or, rather, for the merchant who hired the tunnel from the government for that day, would be allowed to carry one load of goods for themselves, which they could buy at lower prices in Hransnica, the community just outside Sarajevo that had been turned into a major market area. This privilege often saved soldiers' families, but the practice of letting merchants use the tunnel to import goods, together with the plundering or "taxing" of the UNHCR humanitarian aid, provided the basis on which the black market could be established.

Change of Norms

The struggle for daily subsistence in war conditions caused drastic changes in Sarajevans' lives and orientation. Most of the changes directly related to subsistence conditions were temporary, in the sense that the prewar sociocultural norms were left intact, but some of the changes were of a more lasting nature.

"Imitation of life" was a creative way to accept wartime conditions temporarily while preserving the forms of prewar normality. Sarajevans were able to adapt their norms without losing the possibility of going back to prewar norms after peace came. Holding jobs, for example, provided not only some economic benefits and social contacts but most of all a daily routine, which was the best way of fighting the destructive effects of the irregularity and normlessness that the war brought.

In Bosnia, losing weight was traditionally seen as something bad and dangerous, especially among the lower class and the residents of rural vil-

lages. This sociocultural norm probably arose from the population's historical experience of famines and illnesses; people weakened by poor nutrition
were especially vulnerable. After the Second World War, and especially
among the younger urban middle class, people watched their weight more
strictly in accordance with new Western body ideals. During the war, putting
on weight was often considered undesirable and a sign of immorality, but
this attitude was not based on standards of beauty. Rather, gaining weight
was possible only for those who were living well despite the war, most likely
because they were war profiteers. The loss of weight, which averaged between
10 and 20 kilograms, was physical evidence of the hardships and suffering
that the war brought: suffering embodied. But this change of attitude lasted
only during the war. As conditions began to improve toward the end of the
war, people once again became concerned about gaining weight in accordance with Western body ideals. "Now, when the war is over, everyone suddenly gained weight. It is not only because of the food, but also because of a
sort of relaxation of nerves. The metabolism probably works in a different
way now," a young man from Čengić Vila told me in 1996.

The subtle wartime shifts in the meaning of hospitality were difficult to
perceive because generosity to others was a basic social norm both before and
after the war. But hospitality took on new meanings during the war, becoming not simply an opportunity to show respect and appreciation to guests but
also a welcome break in the monotony of the everyday diet. In this way, the
wartime experience of Sarajevans probably resembles the meaning of hospitality to many poor populations with scarce and monotonous food resources. During my fieldwork in Sarajevo, I twice became embarrassed by
people's hospitality. The first time, I did not want to believe that I was treated
as a guest by my host family. They felt like family, so I was not aware that
when I was around they were serving better food than when they were alone.
I would not have been so embarrassed had I realized that they too enjoyed
eating better, taking my presence as a sort of an excuse. This became obvious
to me in another embarrassing episode when a friend invited me and two
Sarajevan friends for dinner one evening. As we walked toward his home, he
pointed proudly to the fresh chicken, green salad, and potatoes in the two
carrier bags. I knew how precious this food was and realized that it must have
cost him quite a fortune; it was one of the first weeks during the whole war
when you could buy chicken, salad, and potatoes at the market. I started
telling him that he should not have gone to so much trouble just because he
invited us to dinner. He looked at me, confused, and said, "I have been
dreaming of roast chicken, fresh potatoes, and green salad for two and a half

years now!" His remark sums up everything that can be said about food in wartime Sarajevo.

These were temporary changes in people's way of life, and by imitating prewar norms Sarajevans preserved them and were able to go back to them as soon as circumstances allowed. Holding on to prewar standards of normality was a way of resisting the humiliating conditions that threatened their health and lives. Other changes in social norms could prove to be of a more durable character. These shifts were both welcome and disturbing, depending on the person's position and point of view.

Because young people were the ones who could get employment during the war, economic power shifted from the older generations to young adults. The moral norms governing economic life changed drastically, as stealing and cheating became more acceptable. This shift was a part of a larger transformation in the economic system, which lost most of the social welfare elements that had existed in Yugoslavia before its dissolution and established a "free market" based on wartime criminality. The overlap between the black market and the free market gave those who were in power and were already better situated than most others even more opportunities to increase their wealth, in a war-specific neoliberalism.

The organized, often institutionalized theft that was so prevalent during the war met with greater tolerance than during the prewar period, and this shift seems to have had lasting effects, changing moral norms regarding acceptable and unacceptable conduct in economic life. The corrupt and exploitative capitalism, characterized by patron-client networks[3] among profit makers and by the almost complete loss of rights and security among employees, that is now firmly established would have been intolerable in the prewar period. In 1994, I met a shop assistant in her thirties who worked for ten deutsche marks a month, from 8 AM to 10 PM, seven days a week, with no right to holidays, and who was afraid she would be fired if she complained or was not good humored. As she had children, she was in fact happy to have an income in foreign currency at the time, while at the same time she was shocked by the harshness of her employer. For many Sarajevans these working conditions were unacceptable, but most thought that they would change when the war was over. Unfortunately, while these terms of employment bothered Sarajevans, their critique did not disturb the international promotion of neoliberal ideals of the so-called free market. In fact, the Western market ideology ignored the fact that "free market" opportunities in Bosnia and Herzegovina were based on war profiteering and other crimes.

At the same time, the value of genuine social contacts, voluntary solidarity, and mutual aid rose during the war, and this awareness of interdependency seems to have survived into the postwar period. In this new political-economic climate, some people became hardened into ruthlessness, while others became humbled and learned to appreciate one another.

The constant threat of death created a fertile ground for turning to religion as a way of forgetting the war for a moment and as a source of protective magical formulas. The importance of religion was reinforced by the fact that the primary source of subsistence goods and sometimes money, beyond the UNHCR, was religious organizations. Before the war, most Sarajevans were not religious, but during the siege, they felt forced to choose one religious group to belong to in order to get some food aid. In families with several religious backgrounds this could cause tensions, but at the same time it gave them opportunities to get help from several sources. Thus, religion entered the everyday life of most Sarajevans in an organized and institutionalized way. It became public, in contrast to the prewar way of practicing religion in private. The extent and permanence of these normative changes in the postwar period remain to be seen.

Chapter 4
Tests of Trust

By 1994, half of Sarajevo's 600,000 prewar residents had left the city. Another 150,000 "displaced persons" had arrived, mostly Muslims from villages and small towns in eastern Bosnia. So the population of Sarajevo in 1994 was 450,000, two-thirds of whom were prewar Sarajevans, and one-third of whom were newcomers.[1] The massive turnover in the population brought by the war affected social relations in dramatic and often paradoxical ways, as kinship ties were ruptured, strained, or reinforced, old friendships were corroded by distrust or dissolved by ethnoreligious and nationalist antagonisms, and new friendships and forms of mutual aid were forged under siege.

Only in extreme situations of armed conflict, mass catastrophe, or natural disaster do most people realize how entirely we depend on one another for physical as well as psychological survival. What we seek in our social relations is a sense of security, however real or illusory this security may be. During the war, Sarajevans had to face their own and others' mistrust and selfishness, as well as solidarity and altruism, often at the same time and even in relation to the same person. One of the most important questions existentially, which eventually assumed moral significance, was whether to leave Sarajevo. Under circumstances in which it is impossible to foresee the future or even to predict the outcome of a specific act, all decisions appear to some extent arbitrary. Yet, the choices people made were judged by strict moral standards. In the minds of those who stayed, leaving the city seemed like desertion or betrayal, though less reprehensible than taking up arms against it.

Long-established friendships were broken by the stresses placed on interpersonal relations by the divisions of war and the demands of surviving the siege, but Sarajevans established new friendships with surprising speed. When the state and its institutions collapsed, families and neighborhoods provided the necessary aid and protection, a pattern people associated with traditional villages in the past. In families, those who left were mourned and those who remained became closer, while those who failed to show the expected solidarity were condemned. People became increasingly interdependent, heightening both solidarity and mistrust. The poor relationships between prewar Sarajevans and the mainly Muslim newcomers show that national identity was not the strongest bond. Interactions between natives and newcomers were distant, fragile, and sometimes hostile. Belonging to the same national group did not make strangers feel alike, akin, or secure with one another. In fact, natives often blamed the newcomers, together with those who had left, for the loss of what they called Sarajevanness, a local identity that also became a moral quality, whose central component was knowing how to live in an ethnoreligiously blended town.

The experiences of a young man from Čengić Vila illustrate a typical Sarajevan struggle with the unexpected, featuring surprising generosity as well as an unanticipated refusal of help. The problem was obtaining the one hundred deutsche marks he and his mother needed to install gas.

[My godmother] came to our house every day, she saw how my mother was distressed, she saw my [bad kidney] diagnosis, and she didn't offer it to us, but worse, she offered [the money] to some refugee girl. Like, she felt sorry for the girl. That was a terrible disappointment. . . . [She] never said, "I have known you since you were born, I carried you in my arms, here is the money and you can return it [when you can], or not, it doesn't matter." . . . It was logical that if we were close, if we were in some sort of family relation through godmotherhood, that there should be some priority in terms of who you are going to help.

After his godmother failed to offer badly needed help when she had money to spare, the young man became unsure of what to expect from other relations. Eventually he went to his mother's wedding godfather[2] to ask for help, not really expecting any. The godfather reprimanded him for not coming earlier:

[He] held his head and said: "But who is going to help you if not me! Why are you restraining yourself?" And then his wife said: "You are crazy, you should be spanked on your behind, what did you do, why didn't you come to us? If we have, we shall give to you. Even if you'll be indebted to us for a hundred years, better to be indebted to us than to someone else." I just sat and listened, and when they were finished I started crying, because we'd known each other earlier and I knew they were good people, but you know, during war people change.

The neighbors, too, assisted the young man and his mother with the gas installations. The fact that the mother was Serbian and the deceased father Croat proved to be insignificant, as he told me that the neighbors who helped the most were Muslims. These experiences reassured people that some prewar social norms were still valid: godparenthood as an unquestionable bond of solidarity, and neighborliness as more important than nationality. When social relations were reshaped according to new, wartime priorities, there was no way to know what to expect from old relations, and this unpredictability was in itself destructive. At the same time, unexpected altruism renewed hope and restored people's faith in humanity. The young refugee woman who received one hundred deutsche marks from the young man's godmother was surely encouraged by this act of solidarity.

The young man himself was happily surprised when a neighbor, whom he had avoided since they had quarreled over a banal thing before the war, suddenly came and said: "There has been no bread in the town for a month and I don't know how you manage; you are a young man. Here is a bag of zwieback." "I first started to apologize for what happened before the war," the young man continued, "but he said that it was not important, the important thing is to survive. So, there were incredible situations. There were a lot of nice things." The imperative of "survival" could be used to justify both selfish and altruistic acts. In Sarajevo under siege, people were forced to reconsider their priorities in human relations, though not always in systematic, consistent, or even rational ways.

The help that people offer to others in extreme situations often has no explicable motive; neither personal nor mutual advantage seems to be involved in these uncalculated acts. People who help others in crisis seem to act upon an ethic that seems natural to them. They often say that it never occurred to them to do anything else and that anyone else would have done the same in their place, although they probably know that others did not.[3] Scholars have scrutinized instances of altruism in other situations, especially after the Second World War (for example, Bauman 1991, 1992, 1993; Levinas 1999; and Staub 1992, 2003). In an interview on Swedish television, Zygmunt Bauman discussed research about people who risked their lives to save someone else's. No particular pattern of social or cultural affiliation emerged among people who acted this way. Bauman drew the conclusion that there are always people who act from their conscience and that this deeply felt personal morality has nothing to do with culture and society. He sees this ultimate morality as humankind's only hope in the contemporary predicament informed by multiple and often contradictory ethical norms. While Bauman sees a problem in moral pluralism, the Sarajevan example shows that what undermines ethical norms is violence and fear rather than competition between ethical systems. The fact that people have to be convinced under existential threat to mistrust or hate the ideologically differentiated "other"

proves that trust and concern for others are the given in successful social relations. Uncalculated altruism is a premise of social action, while selfishness
entails calculations and predictions that are difficult if not impossible in
wartime circumstances.

Sarajevans said both that people changed during the war and that they
showed their "real" character, whether selfish or altruistic. This contradictory
notion arose when people tried to make sense of others' unexpected acts.
Both run counter to the pervasive feeling that life in wartime was surreal, an
"imitation of life." Perhaps this is the essence of life in war: it can feel both
intensely real and strangely surreal. For example, you may go out to meet a
new friend after a strenuous day of household chores and be acutely aware of
the risks you are running; yet the surrealism of never knowing what tomorrow might bring heightens the reality of the pleasure you feel in sitting in the
café and your deep sense of connection with a friend. You do surreal things
and feel them more intensely than in peacetime, and it is exactly this intensity
of experience that makes you feel more real.

To Leave or Not to Leave

The question of whether to stay or attempt to leave occupied the minds of
most Sarajevans. Arguments for and against leaving changed over the course
of the war, but the dilemma existed at the beginning in 1992 as well as at the
official end of war in 1995–96. During my fieldwork I met people who left at
various points during the war. The primary considerations in all of the cases
were similar: personal security, confidence in the possibility of starting a new
life abroad, judgment about the political situation in the future, and concern
for family members from whom the person would be separated either because they would stay in the war, or because they would be alone in a foreign
world. Some people who would have left Sarajevo had there been no one else
to consider did not want to leave behind members of their family who did
not want not leave or were unable to leave. A man from Dobrinja told me:
"Even if I could have found a place [for them] in the town, I couldn't have
left my parents there—they were old. It would not have been human."

At the beginning of the war people considered only the physical dangers
when they decided to separate temporarily. Nobody thought about the effects that a protracted separation would have on their relationships. I heard
many times, in Sarajevo as well as from refugees abroad who had somebody
left there, that had they known that the war would last for years, they would

never have departed. Many people decided to stay because of the same belief that the war would not last so long and be so destructive.

The former Yugoslav People's Army (JNA) helped people with flights out of Sarajevo, taking the elderly, women, and children out of the danger zone for "humanitarian" reasons. Most of the Sarajevans I met in Zagreb or in Sweden told me that they left on the last plane or the last bus. "Belgrade looked like Saigon those weeks," a middle-aged woman told me in Zagreb during the autumn of 1993. This story communicates the sense of desperate emergency in a world dissolving into chaos felt by those leaving in those early days, before the siege of Sarajevo was established. It also conveys the fact that there was not enough information to make a rational decision as to whether to stay or go, let alone to evaluate what it would mean. In this light, the negative judgments that Sarajevans who stayed made in retrospect about those who left reveal the need to justify their own choices. Perhaps they express bitterness toward those who escaped the city not only because those others did not share their suffering and loss of a decent way of life but because they are ashamed of things they themselves did during the siege.

When it comes to the former JNA's assistance with the exodus, I heard a man in Sarajevo speculate that although Sarajevo was never "cleansed"[4] like some other parts of Bosnia, the "cleansing" was done indirectly at the beginning. By splitting families, the Serbs knew that the men who stayed behind would not last long before leaving the town to join their wives and children. In many cases this was exactly what happened. But leaving men in the town also meant leaving soldiers there, ensuring the necessary conditions for war. Yet another moral contradiction of this war is that in some circumstances humanitarian assistance facilitated armed conflict and "ethnic cleansing." The same problematic situation occurred when the United Nations helped to evacuate Croats and Muslims from Serb-occupied territories, as well as with the international post-Dayton assistance to resettle Bosnians in nationally "right" parts of the country, rather than their homes.

The initial phase of local patriotism, which involved anger, defiance, and a shared sentiment that the town must be defended against the "jerks" (*papci*) up in the mountains, soon turned into disappointment and emotional exhaustion. The Sarajevan art group Trio commented on the situation by changing the name of the Beatles' album, *Sergeant Pepper's Lonely Hearts Club Band,* into *Sarajevo's Lonely Hearts Club Band.*

Over the course of the war, as people realized what profound consequences separation entailed, they reevaluated the question of leaving. During the ceasefire in 1994, some of those who left at the beginning came back to

Sgt Pepper logo redesigned by "Trio" - Sarajevo

Figure 15. *Sergeant Pepper* logo redesigned by the Sarajevan design group Trio to express the feelings of the men who were left alone when women and children were evacuated at the beginning of the war. Bought in March 1995; reproduced courtesy of Trio.

rejoin their families, particularly wives and children whose husbands and fathers remained in Sarajevo. Others took advantage of the opportunity to depart. There was a popular joke at that time: If the siege were lifted, everyone from the town would try to leave, and all those who had fled would try to come back. When they met halfway, the people leaving and the people coming back would comment about each other: "Look at those idiots!"

As the situation in Sarajevo did not improve after 1994, more people decided to leave, and this exodus continued even after the official ending of the war by the signing of the Dayton Peace Accords on December 14, 1995. These people knew the conditions; they had to give up forever the right to come back. Most who left at this stage were those whose families were already abroad, people who could organize a flight for the whole family, or young people in search of better prospects for adult life than postwar Sarajevo seemed to offer.

My first visit to a home in Sarajevo was to the parents of two brothers I had met in Zagreb. Their mother greeted my colleague and me as if we were her own children. She made roast chicken with potatoes and soup. Although I had some 10–15 kilograms of food and other things that their sons had asked me to take to them, I was overwhelmed. While we were chatting, a doorbell rang; after a while the mother came back in tears. It was a neighbor whose son had just left the town for good. The neighbor was totally devastated and only now could she share her grief. People could not say that they were planning to leave because that might jeopardize the whole plan. They could not say goodbye to friends and neighbors and explain their decisions. It was impossible to take any possessions because even that could arouse suspicion. The couple we were visiting would not let us leave; they wanted us to stay with them while in Sarajevo. Eventually a young man came in, who was introduced as a neighbor and a friend of the couple's sons. He was very nice, and when we managed to persuade the mother that we had to go, he helped us find our way. He had been in the army with one of the sons but had managed to transfer to the police forces so he could stay in Sarajevo and did not have to fight on other Bosnian fronts. His patriotism was declining rapidly as he saw that with the ceasefire he was still living the same miserable life as he did earlier in the war, while some other people were becoming extremely rich. After years of active service he was also thinking about leaving the town and his family and starting anew, so he was eager to hear how his friends in Zagreb were doing.

The departure of young people in their twenties and thirties was a heartbreaking problem for families in Sarajevo. Most of the young adults found some sort of work during the war, especially after the ceasefire in 1994. However, only those who saw their jobs as meaningful steps to future careers planned to stay. A young woman in Čengić Vila explained her dilemma. The idea that during the past two years of the war she could have probably established herself abroad was painful when she looked at her life in Sarajevo. At the same time, she was hoping that the worst of the war was over. She was very attached to her family and would have worried about their well-being in Sarajevo. She realized that leaving everything behind and starting from scratch somewhere else required an adventuresome temperament, and she was not really the type. She would always have felt like a stranger and a burden to someone, and when the war was finally over she would feel ashamed for leaving and want to return. As a medical doctor, she had meaningful work in her profession and the possibility of a good career.

These attitudes were shared by many Sarajevans. This young woman felt ambivalent toward those who had decided to leave. On the one hand, she understood that everyone had reasons for leaving, but on the other hand, she felt that people should have stayed and made some contribution during the war. Similarly, she thought that people should come back after the conflict ended, but also that they should not have the same rights as those who had stayed, for instance when it came to employment. The notion that those who stayed should be given better opportunities in the postwar period was widespread and came into direct conflict with the political aim of promoting as many returns as possible.

I heard many people describing their friends who had left and gone abroad. In these stories, the most important information was where they were, why and when they left, whether they called or wrote through the Red Cross, and how they were doing in exile. "Generally, all departures were secret," a middle-aged man told me in 1996: "If he was a Serb, if he was leaving, someone might have obstructed it. The others I believe hid this because they felt that leaving was not all right. . . . All of my close friends, with one exception, left that way. . . . Even my best friend left without calling. . . . Perhaps he couldn't call, perhaps he left suddenly. But he didn't call during the whole of the war. Probably he doesn't wish to call." Sarajevans knew how dangerous it was to talk about plans to leave, yet they experienced these departures as betrayals and blamed those who left without bidding them farewell and explaining why they were leaving.

If friends made contact from abroad and their reasons for leaving made sense, they might be grudgingly forgiven. Those who stayed were not aware of the enormous guilt and fear of being rejected by their closest friends that those who left often felt. These contradictions arose from a conflict in which people felt forced to make decisions for which they were held responsible;

those who made different choices, or simply ended up in different places, found it difficult to comprehend one another.

Nobody who escaped the physical dangers of this war was immune to survivor's guilt. Those who fled the town felt profoundly guilty relative to those who stayed behind, even though they could justify their own reasons for leaving in practical and moral terms. This irrational, yet profoundly disturbing sense of guilt also affected people in the surrounding countries who saw what occurred and did nothing to stop it, the so-called bystanders. Often, they engaged in humanitarian work as a result of this guilt.[5]

Survivor's guilt is common to all situations in which moral norms are dissolved and people make the best choices they can in hopes of survival. This sense of guilt generated conflicting emotions that were difficult or even impossible to resolve. Those who stayed wondered whether the friends who had left had changed: did they betray their common Sarajevanness, did they become nationalists on the enemy side, or even worse, did they join the armed forces who also physically destroyed Sarajevo, and did they kill? Those who had departed felt so guilty about leaving others behind that they were sometimes unable to rationalize their own decisions in the face of the others' assumed accusations. At the same time, they wondered similar questions about those who stayed: did the war change them, could they ever be friends again, did they become nationalists, and did they kill? Conceding the terrifying randomness of individuals' fates threatened to make life meaningless. Those who stayed needed to justify their own choices, to make staying worthwhile, despite the existential danger, pain, degrading life conditions, and behavior of which they often were profoundly ashamed. Those who explained why they had left and somehow managed to keep in touch were often understood and still seen as friends.

Leaving for the Serbian side was worse than fleeing somewhere else. People felt it was essential to know what men were doing, to clear them of the worst possible crime in the eyes of Sarajevans: shelling Sarajevo and shooting Sarajevans. Betrayal of Sarajevanness by leaving the town was bad enough, but men who fled to the other side and were seen in the Bosnian Serbs' forces were considered *četnici* (pl.), a label that meant not only Serbian soldier or Serbian nationalist but also a bad or evil person. Any male friend who went over to the Serbian side was condemned as a *četnik* (sing.) until proven innocent. Any social relation with such people was impossible, and the breach was often irreparable. Even a young female doctor of medicine who still held to the prewar ideology of cross-national solidarity condemned those on the Bosnian Serbs' side: "Some of my colleagues from the faculty [of medicine] went over to the other side. . . . Our profession is such that those who left, both men and women, were not carrying weapons. But nevertheless, . . . they chose to work only for one nation. And they could have stayed here. Here I work for everyone; and they work only for one side."

All who left without keeping in touch were suspected of prewar conspiracy against the Bosnian and Herzegovinian state. Yet everyone knew how unclear the situation was before the fighting broke out and how disoriented people were in the beginning. In retrospect, people's own paralyzing lack of knowledge about what was going on was transmuted into suspicion of those who seemed to have known in advance what was going to happen. The violation of trust seemed absolute. For instance, a young man of Croatian family background had asked a good friend of Serbian family background about the digging that was going on in his neighborhood, Nedžarići, right before the war, and the friend answered: "Oh, nothing! To hell with them, they have started to install gas now." "And when the war started," the young man continued, "it turned out that Nedžarići . . . was a fortification! These were the trenches that were connected to the military barracks. . . . The interesting thing was that no one here knew about it. I want to tell you how perfidious it was, to do something without anyone knowing!" Another friend of his had tried to warn him that something bad would happen, but he just laughed at him. This young man thought that those Serbs who left nice cars and apartments must have been promised that they would get everything back after Sarajevo was conquered. "Because that was the only reason why someone could have left all that," he concluded.

Ostracism was a powerful weapon of moral condemnation, especially when there was no reliable information and contact was lost. The remaining members of a family generally made sure to break their relations with people who were suspected of going over to the other side. Often, that was more a response to the nationalistic pressures surrounding them than a personally motivated act. Eventually, when reliable information was available and communication was reestablished, not having borne weapons, not having shot at the town, and not having killed became crucial for the possibility of moral acceptance and reconciliation.

Families and Households

"You could take just one family, any family in Sarajevo, and describe their destiny. That will give you the best picture of what this war has done to each one of us." My host often made this suggestion, highlighting the painful separations that scarred all Sarajevans. Indeed, I cannot recall meeting any person whose family—a term that, in Bosnia, includes not only parents and children but those whom Western Europeans and Americans would call extended family, such as grandparents, aunts and uncles, and cousins—was not torn apart, most often because some members had left the town, but also because some had been killed.

The remaining family members often lived in the same household and became the primary source of security. In March 1995, a young woman described her family: "I have my father, mother, brother, and me. A family of four, but [also] my grandmother and my aunt [were part of] it. The six of us were here through the whole of the war." She explained that "in Sarajevo it was difficult to be alone. . . . Not for practical reasons. Not because there was no one to fetch water for you, not because there was no one to fetch bread or something like that, but simply because you needed someone in order not to feel alone. For example, if it happens, [being hit by] a shell doesn't [necessarily] mean dying, but being wounded. When you are wounded you are helpless. And when you are helpless and alone, then it is a tragedy. You know, it was enough to feel some security." Being responsible for others did not feel burdensome: "For instance, I was with mothers who had their babies. A baby one, two, five months old doesn't mean help in any way, it means a huge responsibility, isn't it so? But still they felt safer than somebody without anyone."[6] Even being crowded together was a relief: "We didn't use any *apaurin* [a sedative] in our home. . . . I could say, in a way [giggling a bit embarrassedly], that we were *apaurin* to each other. . . . Of the six of us there was always someone . . . to talk to, someone to shout at, someone to laugh at, to make it lighter. And you don't need anything else."

Not only did the state have no power to protect people, provide social services, or uphold basic human rights, but people had to protect themselves from state policies, especially military mobilization. Household members were the only people who could be relied upon in the life-threatening situation that prevailed during the siege. People who lived together shared their thoughts and plans, political attitudes, and existential experiences. Household members were the only people who cared so deeply about one's life and well-being that they could be trusted no matter what.

Perhaps it was because household members were the only entirely trustworthy people that homes were perceived as the only really safe places. People regarded their apartments and houses as safe from other people's anger and aggression, from snipers shooting outdoors, from armed gangs who kidnapped people to make them dig trenches, from police arresting people after the curfew, from cold and hunger, and in the end also from shelling. Of course, many apartments were exposed to snipers, people were taken away from their apartments as well as from the streets, and it could be very cold at home, but nevertheless home signified security. A young man from Čengić Vila explained the emotional logic, which he recognized was not rational: "The moment I heard the first siren or the first shell, I started to go home, instead of waiting for that wave of shelling to go over. . . . I ran home because I had a feeling that in someone else's apartment I wouldn't know where to hide. . . . Although the same could happen in my apartment, psychologically I was safer at home." He also knew that if he took refuge elsewhere his family would get worried, not knowing where he was, so this resulted in a paradoxical behavior: "I started going home exactly when the shooting started."

The division of household duties during the war bore some resemblance to the customary division of labor by age and gender: the adult males did errands in town and took on the physically heavier work, which included supplying water, fetching humanitarian aid and any parcels sent from abroad, going to work if they had a job, fixing papers with the authorities if necessary, and buying or bartering for food and wood. However, because most of the adult males were mobilized and periodically unavailable for household chores, in practice the adult females of the household did most of this work. Children and the older members of the household were exempted, as was the person responsible for cooking. Usually the cook was the mother of the family, not the oldest female but the one who was responsible for the household before the war.

A young man living with his mother described how the two of them managed, highlighting the psychological as well as practical importance of living with someone:

[My mother] was responsible for cooking, and making the fire. Everything else as far as the physical chores were concerned was done by me. . . . I fetched the water, I fetched the wood, I always went to the town when something had to be fetched—a parcel or something else. . . . And my mother was in the first place responsible for the basics: raising the morale and psychological [condition] [laughter], because she is an incredibly high-spirited woman. [That was the most] important thing: she was not afraid. . . . I was very much afraid. So the moral and psychological support that she gave me was more important, I think, than what she cooked.

Most households were enlarged during the war, not only because of the destruction of many apartments but also because it was easier to take care of relatives who were living together rather than separately as they had before. During the winters, everybody spent their time and slept in the same room; the room used for cooking was the only warm space. Sleeping arrangements were very flexible. When shelling escalated, beds were moved to the more secure parts of the apartment.

Generally, the larger households seemed to be better off because there were more hands to help with the chores, and scarce food and financial resources could be used more rationally. Often the household was supported mainly by one of its younger members who managed to get a job with some humanitarian organization or the UN because of his or her knowledge of foreign languages and computers. These jobs paid salaries in deutsche marks, with which people could buy necessary articles on the black market. According to an official with the European Union, in 1994 5 percent of the population earned foreign currency by working for foreign organizations and 15 percent of the population had it sent to them by relatives from abroad. Most of the remaining 80 percent probably got their share by belonging to a household.

Parents and Children

During my first stay in Sarajevo in 1994 my host told me about a dream he had had recently. He was trying to cross the border between the government-held territories and Republika Srpska in order to go see his daughter. He did not know how to make both sides understand that he was just a harmless civilian crossing no-man's land, so he made a banner. On one side it said, "I am just going to see my daughter. Coming back soon" in Latin letters, while on the other side the same text was written in Cyrillic letters. As he crossed the border he tried to hold the Cyrillic side turned toward the Serbian side and the Latin text toward the government side. But the wind started to blow, and it kept turning the banner the wrong way round all the time. He fought the wind, trying to turn the banner, but the wind was too strong. He awoke sweating.

He told me that before the war he used to look at the photographs of children that held the central place in some old lady's home. The children had emigrated to Australia or America, and these pictures were all she had left. He always thought this was tragic—something that could never happen to him. "But now," he concluded, "we are doing the same." My hosts had photographs of their daughter and other family members who were in exile on the bookcase in their living room. All of my hostess's relatives were in exile. They told me that I brought them a spark of youth that had departed from their home with their daughter. I asked whether they considered leaving Sarajevo and joining their family in exile, but they just said that they could not. One day my host pointed out a man standing in the window in the building across the street. "You see that man? That is Dudi. Dudi is a very nice person, everybody likes him, but you can see that he is somehow lost, he is not feeling very well. Sometimes I exchange a few words with him, about the weather, but you see Dudi is Albanian, and he doesn't speak Serbo-Croatian. If I left Sarajevo, I would be like Dudi." "People are different," he continued on a different occasion; "they are like plants. There are some plants that you put into new soil and they bloom, but others just wither."

Many Sarajevans over forty felt that they had no chance of starting a new life from scratch abroad and that their life as refugees would be even worse than their life in besieged Sarajevo. At the same time, they wanted their children to be safe, so they made the painful decision to send them away for the duration of the war. A woman who had a teenaged son and daughter initially decided to keep them with her. But as the war went on, her son approached sixteen, the age at which young men were conscripted and were no longer allowed to leave. She recalled how she got her children out of the town:

> I managed . . . to get an invitation from Italy so that he could participate in a [chess] tournament. . . . I asked in my old firm and they sent me on a business trip, to do some work for them, because they knew I had children, and that it was difficult, and that my husband had left. . . . I thought of leaving only with my son but at the last moment when I was applying for a visa I saw that I could apply for a minor child, so I applied also for my daughter. Sarajevo had again been heavily shelled, gas was cut off, and I was going to be away for a month, so I was worried that something could happen to my daughter, so I decided to take her, too. . . . I left the town, and then I decided to leave not only my son but also my daughter abroad, with some relatives. . . .

They traveled to relatives in Holland. "There was pressure on me to stay with the children," she said, "but I knew that my cousin with his wife would care for them as a brother, as a parent, until I could see what was going to happen." She returned to Sarajevo because she could not imagine herself starting from scratch in a strange country at the age of forty and because she could keep her job and her apartment, so her children might have a home to return to after the war.

Like many other parents, she tried to see the positive sides of this painful separation. Children who lived abroad for some time would not only escape the dangers of war but also get a good education that would be valuable when they returned. But nothing could be planned in advance.

I wanted to leave my son as long as it really wasn't peaceful. . . . Because I am a mother in the first place, and only after that a patriot [embarrassed laugh]. I don't want my child to die for any country. Everyone will tell you that. . . . I left my daughter because this year is a crucial one.[7] I have stayed, and I shall endure. But I will try to go and see them by the end of the year. If the situation is better I will bring my daughter back. If there were to be complete peace I would bring back my son too, but never mind. I am not sorry for my son, because I had wished to send him abroad for education after secondary school. . . . And as to whether he will come back, well . . . I am in a way saving these roots so that my children can return. And if it becomes terrible here, worse than it is, and if I have no other choice, I will leave all this and go to my children.

Parents would also rationalize that young people's employment abroad made them more useful for their country than if they had stayed at home. Eventually, they realized these children were unlikely to return.

Husbands and Wives

Sending children away for safety while parents keep the home fires burning occurs not only in wartime but at other times of economic and political crisis as well.[8] The separation of spouses was a more war-specific phenomenon.

The war was very hard on marriages. Couples who decided that one spouse, usually the wife, would leave with the children were in the most difficult situation. Marriages that remained intact were those in which the other spouse followed the rest of the family as soon as possible. In many cases this took several years. After the ceasefire of 1994, some women and children returned in hopes that the war was over. Reunions were sometimes difficult, and some couples divorced when they realized that two years of completely different living conditions had made them drift too far apart. Others never managed to reunite and divorced during the war. Some refugee women found a new husband abroad, while some men, left alone in the town, eventually found another woman.

For so-called mixed marriages,[9] ideological and national differences were devastating, since most of the "mixed marriages" in Sarajevo were between Serbs and Muslims, the two groups that were defined as main enemies during the war. A fatwa by the head of the Muslim community, Reisu-l-ulema Mustafa ef. Cerić, described "mixed marriages" as unnatural and compared the children of these marriages to rotten eggs. In an interview for the Croatian weekly *Globus* on September 19, 1994, the president of Bosnia and Herzegovina, Alija Izetbegović, called this fatwa "hypothetical" but did not renounce its contents (Izetbegović 1995:94). Although before the war the main problem faced by "mixed" couples was opposition from their families, during the war fear and the changed sociopolitical attitude toward national identity became the primary cause of tensions.

A Muslim woman who married a Serb in the 1970s told me that her father did not talk to her for seven years. After the premature death of her brother, her father came to terms with her marriage and accepted her children, but he never forgave her completely. She remembered him telling her: "He [the husband] is a nice man, I can't say anything against him, but you shouldn't have done it." Her mother was not opposed to the marriage, and the woman tried to find explanations in their family history. During the Second World War, her mother's Muslim family had managed to escape from Chetniks only because some Serbian neighbors helped them. Her father, in contrast, was from a highly educated Muslim family of religious scholars and judges who were more mistrustful of the Serbs. Her husband's family was open-minded concerning national differences, perhaps because they too had a positive experience of cross-national bonds. Her husband's father died as a partisan, and after his mother died when he was fifteen, a Catholic woman took care of him and became his second mother.

The main factors that destroyed the majority of well-functioning "mixed marriages" were the differences in opinion as to who was politically responsible for the horrors of war and the fear of being associated with the enemy by others. In the case of people who left for the enemy side, it was crucial to know that they did not take up weapons. For those who stayed, the only way to keep a "mixed marriage" intact was to hold firmly to a non-nationalistic ideology, as my hosts did.

The story of a Muslim woman who divorced her Serbian husband during the war illuminates the havoc that a war framed in nationalistic terms wreaked on "mixed marriages":

My husband was . . . a Serb, and even before the war, during the war in Croatia, he had his opinion that the Serbs were threatened. . . . At the beginning of the war . . . he blamed Alija, but by blaming him he blamed all of the Muslim people, because we wanted freedom, sovereignty. It didn't mean that if we separated we would fight with them. Of course, . . . there were some threats here. If nothing else it was said that all Serbs were Chetniks, that all of them should be slaughtered in the same manner they were slaughtering, that revenge is best, and so [on].

She understood his fear at the beginning, and tried to protect him from doing military service through her connections. He was almost fifty years of age, but he continuously received draft notices and was called to dig trenches. She wanted him to condemn the Serbs, which he would not do, and their relations became more and more unfriendly:

I don't know. I could not understand why he simply couldn't condemn Karadžić and Milošević. . . . Before that we had some disputes, but I think we could have solved them. . . . He repeated that he would leave, and I told him to go if he wanted. . . . Muslims and Croats were also fleeing, but Serbs fled in masses. Somewhere in October 1993 I raised charges in matrimonial court. I told him . . . "If you want to leave, then leave, but you shall leave divorced." . . . Because there were cases of mixed marriages where the husband fled to the other side and became a Chetnik troop commander, a *vojvoda*. . . . And of course people would tell me that I was a Chetnik woman, and that my children were Chetniks. One has to survive in these surroundings.

She understood that her husband would never take up arms against the city: "He was not a man who would kill. He was a hunter, and I know, because his hand would shake when he shot at a deer. He wouldn't kill, but he supports their [the Serbs'] ideology. . . ." Yet she felt compelled to separate from him and treated his departure as inevitable even before it happened.

When the divorce case was heard, the husband "told the psychologist and the social worker that he didn't want to separate. But he didn't speak with me at all, he didn't approach me like a man, like a husband. Nothing, like cat and dog. It was hard for some time." Their children didn't like it and said they felt sorry for him. He wanted to take their daughter with him to Belgrade, but she refused to go. "So the court gave me custody of both children because the apartment was in my name. So I had the apartment, I had work, . . . and even then he said that the judgment was on national grounds because the judge was also a Muslim."

Finally, he "decided to leave. I wished him good luck, good health and long life. . . . He called the morning that he went over. . . . He was in Grbavica. They interrogated him there, I heard. They wanted to send him to the front at once. But I heard that he didn't want to leave Grbavica. He wanted to send parcels to the children, because . . . when it came to food, the situation was much better there. . . . And he really sent parcels. When he saw that

Figure 16. Crossing the Bridge of Brotherhood and Unity (Most bratstva i jedinstva) between Serb-held Grbavica and the government-controlled parts of the city center. February 1996, before the reintegration of Sarajevo. Photo by author.

I had prepared to take the children out of Sarajevo, he decided at once that he was leaving, too."

At the time of the interview in March 1995, she still felt badly about the divorce, although she was certain that she did the right thing in order to protect herself and their children from accusations of being Chetniks. She managed to send him his most valuable personal belongings. They kept in touch by telephone, although mostly through the children. She heard that he accused her of divorcing him during the war, and she knew herself that even her own father who was against this marriage would not have approved. Their well-functioning marriage was destroyed by the war and its nationalistic ideologies. With a mixture of regret and resignation, she concluded: "I tried to be fair toward him. . . . When we talked to each other I talked to him normally, without emotion. . . . I think that in peace it would have been very hard for me to separate from him."

Because of ideological pressures, young couples who married during the war were mostly of the same nationality. Ironically, younger people were not strongly attached to the religious traditions on which Bosnian nationalities were based. This generation increasingly saw themselves as Sarajevans,

Yugoslavs, Europeans, and citizens of the world, and some of them kept their opinions regarding these matters during the war. In March 1995, I became friends with a young couple who had met two years before the war, went through the war together in Sarajevo, and married in 1996: she was of Muslim ancestry, and he was from a mixed Christian background. They applied for visas to the United States, which still had a quota for "mixed couples", and by 1997 they were living in California. They managed because they were not afraid to confront their families and neighbors.

She: There were situations . . . where these mixed marriages had a hard time. Primitive people around them could say that they were traitors.

He: It depends how you meet the neighborhood, because the gossip is usually spread in the neighborhood. Perhaps somebody said something about us behind our backs, but there was nothing said to our faces. In the first place, this was because we were really acting correctly, and secondly, because we let everyone clearly know that they should not mess with us . . . so that no neighbor would start reproaching [my girlfriend] that she is together with a Vlah [derogatory term for an Orthodox person].

Prejudice and harassment of "mixed" couples made many young people disillusioned about their future in a more nationalistic society. One young man, who later left Sarajevo, told me in 1994:

A mixed marriage in this place now can exist only if one party absolutely does not care [about his or her nationality]. That is very hard to find nowadays, but that is understandable, as so many people have been killed. . . . Recently the mother of our chauffeur left because of that. To spend forty years in marriage with someone and then leave him. That is not very easy. He is Muslim and she is Serbian. She went to Serbia, she is a real Serb born in Serbia. One of the sons married a Croat girl and went to Croatia.

He found the sundering of family ties by national loyalties extremely disillusioning. "The fear about physical survival kills emotions in you.[10] Which, to be concrete, killed my wish to continue the species. I was never a guy who absolutely had to have children, but in these surroundings I definitely won't. And I hope I do not marry a woman from these parts."

Another young man of Croatian background whom I met was dating a girl from a Muslim family. She told him that her parents would never allow her to date a Croat, but she had no major prejudices about nationalities, and when they argued about politics, they turned it into a joke. He understood her parents' viewpoint because he knew that she had lost seven family members in the war; an uncle was killed by Croats in Mostar, and his wife and two children were expelled. His maternal grandmother, too, was against marriages between different nationalities. So, even after more than a half a year, he still presented himself to the girl's family by a Muslim name that he had invented. As he did not want to leave the country, he adapted his behavior in accordance with new animosities between nationalities, while keeping his prewar view that nationality was not an important factor in a relationship.

Neighborhood

The tradition of neighborliness in Bosnia and Herzegovina holds unique meaning in this multiethnic society. Because of the long history of living next door to people of different religions, customs, and social positions, the concepts of neighbor (*komšija*), neighborhood (*komšiluk*), and neighborliness (*komšijski odnosi*, literally neighborly relations) came to represent a special bond of interdependence and trust between unrelated people. This bond was stronger than any religious, political, or social factors that separated them and could not be jeopardized by them. A middle-aged man offered this explanation of why a death announcement (*osmrtnica*) lists neighbors (*komšije*) among the grieving. "There is a very ancient story about it: A man was selling his house, which was objectively worth a hundred gold coins. But he wanted two hundred for the house. When the buyer asked why the price was two hundred when it was worth only one hundred, the answer was: 'The neighbors are worth as much as the house is.'" My host explained the difference between neighbors in the modern context (*susjedi*) and traditional neighbors (*komšije*):[11] "*Susjed* is to say good day, good evening, to give greetings on the street, and so on. *Komšija* is good day and good evening, but also brings water to an older woman, brings her bread, can be a sort of extra hand to her, and can help her as much as he can without sacrificing his own well-being." As in any society in transition from face-to-face social relations to urban anonymity, the term *komšija* was used to encourage solidarity between unrelated people. My host, for instance, called a shopkeeper *komšija* to establish some familiarity with an unfamiliar person and turn a brief encounter into a connection he might call upon right then or in the future.

In modern towns like Sarajevo, the circumstances of prewar life often made the neighborhood an institution of diminishing importance. People spent their days at work and their free time within the family circle, with friends, or downtown. Some neighbors became friends because of mutual affinities, not simple proximity. A middle-aged woman who lived in a modern apartment complex recalled: "In our family the gatherings [*sijela*] were confined to a smaller number of close friends who go back to our school and university years. . . ." In the evening on weekends, she said, "we would bring out a rich meal, of every possible origin." She described the art of having a social gathering (*sijelo*): "Bosnian gatherings begin in the evening (*akšam*) . . . the first twilight. Then the food (*meze*), drink, and coffee are brought out, and people sit and enjoy (*ćeifiti u rahatluku*) . . . With food (*meze*), one doesn't get drunk, but just a bit caught by *ćeif*, and *ćeif* is a special pleasure when one relaxes and is not bothered by anything. . . . *Rahatluk* is a very similar thing. To live in *rahatluk* means to live relaxed, peacefully." I spent quite a few late evenings in this family's home, especially during the spring of 1996. Even though they were a modern, business-oriented family, they knew how to offer the pleasures of relaxation, *ćeifiti u rahatluku*, and they generously extended their hospitality to me.

During the war, as work opportunities disappeared and every outing meant a long journey filled with risks, people's lives became concentrated around their homes. Neighbors met on the staircases and in the cellars during periods of heavy shelling, while cooking outdoors, or while waiting in water queues. Gradually neighborly solidarity based on close everyday living, an aspect of Bosnian cultural tradition that had not quite been forgotten, reemerged. Prewar neighbors started meeting for coffee and conversation in order to make the time pass and satisfy their need to socialize.

We organized gatherings [*sijela*], mostly at [the apartment of] this woman who lives alone, on the third floor. . . . We'd brew coffee and then we'd all turn our cups and tell fortunes from coffee [grounds]. . . . I don't believe in anything, and especially not in a cup. But, you know, there were moments when they were predicting a bright future for me, you know, so I fed on those lies. Then we told jokes, laughed, laughed ourselves to tears. Without any purpose, we sat in the dark. . . .

They shared the scarce resources that were at their disposal: "A few times we were also at another neighbor's when she would receive parcels from her husband, from Serbia, and the parcels were really rich, with sausages for instance. . . . She would fix a big dinner and invite all the neighbors." The custom of paying visits on others' religious holidays was yet another way to strengthen trust among neighbors of different ethnoreligious backgrounds.

Neighbors protected one another from outside threats, especially at the beginning when armed groups in search of hidden weapons searched homes and people were harassed on the suspicion that they were Serbian spies or sympathizers. A young man, the only child of a Croat father from the Catholic tradition and a Serb mother from the Orthodox tradition, told me that his Muslim neighbors must have protected him during a search:

Some of the Muslims in our neighborhood probably said not to touch us. The family living across from me was also Serbian, and they said not to touch them, that there was nothing there for sure. They came only to our doorstep, they didn't go in but asked for our identity cards and said, "Do you have any weapons?" Just in order to do what they had to, to have knocked at the door. They went into everyone else's apartments, but not ours. And then my mother said of course, "We don't have any weapons. Where would we get them from? We are actors. We fight only with wooden weapons, wooden swords, guns," and so on. I mean, there was a bit of joking and everything, but basically it is not pleasant.

Later in the war, however, someone must have reported to the police that there was a young man at home, and the police came to check why he was not mobilized. After checking his documents, the police left, but he still felt upset because he was suspected. He never knew whether a neighbor had reported him, and he did not ask anyone. He did not know what the neighbors really thought about him. The most important thing was that they did not show whatever hostility they might have felt, except for some children who made insulting comments.

Mistrust did appear between neighbors in these conditions of existential interdependence. Hiding in cellars was a stressful experience conducive to conflict as well as solidarity. Tensions between neighbors seemed to be mostly about what leaders or groups were responsible for the war. In Muslim-dominated surroundings, Serbs were suspected of collaborating with the enemy side, or at least of sympathizing.

A Muslim woman told me that in the beginning of the war it was suddenly impossible to know who was your enemy and who was not. This uncertainty was strengthened by rumors of neighbors killing neighbors and friends killing friends in other places in Bosnia and Herzegovina, although nothing like that happened in her own neighborhood. In a prize-winning documentary, *We Are All Neighbors* (1993), Tone Bringa captured the slow but efficient way in which the lack of information left the villagers with only the rumors of "ethnic cleansing" to orient themselves. In this atmosphere of nationalistic propaganda, we can follow step by step how lifelong neighborly trust dissolved. The film ends tragically in "ethnic cleansing" of Muslims by the HVO, while Croat Catholic neighbors just stand by. The sequel, *Return-*

ing Home, shows that life after "ethnic cleansing" is possible, although relations across ethnoreligious lines remained cold and formal and people's sense of national identity and religiosity had increased considerably. The *Sarajevo Survival Guide* makes its own satiric but sharp comment: "Rumors are the most important source of information. They spread with incredible speed and often mean more than news transmitted through official channels . . . Rumors are spread by all: housewives, university professors, teenagers, doctors. No one is immune" (Prstojević 1994:29). The stories I have heard from refugees who experienced "ethnic cleansing" in the war, however, included both instances of betrayal by neighbors and of people risking their own lives out to loyalty to neighbors.

Silence was another manifestation of mistrust. A Muslim woman told me of a young girl in her neighborhood whose father was a Serb and whose mother was a Muslim. The girl heard two Serbian neighbors say that the situation would get easier when the Chetniks entered the town. They thought that they could speak like this in front of the girl because her father was a Serb. In front of Muslim neighbors, in contrast, they were silent, and the Muslim woman was annoyed because they would not condemn Karadžić and Mladić for the siege and all the suffering: "We were still behaving normally with these neighbors, but there was already a certain amount of fear. You could see that they were also suffering, that they didn't have anything, that they were also threatened, but it was simply irritating that when a shell exploded, and we would unconsciously curse their Chetnik mothers, these people would just keep silent." A Serb woman in the same neighbourhood told me that it was hard for those who took it personally when shells were falling and people were cursing the Serbs: "In that moment he [any neighbor] doesn't think about me, but he thinks about his child," she explained; "I cannot take that personally."

At the beginning of the war, suspicion that people in Sarajevo might betray the town to the enemy was used to justify repressive but ineffective military actions. For example, telephone lines were cut off by local military units so no one could tell the enemy where the military positions in the town were. This reaction was not very rational, because the Serbian forces had such a good view of the town from their position on the hills that they hardly needed anyone to tell them where the troops or headquarters were. The armed men who conducted house searches said they were looking for Serbian spies or weapons, but often they were looking for valuable things to plunder from the frightened owners. A Serbian woman living alone with her aged mother told me: "One evening I was taken for twenty-four hours, from

11 PM. till the dawn, for interrogation,[12] not because of [nationality], but in order to take a Renault 5, a new one. . . . It was my friend's car, a friend who had left, and I had the key, so that was the reason, not because of me. When it comes to nationality I didn't experience any unpleasantness."

A young man of Croatian family background who was mobilized in the Croatian HVO troops and who lived in one of the central parts of the town with a mixed population, witnessed some incidents in his neighborhood, although he himself never had problems. Everyone in the neighborhood who was not Muslim took down their surnames from the doors, but he left his father's name although it was obviously Croatian. The gangs who went around the apartments would come to him and ask him where the Serbs were. He would not tell them, but when they asked where certain people lived he would tell. He gave me a fairly reasonable explanation of why some of the Serbs actually had weapons in their homes:

Most of the weapons were found in Ciglane. There were mostly buildings where military officers' families lived. Weapons were distributed, and when someone gives you a weapon you'll probably take it, especially when the army is giving it out, you think you have some good grounds for taking it. If I had been a reserve officer and was told that I had to have a weapon, I would have taken it. But, the plan was to arm [Serbs], in order to have strongholds in the town when it [the conquest] began. The other thing is that people were not at all ready for it. Most of them who got weapons thought like everyone else: I don't want to shoot, I might get killed. But, weapons existed.

He thought that the Serbian military-political leadership planned a conquest of Sarajevo and prepared support from inside the city by arming Serbs who were JNA officers. People did not necessarily understand what was going on and continued to accept things as they came, including weapons when they were distributed, with a sort of opportunistic inertia. Then armed conflict began, and armed gangs plundered everyone under the pretext of Muslim resistance toward conspiring Serbs.

In the spring of 1996, after the fighting had ended, I got acquainted with some of the people living in "Loris," a large apartment house in Hrasno, right on the border with Grbavica, a central part of town that was still under Serbian control. The whole building was the front line, and it was amazing that any civilians there survived. Bosnian army (ABiH) units became a part of their daily lives, and they developed friendly relations with soldiers who were placed there. The building had been a battlefield. We could walk through it from one end to the other because holes had been blown in the walls that had previously separated staircases and apartments. As I followed a friend who

Figure 17. A street in front of the modern apartment building "Loris" in Hrasno, on the front line toward Serb-held Grbavica. Sarajevo, May 1996. Photo by author.

lived there through the building, I became numb from seeing the devastation. Some deserted apartments had been shelled and almost completely burned. In others everything was a mess, but I could see the possessions of the departed owners: saucepans and coffee cups, smashed porcelain, heaps of clothes, old letters and postcards. It was macabre that private belongings were so nakedly exposed. An important border of privacy had been trespassed, domestic integrity had been violated, in a symbolic social rape of family life—all of this in a culture that cherished the custom of visiting others' homes. Sarajevans were very disturbed by the thought that former neighbors plundered what remained in the abandoned apartments. Fear of looting was a major reason why many did not want to leave and felt it impossible to return. To live again with the neighbors who did this sort of thing seemed untenable. Sarajevans were ashamed that this had happened. Until I came to "Loris" I had met only people who condemned people who plundered their own neighbors. But in this environment, where destruction was so overwhelming, I suddenly understood those who remained in the building, who told me how they scavenged whatever they could find in the deserted apartments of their former neighbors. It was a matter of survival with scarce resources; they took tools, essential parts, furniture to block a window facing the Serbian side. What others saw as a deepest betrayal, these people saw as a loan from those who did not need the items any more. This violation of prewar neighborhood norms seemed natural, logical, and even normal on the front line.

The ways *komšiluk* worked during the war reminded people of the role that neighborliness traditionally played in Bosnian villages. Those who did not appreciate returning to an older, rural way of relating joked about it, in a typical Sarajevan fashion: "Now we have Golden Lilies (*zlatni ljiljani*, Turk's cap lily, the symbol of the ABiH soldiers), Silver Bosnia (Bosna Srebrena, the old Catholic seat in Bosnia and Herzegovina), and the Stone Age (*kameno doba*)." Others saw the revival of *komšiluk* during the war as a way of resisting the dominant nationalistic discourse, because *komšiluk* as an institution effectively denied the primacy of national bonds. Knowing how to relate across ethnoreligious boundaries and seeking primary security in the *komšiluk* rather than among national brethren was one of the basic elements of Sarajevan and Bosnian identity.

As living conditions improved, the wartime pattern of socializing moved back toward the prewar one. Already in 1996 neighbor women were not gathering to tell their fortunes; people were occupied with their own plans and worries for the future. Socializing again included friends who lived beyond the neighborhood, since the military situation allowed people to move around with less danger.

IDPs, the New Neighbors

Generally, prewar neighbors took care of one another, while newcomers were left out. Most new neighbors were internally displaced persons (IDPs) from other parts of Bosnia and Herzegovina, who often had social networks with people from their hometowns, as well as more direct relationships with humanitarian organizations, including the UNHCR.

Many a Sarajevan regarded the people who had been displaced from rural communities as a threat to their way of living. A young Catholic woman explained: "Look, I feel sorry for these people because I know that these places [Srebrenica, Goražde] are shelled, that they are besieged. But I am allergic to them, when I see them I want to puke. . . . It is no longer only primitivism. It is insolence, do you understand me? . . . Everyone here in the top positions in the district is from Goražde, so they simply assign a flat to their fellow Goraždan. Yuck." The practice of officials favoring other IDPs was particularly objectionable, seeming to supercede the rights of lifelong Sarajevans. "That is why I'm telling you I have a feeling of panic and terror that Sarajevans should start their own party," she continued. "And you know, I saw the graffiti on the buildings [that was] inspired by this situation: 'Serbs come back, you are forgiven for everything!' You know, that is a change . . . from the beginning of the war when they [Serbs] were blamed for this and that. People are saying, If only our old neighbors would come back I would be overjoyed, because this is terrible."

Newcomers always have to be socialized into a neighborhood; urbanites often fear the influence that rural migrants might have on their bourgeois values and way of living.[13] But when the influx occurs on such a large scale as it did in Sarajevo, not only involuntarily but under conditions of siege, longtime residents feel especially threatened. The way of life of newcomers to Sarajevo was perceived as more primitive. Rather than merely feeling superior, however, Sarajevans feared that the newcomers might solidify the primitive style of living they themselves had been forced into by the circumstances of war. This source of antagonism was compounded by the fact that the immigrants were Muslim and often much more religious than the urban dwellers. In the changing political and religious climate during the war, the demographic and cultural reinforcement of Bosnian Muslim identity meant that the secular, pluralistic, and tolerant society of prewar Sarajevo would be even harder to reestablish. The rapid, forced migration collapsed the previous distinction between Sarajevans and rural Bosnians, accentuating the problems that arose because of the number of immigrants, their rural origin, their ethnic homogeneity, and their religiosity.[14]

Out of this animosity, two old non-national, but highly loaded moral labels began to be increasingly used by old Sarajevans in order to differentiate themselves from the new ones: *raja* and *papci*.[15] With contempt and moral indignation, the old Sarajevans increasingly identified the newcomers as *papci*; they were "primitive," greedy, emotionally insensitive, badly educated, and bad mannered. *Raja*, in contrast, the old Sarajevans, were the people one liked, most often because they resembled oneself and shared one's moral beliefs.

Sarajevska Raja

Friendships in prewar Sarajevo were formed by free choice on the basis of common affinities. They could become deep and strong, even equal to bonds of kinship, which was often imagined as a "blood" relationship. The younger generation spoke of *raja*, the circle of friends and acquaintances they liked and went around with. Most were simply friends, but people had one or two close friends, also called "real" friends, among them. Adults used *raja* more generally for people with the same moral beliefs whom they liked, whether neighbors, colleagues, or acquaintances. A real friend was very special. My host described his close relationship with his best friend, who also was his wedding godfather (*vjenčani kum*):

Friend is a very deep category for me. I mean, I didn't choose my brother or my sister. God gave them to me, as people say, and they are mine. But I have chosen my friends. Out of five hundred thousand Sarajevans, I chose my friend for myself. . . . I am talking about a friendship that started at the age of twenty-four or twenty-five and has never been broken till this day. This friendship also resulted in relations between our children . . . and we really lived as one big family in separate houses.

But his friend lived in the part of Sarajevo that was under Serb control during the siege, and they remained in contact mostly through their children who had fled abroad. "I haven't lost him, that is, I cannot allow myself to lose him, because he is too precious to me. He is somewhere there on the other side due to the circumstances, not because of his personal beliefs. He is in the group that is labeled as aggressors against me." But everything my host had heard from and about his friend suggested that he had not become his enemy. "He also dreads that this thing that happened to us could break our friendship. These friendships are . . . a tradition here. . . ." He continued to tell me "a true story about this sort of friendship in the Second World War":

There were Jovo and Mustafa,[16] and Jovo was banished. Jovo got on his horse and took the gold he had and threw it from the horse to Mustafa and said, "Mustafa, take care of this for me. If I come back, you'll give it back to me." . . . The war ended. Jovo comes back and Mustafa throws to him his parcel and says, "Here is what you gave me. You didn't count it when you gave it to me, I didn't count it when I received it, so it is as you gave it to me." These are the friendships that people make no matter what happens. Because people are first of all people, and as they say, no one chooses their nationality and religion.

I remember the first day when the part of the town where this friend lived was reintegrated with the rest of Sarajevo under the Bosnian government's control. As people and authorities from the government-controlled part of the town prepared themselves to enter it for the first time since the war had started, some for official reasons and others out of curiosity, my host wanted to be the first one from this side to visit his friend. It was not because of the formality or symbolism, but because he was worried that his friend might encounter unpleasantness from the people and authorities of the Muslim-dominated government's side. I have never seen my host so nervous; he seemed uncharacteristically upset as he anticipated their meeting. Through four years in war-torn and besieged Sarajevo, he was a master at making light of distress: when all supplies were cut off, he made theater out of preparing coffee on the balcony; when we had to run between the houses to protect ourselves from snipers, he acted as if it were a game of hide-and-seek. I think this was one of his most difficult days. Several days later, we went together for a family visit, and as far as I could judge the friendship was intact, although the two had gone through individual horrors that they probably would never be able to compare.

Tying dear friends to the family, crossing boundaries not only of kin-ship but also between different ethnoreligious backgrounds, was a well-established tradition in Bosnia and Herzegovina. Godparenthood (*kumstvo*) took two equally important forms: to a newborn (*kršteno kumstvo*), and to a bride and a bridegroom (*vjenčano kumstvo*). The bride and the bridegroom each had a wedding godparent, who was often their closest friend. A godparent to a newborn child provided security for the child if the parents died or became unable to provide for the child. Often a member of the family who was especially close to the parents would be a godparent. If the child and the godparent were of the same Christian denomination, this relationship (*kršteno kumstvo*) was formalized at the child's baptism. In Bosnia and Herzegovina, where people of different religions often forged close friendships, a special kind of godparenthood developed: *šišano kumstvo*, haircut godparenthood. When the child was about a year old, the godparent cut the child's hair. This tradition, which was not religiously based, became popular in Bosnia and Herzegovina after the Second World War when many people became secular and lost, or gave up, their previous religious traditions.

Losing and Making Friends

The loss of very close friends hurt Sarajevans, and the sundering of friendships changed the social fabric in a decisive way by shaking the idea of friendship at its very foundation: trust and help in times of need. Friends were lost because they did not help in critical situations, because they left town and did not stay in touch, or because they betrayed the values that were central to a specific friendship.

A young woman physician whose prewar friend I met in Sweden was left without a close friend. As far as she knew, only one had been killed, in 1994. The rest had departed, though only one was on the Serbian side. She kept in touch and was aware of their whereabouts as well as their reasons for leaving. She made new friends during the war, but she kept the fragile bond to her prewar friends through their parents who had stayed. "You know, when you get used to someone, you simply miss your friend. Because, after all, we have [pause], all right, even at this age you can make new friends, but it is different when you have known someone for years. . . . When she calls me she knows how I feel, and I know how she feels [just by hearing the tone of her voice]. These are the things that one misses."

With friends, as with close family members who had left, keeping in touch was seen as a continuation of a friendship. The theme of friends who left without notice and never called or wrote was prevalent in Sarajevan friendship stories, causing strong feelings first of betrayal and then of bitterness and moral contempt, which eventually became emotional indifference. Characteristically, people would say that they did not know anything about such a friend, although in most cases they did know something, because information was spread through other friends, acquaintances, and relatives. Refusing to talk about a lost friend was a way to mark the break in the relationship. An exchange I had with a young woman typifies this attitude. She said, "A friend of mine left. I studied with her for six years. We used to spend all our time together, and she never called me. Never." I asked, "Do you know where she went?" She answered, "I don't know. I know only that she was in Dobrinja, the last suburb toward the Serbs. I know that the suburb had completely burned down. . . . I mean, I stayed at the same address. Whether or not she could know that is not important, but she certainly could have tried to write a Red Cross message. But she didn't. I have heard that she is somewhere in Serbia, in Čačak, and that she didn't make it very well there, and I am sorry, I am honestly sorry. . . ." She expressed regret for her friend's sake, because her friend's departure had terminated her education and ruined her career prospects. She concluded, "That means, one human life is destroyed. I mean, she was a gifted student. . . . And really, if this madness ever comes to an end, and if I am ever able to go to Serbia or send a message, I'll really look for her. I'll really look for her, just to ask her why she didn't call. . . . Three years have passed, I mean, if there was some anger it abated. . . . It was a free choice. I could have left too. I really could have. But I didn't leave."

Lost friends were not condemned for their cowardice, for choosing safer lives and better material conditions, or even for betraying the country and its ideology. They were condemned for having betrayed the social codes of friendship, the city, its citizens, and the urban life they shared. Those who left were traitors to the Sarajevan spirit, which I refer to as Sarajevanness. This sentiment was expressed in many war songs by popular artists. One of the most popular, "Sarajevska raja," quietly but pointedly condemns a friend who fled abroad:

Sarajevska raja
(muzika/text: Hemda)

Sarajevan *raja*
(music and text: Hemda)

Ljubio sam jednu malu sa Baščaršije
ljeto dodje a ja tužan ne mogu bez nje
U Parizu, Beogradu druže jedini
Volio bih i ja s tobom sada šetati

I loved a girl from Baščaršija,
Summer came and I was sad without her.
My only friend in Paris and Belgrade,
I would also like to stroll there with you.

Sarajevska raja,
dok gradovi Bosnom gore
daleko ste bili
kad je teško
Sarajevo ostavili

Sarajevan *raja*,
while Bosnian cities burn
You were far away.
When it was difficult
You left Sarajevo.

Volim tvoju pjesmu staru jer
      me podsjeća
na pijane noći naše
behar proljeća.
Ovo nije tvoja borba drugi ratuju
Ipak druže ti si tamo a ja sam još tu.

I like your old song because it
      reminds me
of our drunken nights,
of the blossom of spring.
This is not your fight, others are fighting,
Nevertheless my friend, you are there and
I'm still here.

Kad se vratiš jednog dana pozdravit
      ću te
ništa više neće biti k'o što bilo je
Nemoj biti tužan tada niko nije kriv
Spasio si svoju glavu ostao si živ.

The day you'll come back I'll
      greet you
[But] nothing will ever be the same.
Don't be sad then, it is nobody's fault.
You've saved your head, you've stayed
      alive.

(Miličević 1993:15, my translation)

While facing the painful loss of old friends, Sarajevans forged new friendships with people from work or the neighborhood who shared the most difficult times. A young woman described the friendships she made early in the war when she worked in the bakery:

These are special friendships. . . . We were together there for a year and a half . . . [sometimes] for twenty-four hours together. And together we experienced the worst, those heaviest shelling times. . . . There is something that binds us after we shared our fear, hid together, ran together, waited for the negotiations together. . . . We joked with each other, made some practical jokes, we worried about food, and how to organize meals. So I brought one thing, and other people something else, and we gathered food. We made small banquets for dinner, somehow. . . . That is something special, something that can't be described to someone who hasn't experienced it. I think that these will be special friendships, although we don't socialize now with the same intensity as when we worked together. I keep in touch with some of them, and we see each other now and then, we go out for coffee. And there is always something that binds us. You know, you fight for your life together, literally for your life.

War friendships and support within wartime neighborhoods were established in a similar way. People were forced to spend time together because there was no other way of socializing. They shared hardships, helped one another, and tried to make life as bearable as possible by organizing simple *sijela*, social gatherings.

The new war friends were those you could entrust your life to, who were there for you when you needed help the most. They were willing to make sacrifices in order to help you. These friendships were a new type of social relationship that emerged during the war. War friendships were intense and quickly formed, in contrast to the peacetime, long-term processes of getting to know each other and gradually building mutual sympathy and trust. A young woman explained:

There are people whom I met only during the war, but I am in a stronger relation to them, or more dependent on them, than toward the people I knew all my life, but who had left. . . . You are with them all the time. When it was shooting, when it was quiet, when you didn't have water, when you had electricity, when you had no gas. . . . You experience that intensely, that's why one binds oneself to these people much, much more than before the war. . . . Here, you socialized in order to survive. Not to enjoy [yourselves], but to survive.

During the relatively short time that I spent in Sarajevo, I made some friends to whom I became as strongly attached as any of my peacetime friends outside of Sarajevo. These intense friendships were formed because of the war conditions we were sharing. Similarly, I acquired a war family. The warmth they shared with me—as if I were the child they missed—induced the feeling I often had of substituting for the absent family member when I met parents, siblings, or friends of refugees I knew from Zagreb and Sweden. In the beginning, although I enjoyed this kind reception, I felt badly about the situation. I felt guilty about being in a privileged position, having freedom of movement that these people, although deserving it by all standards, did not have. I also felt badly about receiving all this emotional attention that I did not deserve, except by knowing the persons who were so much missed. But after some time I began creating a new social and emotional network, and by talking with people I realized that these new bonds were common during the war.

Does "Sarajevo" Still Exist?

During my trip to Herzegovina in the spring of 1993 I met a young man, a native of Sarajevo from a Croatian family background, who was on sick leave in the hotel where I stayed in Neum. The hotel functioned as a refugee camp, as the seat of the Croatian branch of Mostar University, and as the Center for Herzegovinian Croats. I was under the impression that the young man was not so much physically ill as he was sick of the war. We talked for a while, and when I heard that he was from Sarajevo I asked him about the situation there and why he left. He said that he could not stand the fighting so he ran away, over the mountains, to Herzegovina. There he decided that it was better to join the Croatian troops in Bosnia and Herzegovina (HVO) than to be listed as a deserter. But he was not interested in military life and fighting. At the time when I met him he was mostly resigned. "There will never be a Sarajevo again," he told me. "The town may survive and be built up, but because of the people who left, life in it will never be the same. Because these people and the town life were Sarajevo."

In a way he was right: the war transformed the town, its people, and its culture. In 1995, after the NATO bombing of Serbian strongholds around Sarajevo, people for the first time started to believe that the fighting might end. At that hopeful moment, my host told me that he did not have a friend to go to for a conversation any more. A young working woman told me that it used to be hard to meet somebody in the town even before, but after the summer of 1995, she could walk on the main street without meeting a soul she knew. When I asked people to tell me about their friends and what happened to them, the most common answer was that all of their friends had left. The prewar Sarajevan population was often seen as the bearer of "Sara-jevan spirit," a way of life produced by a centuries-long melting pot of vari-ous cultures and religions, free-spirited and traditional at the same time. The most important ingredient was the sharp and self-revealing sense of humor, which allowed this blended concoction to function as a pleasant, even beloved social milieu. Without that spirit, many people felt that Sarajevo never could be itself again.

PART II

Ethnonationalist Reinventions

Chapter 5
Political and Economic Transformation

Over the course of the war, Sarajevans were increasingly divided along ethnonational lines into Muslims, Serbs, and Croats. Ethnoreligious identities became politicized and grew more salient in everyday life. Many Sarajevans consciously resisted this process, defending the secular, ethnically pluralist culture that had characterized the town, but even they found themselves acting in accordance with the new emphasis on religion and nationality—or, ironically, reacting against nationalism in a way that reinforced those divisions. Family members, friends, colleagues, and neighbors were judged by new, wartime standards, as people almost invariably tried to understand whether or not others' actions were influenced by their national identity. For example, a Serb, who belonged to the group that was officially defined as traitors and aggressors, would be seen as a bad person if he or she acted "like a Serb": if he or she had hidden weapons in order to take over the town, placed Serbian solidarity above solidarity with Sarajevans of diverse ethnoreligious backgrounds, or violated the norms of mutual aid that became a vital, though beleaguered value of local culture in a city under siege. But a Serb who did not act "like a Serb," who in some way proved to be a good person, became a good Serb—and still a Sarajevan.

What political forces made ethnonational identities more salient, and how was the structure of society reshaped in accordance with those identities? What were the position and policies of the Bosnian government toward Sarajevo's citizens as well as other nations emerging from the breakup of Yugoslavia? What consequences did international involvement in politics, warfare, and diplomacy have on the city? The transformation of Sarajevan society took place in the fabric of everyday existence, not just the realm of high politics and the crucible of warfare. What happened to the language under the rising pressure of nationalism? What symbols were superseded, and what signs of the times emerged? What did Sarajevans think about the new meanings of ethnoreligious identity, and how did they negotiate across new national lines of division?

I begin by explaining two key terms: "ethnoreligious background" and "ethnonational identity." I use "ethnoreligious background" rather than the more conventional formulation, "ethnic identity," because it fits the specific sense of group belonging that existed in Sarajevo. Before the war, people's feeling of identification with a particular ethnic background was based on religious traditions within the family. Prewar Sarajevan society was predominantly secular, and ethnoreligious background was not a strong factor by which people were differentiated, especially in public and social life. The term "ethnic identity," in contrast, assumes that ethnicity is a defining feature that pervades people's daily interactions.

Similarly, I use the term "ethnonational identity" in order to specify a type of national identity that was based on ethnoreligious identity. In the Sarajevan context, it is essential to understand that the meanings of national identities were emergent rather than preexisting. The reorganization of life around ethnonational divisions was a process that Sarajevans found deeply disturbing. Many families included members from different ethnoreligious backgrounds, so some people were reluctant to identify with a specific national group, and others had a certain leeway in choosing what national identity to declare. Most Sarajevans were generally comfortable acknowledging their multiple ethnoreligious ties. Some were discomfited by what they perceived as others' opportunistic assumption of ethnonational identities, while others treated it as necessary in order to survive in the war.

In the protracted crisis into which the war plunged Sarajevans, people's search for security became primary. Whatever enabled them to feel more secure was precious, however tenuous the security it actually afforded. The sense of security provided by a feeling of belonging to a group, which was not so important in the stable circumstances of peacetime, became crucial under the conditions of the siege. The emotional charge that group belonging carried could be experienced as a difference between life and death, and therein lay its immense political potential. Those who had not identified strongly with their ethnoreligious background found that it became more salient over the course of the war as they searched for people whom they could trust. This shift was not merely a matter of the political exploitation of ethnonational identities, but was produced and reinforced by the war itself.

National identities in the former Yugoslavia have been in transition since the Second World War, when a compromise was reached between two countervailing tendencies: to strengthen the national identities of South Slavic peoples entering the Yugoslav federation, and to promote a feeling of common identity. (*Jugo-slav-ija* means south-Slav-land.) Both of these political visions have coexisted in this region since nation-building processes began in Europe during the nineteenth century. The differences between the nations that became members of the Yugoslav federation—Slovenes, Croats, Serbs, Montenegrins, and Macedonians—were respected, and each people was given a republic in which they constituted the majority. At the same time they were united in one federal state, with a political ideology of "brotherhood and unity" (*bratstvo i jedinstvo*) that aimed at eventually uniting them all into one nation as Yugoslavs. This ideal was symbolically expressed in the Yugoslav coat of arms by six torches whose flames united at the top.

The federal republic of Bosnia and Herzegovina, however, had no singular ethnoreligious majority, and there was no ethnonational group called "Bosnian" or "Herzegovinian." I am often asked why this was so. In many ways, Bosnia met the conventional European criteria for nationhood: Bosnians identified as Bosnians and were identified as such by the surrounding national groups; they had a sense of shared culture, history, and destiny; the name had existed for centuries. The answer is yet another political compromise. Both Croatian and Serbian politicians have long asserted political and territorial claims over Bosnia and Bosnians. Historically, the residents of Bosnia did not have the opportunity to declare themselves Bosnian as a national identity. Those of Catholic family background had to declare themselves either Yugoslavs or Croats, with whom they shared this religious background. Similarly, Bosnians of Orthodox family background had to declare themselves either Yugoslavs or Serbs, because of their shared Orthodox background. But where did this leave those of non-Christian family background, the overwhelming majority of whom were of Muslim family background? The more extremist Croatian and Serbian politicians claimed that Bosnian Muslims were "really" Serbs and Croats who had converted to Islam during Ottoman rule; thus, the whole republic could be divided between Serbia and Croatia. The politicians of Muslim background, however, claimed that they were neither Croats nor Serbs and asserted that they had the same right to a national republic as the other South Slavic peoples. In 1974 it became possibile to declare oneself "Muslim" in a national sense, as well as Yugoslav. The republic of Bosnia and Herzegovina became home to three constitutive national groups: Muslims, Serbs, and Croats.

This compromise produced incongruence in the terminology for ethnonational identities in the former Yugoslavia: all the other national labels are the names of peoples and territories; only "Muslim" is the name of a religion. This terminology was changed during the war: the label "Muslims" in a national sense has been replaced by "Bosniacs." Those of non-Muslim background object fiercely and ridicule the new name, because "Bosniacs" sounds like "Bosnians" and they are afraid that the world will think that all Bosnians are Muslims. In this book, I use the terms Muslims, Serbs, and Croats because these were the national labels used by most Sarajevans when I did my fieldwork during and right after the war.

The political project that was undertaken in the former Yugoslavia after the Second World War was to make Slovenes, Croats, Serbs, Macedonians, Montenegrins, and Muslims eventually identify as Yugoslavs, which they increasingly did. People of mixed ethnoreligious backgrounds, as well as those who wanted to stress their sameness with rather than difference from people they were living with—in their families, neighborhood, social circles, the Yugoslav Republic of Bosnia and Herzegovina, or the state of Yugoslavia—declared themselves national Yugoslavs.

When political mobilization began during the late 1980s and the 1990s, Yugoslavia had been in a serious economic crisis for at least a decade. People were tired of communists and their economic policies and wanted something new. That the most successful political mobilizations went along ethnonational lines was probably due to the fact that Yugoslavs were politically represented through their national republics, which sent representatives to the federal parliament. Any appeal for a change, whether economic, cultural, social, or political, had to go through the national republic. For example, peasants in northeast Croatia and northern Serbia who had the same problems and interests could not unite politically in their demands; rather, they were presented in the federal parliament as Croatian and Serbian demands. In sum, nationalism was a constitutive element of the former Yugoslav federation (see also Magnusson 1993: Bowman 1994:152).

The political mobilization of Muslim, Serb, and Croat national causes within the former Yugoslav Republic of Bosnia and Herzegovina was often met with resistance and disbelief. This "nationalist road" cut through not only towns and villages but also neighborhoods, workplaces, friendships, and families. The question of identity was a problem since Bosnians identified themselves and were identified by others not only as members of their particular national group but also regionally, as Bosnians. They were known for "tolerance, good will, and conscious desire for co-operative and civil relationships" (Sorabji 1993:33–34, in Bowman 1994:161) among themselves. For them, knowing how to live well in the sociocultural milieu that blended several nationalities with their ethnoreligious differences was an essential part of being Bosnian (see also Bringa 1993:75).

When the war started in Sarajevo in April 1992, the first victims fell

Figure 18. A memorial plaque from the period of Austro-Hungarian control shows that as early as 1912 there was a joint mayoralty in Sarajevo held by three persons: one with a typically Muslim name; one with a typically Catholic, Croatian name; and one with a typically Orthodox, Serbian name. The text is written in the three major Bosnian scripts of that time: Latin, Cyrillic, and Arabic. Sarajevo, March 1996. Photo by author.

while demonstrating in front of the Parliament in Sarajevo against the nationalist politics that were ascendant (see Magnusson 1993:23). When I talked to a young woman who had participated in the demonstrations she remembered one banner saying: "If you want to divide us, you can divide us only into *raja* and *papci!*"—decent people and jerks.

The war government of the Muslim-dominated side of the town where I worked was quick to name the official "first victim" of war. Significantly, the choice fell on a female student of Muslim family background, Suada Dilberović, who had participated in the demonstration and been killed by a sniper hidden in the Holiday Inn. The anti-nationalistic feelings that prevailed in Sarajevo before the war were already being reformulated as the innocents of one nation being crushed by the brutal hands of the other. The snipers were Serbs.

The question of why and how the feeling of being Bosnian and belonging together regardless of differing familial ethnoreligious backgrounds eroded into mistrust and marked differentiation between distinct ethnonational identities is certainly an important one, and many scholars have tried to describe and explain formation of national identities in Bosnia. But another, more structural change in Bosnian society began before the war and was accelerated by it: the nonnationalistic social welfare state of the prewar era was rapidly being transformed into a capitalistic society where the elite would thrive while the masses would barely survive. In many ways, this system shift was connected with the political resurgence of ethnonationalism during the war. Many people became concerned that members of the dominant ethnonational group—in Sarajevo, Muslims— would become privileged not only culturally and politically, but also economically.

This political economic transformation was most obvious in the new conditions of employment that emerged during the war, when people were desperate for paying jobs. Working hours depended on the employer, and could extend to sixteen hours a day for a miserable salary with no benefits whatsoever. There were no trade unions, no maternity leave, no sick leave, no holidays, no additional compensation for night and holiday shifts, and no guarantee of continuous employment. Suddenly, workers had neither security nor rights. These terms were no worse than the general conditions of life under the siege, and they had to be accepted. The source of the initial investment in goods and machines made by these new employers was also highly questionable. Sarajevans believed that all of the businesses that began in 1994 and flourished through 1996 were based on war plunder or smuggling.

Notably, international observers and institutions concerned about the multifaceted conflicts in the former Yugoslavia remained silent about this shift in the socioeconomic system, while often reporting on the upsurge of religion and the growing power of ethnoreligious identities, and in some analyses religion figures as the single central factor in producing and sustaining the conflicts that eventually escalated into war. Did the system shift from self-ruling socialism to a harsh, exploitative, and undeveloped form of capitalism go entirely unnoticed outside of this region? Was it simply ignored because it suited the exploitative interests of international capitalist economies and institutions, which are dominated by European and American interests? Or was this system shift even promoted by international involvement in the region?

Still, perhaps more important than the international factors was the seemingly paradoxical role of the Bosnian war government in promoting these changes. On the one hand, it declared its ambition to achieve a multiethnic, secularized welfare state, but on the other hand, it promoted a capitalistic society and differentiated among its own citizens according to their ethnoreligious backgrounds.

By choosing to constitute the new Muslim identity of Bosniacs (Bošnjaci), the government reproduced the problems that the former Yugoslav ideology of "brotherhood and unity" had tried to solve. Because the people in their homeland were ethnoreligiously mixed, the new political leaders could not in any simple way promote the idea of a nationally homogenous state. The Bosnian government may have become more inclined toward other Muslim states than it would otherwise have been because of the stunning indifference that the West showed toward the Bosnian war. Many Bosnians were deeply and continually shocked that Westerners, with whom they identified strongly, did not respond to the many-sided, expanding conflict in the former Yugoslavia as they expected and hoped they would. Nevertheless, the Bosnian government did not adopt a policy of Islamization, and it continued to utilize democratic forms because it held onto the conjoined Western ideals of material prosperity and political freedom. These allegiances were reinforced by the region's cultural and economic ties, as well as geographic closeness to the West.

The presidency consisted of representatives of the three major nationalities. Some cabinet ministers were non-Muslims. But they were ministers without portfolio, which in practice meant that political power lay entirely in the hands of Muslims.[1] A political organization for the protection of the civil rights of those Sarajevan Serbs who stayed on the government's side, Srpsko Gradjansko Vijeće, was encouraged by the government. However, the Serbs I talked with believed that this organization actually served as an alibi for the government; they did not feel that it gave them any guarantees of security. The Bosnian government espoused and to a certain degree sustained the ideals of coexistence and democracy, but these ideals were not effectual in practice.

Many people I met in Sarajevo believed in the government's good intentions, which enabled them to think of the new country as the continuation of their previous one. In their eyes, those who broke all moral norms were the "others," that is, the Serbs on the other side, and especially the Serbian political leaders. The criticisms that some people made of the government, as well as the concrete examples of the government's injustice toward non-Muslims, were explained by exigencies of war, which forced the Bosnian government to act against its own good intentions. This rationalization was one of the ways people dealt with the destruction of their previous understandings of political life by their recent experiences. The idea of political normality could be sustained by regarding current governmental practices as a response to exceptional circumstances and only temporarily imposed.

Citizens critical of the Bosnian government's policies interpreted its stated commitment to secularism and inclusivity as a mask, and every occurrence that promoted the Muslim—that is, the Islamic—point of view was taken as a proof of the government's real intentions. For example, several people pointed out to me that Enes Karić, who held a Ph.D. in Islamic theology, was appointed as the minister of education, science, culture, and sports. Their disapproval was based on the notion that religious authorities should not hold political power in a secular, religiously pluralistic state.

The open display of religion on political occasions began after the elections in 1991, when the ethnonationally based parties won and the Muslim party SDA (Stranka Demokratske Akcije, Party of Democratic Action) began to dominate Bosnian politics. Leading SDA politicians started going to mosques. When state television showed government ministers at prayer, my host told me, only a few of the politicians chose to sit on the chairs at the side and not participate actively; the rest knelt in the center. After some time, the politicians began to shift their positions because they were not used to sitting on the floor for so long and found it uncomfortable. Only Alija Izetbegović, the president, and Haris Silajdžić, the minister of foreign affairs, looked to my host like longtime practicing Muslims; the others were so-called newly composed Muslims, opportunists who were using religion for political purposes. He regarded those who sat on chairs from the beginning as honorable; those politicians were not pretending to be believers, and they had the civil courage to show it.

Criticism of political leaders for bringing religion into public life was fairly common at the beginning of the war. People were used to religion being part of the private sphere of family life and unaccustomed to seeing it in politics. Many regarded it as a threat to the secular society and tolerant way of living they were used to. But not everyone shared this attitude, and the leading politicians were quick to formulate a counterargument, contending that the public display of politicians' religious affiliation was normal in the rest of the world, for example, in the United States.

Like most citizens of the former Yugoslavia before the war, Sarajevans did not have much faith in politics, politicians, or the sincerity of their causes. This skepticism is a heritage from the past. On the one hand, until the First World War the region was dominated by the Ottoman Empire, the Austro-Hungarian Empire, and the Venetian republic. People of the region were subjects and had no political representation. On the other hand, during the period of communism in socialist Yugoslavia when the political process was open to everyone, many opportunists got involved with politics for their own benefit. This skeptical attitude persisted during the war but clashed with the war-induced need to believe in something, to have political hopes, or at least an explanation as to why all this was happening. So, people often turned to those who had the power to decide the course of the war: Bosnian politicians and international leaders. Many people became more disillusioned or even disgusted by the political theater, this time on the global level. A young Catholic woman I interviewed in 1995 expressed a typical attitude: "People have lost their trust in politicians of every nation and type. Politics is a whore, and so are politicians. They talk about democracy, . . . all of them work in the name of the people (*naroda*), but the people get nothing out of it. This also happens in Croatia, and after all everywhere in the world. Also in, let us say, the 'most democratic' country in the world, the United States." Widespread disillusionment with politicians did not resolve the question of why the war was going on and, in the case of international politics, why the world was not doing anything effective to stop it.

Given the lack of reasonable official explanations, Sarajevans became convinced that making Sarajevo under siege into a symbol of something terrifying and incomprehensible suited the most influential member states of the United Nations. Turning the city into a symbol of terror quieted Western public opinion because it made it impossible for other people to identify with the people of Sarajevo. After two years of disinformation and isolation, the people of Sarajevo no longer seemed like Europeans. The incomprehensible terror that defined their existence made them appear essentially different. Thus, no serious demands for action—which would have been difficult, but not impossible to undertake—were placed on Western politicians by public opinion at home. A middle-aged woman in Sarajevo told me in 1994: "I think that everybody speaks about Bosnia as . . . [pause] especially of Bosnian women as raped women, as refugees. . . . So the image of the Bosnian woman is something really very, very different from what she is—it is what the world wants to have." This explanation reflects not only Sarajevans' attempts to understand international inaction but also their growing sense of isolation and of having changed so profoundly that they could hardly identify with their war-selves. Had their own sense of identity not been shattered, outsiders' misunderstanding would not have been as painful. The level of bitterness reflected the strength of Sarajevans' own doubts about what sort of people they had become during the war. Contrasting the international image to their own sense of themselves was a way of reaffirming and stabilizing their wavering sense of identity.

Bosnian Muslim and Bosnian Serb politicians were suspected of playing the diplomatic game by either hardening or loosening the siege of Sarajevo. The Bosnian Serbs were understood to use the siege in order to demoralize the population into eventual capitulation. Yet it was puzzling that, although all roads, pipes, and cables went through Serb-controlled land, during certain periods food, water, electricity, and gas came into town. The Bosnian government, people believed, used the same strategy of isolating Sarajevo in order to prove to the world that they were the victims in this war. For instance, in 1994, the closing of the "blue ways" as well as the periodic disappearance of electricity, gas, and water were explained as decisions by the Bosnian government rather than the doings of the Bosnian Serbs.

A feeble attempt to preserve some political optimism was expressed in the concept of the "juridical state" (*pravna država*), which stood for the ideal political order. Together with democracy, prosperity, and women's equality, the rule of law signified the Sarajevan utopia: a society resembling Sarajevans' ideas about Western democracy and the European social democratic welfare state, where citizenship and civil justice would predominate over nationalism, religious identity, and a criminal and ruthlessly competitive economy. In this type of state everyone would have equal rights and duties, regardless of ethnoreligious identity, gender, family background, or wealth. But what they experienced was an enormous deterioration of living standards and working conditions, as war criminals amassed wealth through corruption and violence, and unregulated capitalism brought plunder and exploitation. Politics came to turn on ethnonational identities, and Sarajevans saw threatening signs that religion and politics could become one, as it should be according to Islam. The processes of change of the political-economic system were as paradoxical as the processes of change in national identities: on the one hand, promises of Western secular democracy and social well-being; on the other hand, raw capitalism and an Islamic type of state.

Some Sarajevans treasured the notion of democracy during the war, while others lost their faith in it. The bitter disillusionment surrounding concepts of democracy and justice was directly associated with Western countries and was most obvious within the Muslim population. The years of Western nonintervention against the war in Bosnia and Herzegovina were increasingly interpreted as hypocrisy on the part of the West, which liked to talk about human rights but did not care in the least about a small Muslim population in Europe. The middle-aged woman who criticized the Western image of Bosnian women's victimization continued:

[In April 1994] I was in Washington and I watched ABC. It was Goražde[2] and Goražde all the time. The whole world knew that there were Serbs rolling their tanks and everything toward Goražde. They allowed nine hundred people to get killed and then they prepared a big show about rescuing the injured by helicopter. And they said they intervened. It is funny, really, they sent four airplanes and . . . only one bomb exploded. After Goražde, I said, the world is really so hypocritical. Don't you think so? [I nodded.] Yes. If it were some other people, the world might have helped. As they were Muslims, the world said—well, let the Serbs kill them.

It took some time for Sarajevans to realize that Western intervention was not to be expected. By 1994, the campaign led by the Bosnian government to persuade UN member countries to sell weapons to the Army of Bosnia and Herzegovina had been integrated into the attitudes of Sarajevans. The cause of their disappointment in the West was now described not as failure to end the war, but failure to arm Bosnian Muslims. The same middle-aged woman explained: "What we have learned in this war is that you can only count on yourself. . . . Nobody asked Americans to come here and die for Bosnia. The only thing we asked from the world was to send us some weapons so that we could defend ourselves. Since we were recognized [in 1992 as a sovereign state], we should have had [that] right."

Eventually disappointment in the West soured into a form of contempt, and Sarajevan Muslims in particular were often eager to state their cultural superiority to Western countries. A well-educated, secularized Muslim woman reflected that, although she had been fascinated and impressed during a visit to Paris in 1989, the war made her lose her enthusiasm for France and turn toward her own cultural roots; now she emphasized Sarajevo's distinguished European Muslim past. Although the UN soldiers in camouflage uniforms and blue berets were respected, they were also ridiculed: the Eastern Europeans for their supposed addiction to alcohol and pornography, the Italians for their red caps and feathers that reminded Sarajevans of a fool's headgear. The European Union's observers, dressed in white, were considered pretentious clowns. The Bosnian Christians' betrayal of Bosnian Muslims and the more or less obvious ambitions of Serbia and Croatia to divide Bosnia among themselves were sometimes connected to a general betrayal by the Christian world.

Many people believed that because of Western nonintervention Islam was gaining more influence in their everyday lives than they were accustomed to, or desired. In 1994, a secularized Muslim woman protested to me: "After all, we are European Muslims. . . . Is it not better for us that the world, that Europe, creates a civilized, civil state? . . . But if they [Europe] leave us to these [Serbs], to kill us, to plunder us, then we have no other choice" than to turn to Muslim countries for assistance. The price of that alliance, however, might be the imposition of strict religious customs foreign to Bosnia. "They have no business to come here and force people. We are different," she concluded.

Sarajevan Muslims were frustrated over being forced by the surrounding world to define themselves as either European or Muslim. The European incapacity to accept the fact that increasing numbers of Europeans are Muslims was imposed on Sarajevans, who knew how to be both. Sarajevans feared that the Christian West, instead of helping them to establish a juridical state, was pushing them toward becoming an Islamic state, a *džamahirija*, a term that often meant what "fundamentalist state" does in the West and was used in this sense in the Serbian press. The word itself is related to the Arabic *jamaat* (meaning community, society, or republic), *djumhur* (mass of people), and *djumhurya* (republic).

One Sunday in September 1994 I took a promenade through the old part of town with my hosts. We came to a small mosque that they wanted me to see. My host asked a man in charge of the mosque whether it was possible to go in with guests. The man said that it was all right, but we had to wait until prayers were over. We waited until half a dozen men came out. We started toward the entrance when a man sitting on a low stone wall nearby stopped us: "Non-Muslims are not allowed into the mosque!" He was in his early forties, dressed in a smart dark suit, white shirt, and tie, with a tidy moustache and beard. The man in charge of the mosque, my host, and a man from the neighborhood who radiated authority joined the group and started arguing with the man in the suit. They contended that non-Muslims could not enter the mosque during the prayers, but afterward anyone could go in without committing a sacrilege. The suited man seemed undisturbed and said that no one who was not Muslim could enter the house of Allah; it was written in the Koran, and they should read it. Although he obviously was not from Sarajevo, he spoke the local tongue fluently and evidently had the power to decide. The temperature rose. My host and the two local men became very upset. They told him that all religious buildings in this town had always been open to everybody. It was their heritage, and they were always able to show them with pride to their guests and visitors. Absolutely nothing in the Koran forbids this, they insisted. They were waving their hands and their voices were intense, but the man in the suit was determined and unmoved. Eventually we left. This was the first incident of that kind that I had experienced. Before that I had gone into several mosques. In fact, in Careva Džamija, where I got acquainted with its muezzin (*mujezin*), Staffan, my Swedish colleague, was even allowed to take photographs during prayers. However, in March 1995, when I tried to find the muezzin of Careva Džamija to give him some photographs from my last visit, I was not allowed into the mosque, and I could enter the courtyard only after covering my head with a scarf, which I luckily had with me. I never found out what happened to the previous muezzin, and I still have the photographs.

When I told this story to the only observant Muslim couple I knew, the young woman, who was a teacher of Islam (*bula*), became slightly irritated and said that these missionaries who came here thought that they could teach the local population the proper religion. She protested that in Bosnia they had been Muslims as long as these missionaries had, and that everybody had always been welcome in the mosques. My host and the young *bula*, as well as some other people, referred to the man in the suit as "Arab" (*Arap*). Apparently such people were sent by some other Muslim country, probably Saudi Arabia. They thought this arrangement must have been agreed upon at a higher political and religious level, since it was obviously impossible to go against it. People in Sarajevo—Muslim and non-Muslim alike—resented being subjected to missionaries. The presence of Muslims and Muslim organizations from other Muslim countries in public life was disturbing. Sarajevans were uncomfortable with being obliged to depend on Muslim countries and uncertain as to how much this would change their way of life.

Chapter 6
Language and Symbols

The ethnonational identities espoused by political elites amid the violence of war were imposed upon Sarajevans by a thoroughgoing renovation of language and symbols. Ethnonationalists used the media to promote the adoption of new words and images to define the people. In their daily lives, Sarajevans experienced changes in pronunciation, vocabulary, greetings, and street names; personal names and other symbols of ethnonational belonging increased in importance. Some of these changes seemed troublesome, others ridiculous, but they became an unavoidable fact of life. These symbols of ethnonational identities and changes in language altered the meaning of these identities as well as social relations in Sarajevo.

The Media

Historically, the media has been an important tool for the standardization of language and culture and for constituting nationalist sentiments and national identities in daily life (Anderson 1992). In the wars and genocides of the 1990s in Rwanda, Liberia, and Uganda, radio was used to spread mistrust and advocate mass killings, resembling Nazi propaganda during the Holocaust. In the former Yugoslavia, the media played an important role in propagating mistrust, fear, animosity, and hatred between emergent nations and ethnonational groups. The opposing view articulated by an all-Yugoslav alternative radio and television station (YUTEL) during the initial years of the crisis and war was unable to prevail against the power of national homogenization projects. Energetic and talented young journalists and intellectuals from all over the Yugoslav federation fought for objectivity in reporting and continued communication among the peoples of the former Yugoslavia. Eventually their headquarters, studio, and broadcast station, on a ship in the Adriatic, were closed down. After that only the local media and the media operated by the various republics were left, which were shifted from communist control to control by new national elites. Some independent newspapers and radio stations existed in most republics, but they were drowned in the sea of state-controlled media.

A plaque that appeared on Sarajevo's Titova Street in 1995 represents another paradox of this war. The headline proclaims that the truth is the first casualty of war; what follows is a list of journalists who were killed, implying that journalists were the prime fighters for truth and unanimously opposed to war. However, just one look at the local media shows that, despite the professionalism of some reporters, its major role was the political manipulation of truth. The international media had a more powerful and equally destructive influence during the conflict. By its ignorance and sensationalism, it portrayed the war in the former Yugoslavia as impossible to understand and thus impossible to influence. Until 1993 or 1994, the people were depicted as helpless victims of bloodshed, or alternatively, as raving lunatics and ravaging beasts. This portrayal enabled international diplomats to continue their gambling with newly empowered nationalists.

The media in Sarajevo had a limited influence because the siege made it difficult to broadcast and listen to the media and to publish and distribute newspapers. Information and analyses of the situation were transmitted mostly from mouth to mouth. The only newspaper published throughout the war was *Oslobođenje*, but during the first years it was printed on one or two pages and passed from hand to hand. The few independent weeklies and radio stations did not make much difference. Before 1994, few people had enough electrical power to watch television. As the situation gradually improved, Sarajevans resumed watching television. Several channels were available: Serbian television (CTB), the Bosnian government-controlled channel (RTV BiH), an independent Muslim channel (Hayat), Croatian television (HRT), and Bosnian Serbian television. At the beginning, radio was more important because it consumed less electricity. Sarajevans could hear both the Bosnian Serbs' station (SRNA) and the government's station.

People's opinions about the war and their revived national identities were influenced by the state-run media, but they relied primarily on their own experiences and those of people with whom they came into contact. One night we listened first to the government-run radio and then switched to the Serbian station: the news was identical and presented in the same order, but the name of the enemy and the side identified as responsible for initiating the attack were reversed. Listening to contradictory reports about the same events on Serbian, Croatian, and Bosnian government-controlled radio and television channels convinced Sarajevans that all the media were

Figure 19. "The first casualty when war comes is truth." A plaque on Titova Road, commemorating journalists who had been killed. Sarajevo, spring 1996. Photo by author.

lying. The only truth Sarajevans accepted was one in which they could recognize themselves. Perhaps because of this reason, for the majority of Sarajevans, the local, government-dominated media was most acceptable.

Toward the end of the war, the number of weekly magazines and newspapers published in Sarajevo increased to prewar levels. The major government-controlled or government-friendly dailies and weeklies were *Oslobođenje, Večernje Novine, Avaz, Ljiljan, Svijet, Republika, Corridor*, and *Žena 21*. The independent opposition media published *Dani, Slobodna Bosna*, and *Odjek*. All three of the main religious communities had their own weeklies and magazines: Catholics had *Hrvatska riječ* and *Stećak*, the Orthodox had *Bosanska Vila*, and Muslims had *Preporod, Sumejja, Kabeš*, and *Kevser*.

In March 1995, a young Catholic woman derided the media's supposed independence:

There is the independent television Hayat. I mean, it is ridiculous, it is more than sad that it is called independent. "Alejkum selam, dear listeners, here is the independent television Hayat." As if "alejkum selam" means good evening. You know, that's how independent they are. . . . In the beginning it was radio that was as objective as it was possible to be objective. . . . Then there is our independent television of Bosnia and

Herzegovina—terrible, I mean you really can't use the term "independent." . . . Our television is the regime's television. . . .

Her disgust was shared by Sarajevans of Muslim background as well.

At a meeting of the top committee of the SDA in Sarajevo on March 27, 1995, the leader of the party and the president of Bosnia and Herzegovina, Alija Izetbegović, commented on the criticisms that the leading pro-Muslim newspaper, *Ljiljan*, had made against the television station's manager. Izetbegović stated his conviction that the newspaper should be as objective as newspapers in the West are reputed to be. He presented state television as vulnerable to criticism from all sides, Muslim as well as non-Muslim: "One Catholic remarked to me that it is not right that so much should be said about Ramadan on RTV BiH because it is a common television [station], not only Muslim. We have completely contradictory comments. One man complains that our television is fundamentalist, while another says that one can't even use the greeting '*selam*' on it. What then is the truth?" His commentary situated the government on a middle ground between the Muslim and Christian worlds.

Symbols

During my first day in Sarajevo, a young Muslim man who was showing me the way pointed out the new police uniforms to me. Several days later, as I was going with my hosts to their apartment in Hrasno, we passed a police station, in front of which a police car was parked. Some policemen in new uniforms stood nearby. My host leaned toward me and said mockingly, "Oh, green! How I love green!" Only then did I notice that the uniforms and car were dark green, not dark blue as they used to be. A Catholic war friend joked about her green T-shirt, "I could say that I am adapting!" After a pause she explained that she liked green rather than blue, which was supposed to be the Croats' national color. The color green was the subject of many humorous remarks, but it was one of the symbols of Islam and stood for the profound changes that Sarajevans were experiencing. These joking comments expressed a critique of the increasing presence of Islam in public life.

Secularized Muslim women and men often deplored the threat that Islamization posed to Sarajevan society by commenting how unthinkable it would be that women should cover their heads (*pobuliti se*). The scarf (*šamija*) that religiously observant Muslim women wear is a highly charged symbol of Islamic identity for Muslims and non-Muslims alike. Women customarily covered their heads in the mosques, but during the war it was trendy also to do it on the streets, although perhaps not so much in Sarajevo as in other towns with predominantly Muslim populations. Since everyone was used to seeing some older Muslim women wearing *šamija* and older Christian women wearing scarves, people in Sarajevo were disturbed mostly by seeing the young female students at the Islamic school (*medresa*) in Baščaršija dressed not in traditional Bosnian Muslim garb but in a new fashion from other Muslim countries. Traditionally Muslim colors were vivid and varied, while Christians wore black, grays, and dark browns. The Muslim fashion for 1996 was black and gray, which provoked sarcastic remarks from non-Muslim Sarajevans. What upset people was not only the public display of Islamic identity but that this sort of Islam was visibly different from the Bosnian and Herzegovinian tradition. Sarajevans' preoccupation with Muslim female dress was similar to that among many Western Europeans.

A neighbor of my hosts was a war widow. Her husband had been an officer of the Yugoslav People's Army (JNA), and when Yugoslavia disappeared and the war began he served in the Army of Bosnia and Herzegovina. He was killed, leaving his wife with two school-aged children. He was counted as a *šehid*, a term that in Sarajevo signified a Bosnian soldier who died in the war and was buried as a Muslim, though it was said that the original meaning of the word was a soldier who died in a holy war, or jihad. New cemeteries exclusively for *šehidi* were established in Sarajevo during the war, often beside the old Muslim cemeteries. One of the most famous war cemeteries was on the site of the former football stadium in Koševo, part of the sports complex that was built in 1984 for the Olympic Games in Sarajevo. The cemetery was divided into one section for civilians and another for soldiers. The neighbor told me about an upsetting incident that had occurred once when she went to her husband's grave. She was dressed casually but decently, in her customary jeans and a shirt; the day was warm, but not much of her body was bare. When she came out of the graveyard a decent-looking elderly man approached her and said that he did not want to disturb her, but that in a graveyard she should be wearing a scarf over her head. She tried to stay calm and said that she never wore a scarf and did not intend to start wearing one now. The man replied that she should respect others. She answered that others may wear it if they wanted, she respected that, but most of the widows who visited the graveyard had never worn a scarf. They did not wear it for their husbands while they were alive, she told the man, so why should they do it now? Besides, most of the men who rested there never would have dreamed of their wives covering their heads. With these words, she left the scene. She found the episode very disturbing. It showed that preserving prewar norms and values was going to require a struggle, every day, in many small and unexpected situations.

The problem with the institution of *šehid* was not so much that it implied an Islamic interpretation of the war as a jihad but that it discriminated between Muslim and non-Muslim soldiers. After the government's attack against the gang leader Caco, the dead policemen and soldiers were buried in Sarajevo's central park, alongside a few old Muslim graves, as a memorial. But not all of the policemen were buried in the park, because only *šehidi* could be buried there, and some of the young men who died were non-Muslims. They were buried in ordinary civilian cemeteries. The graves in the central park became a symbol of discrimination between Muslims and non-Muslims.

Street names signaled the shift toward ethnonationalism in Sarajevo. When the blue signs in Cyrillic and Latin script were replaced by dark green plates in Latin script, introducing the new official color and erasing the prewar equality of Eastern and Western scripts, also the vast majority of non-Muslim street names were changed into old or new Muslim ones. But also streets named after partisans and communists of Muslim background were renamed;[1] the shift in ideology was not only from "brotherhood and unity" to nationalism but also from socialism to capitalism.

Street names have always been a way of marking civic space with the current state ideology. Streets were renamed throughout Yugoslavia after the Second World War, and the generations who lived before that time occasionally used the old names, which sounded archaic and confusing to those who were growing up in the new country. During the dissolution of the former Yugoslavia and the constitution of the new nation-states, the names were changed again. Sometimes the old names were taken back, but more often new national heroes were commemorated instead. So Sarajevo was not unique in this respect.

In the part of the town controlled by the Muslim-dominated Bosnian government, the name of the main pedestrian street was changed from Vasa Miskin's Road, an uncontroversial writer, to the old Muslim name, Ferhadija. The mosque on that street was also called Ferhadija, as was the destroyed mosque in Banja Luka, which became one of the symbols of Serbian physical erasure ("cleansing") of all that was Muslim. Njegoš's Street was renamed Aleksa Šantić's. Njegoš was the greatest Montenegrin poet; as Montenegrins were often half-jokingly described as the only pure Serbs,[2] the name was definitely not acceptable to the new Muslim regime. Aleksa Šantić, whose name gives away his Serbian roots, is a famous Bosnian poet who wrote some of the most popular Bosnian poems, including "Emina" and "Ostajte ovdje." Perhaps he was memorialized by the new regime because the girl in the first poem has a Muslim name, or perhaps because of the romantic, patriotic message of the second poem: "Ostajte ovdje" means "Remain here," and during the war a melody was composed for the poem and it became a very popular song. Although some streets named after non-Muslims remained,[3] a look at the map with both old and new street names, which I bought in 1995, clearly shows the shift from partisans and communists to Bosnian national heroes and old Muslim symbols.

Greetings

Positions with respect to different nationalist ideologies became most obvious in everyday greetings. Where I lived, I greeted all neighbors with the old prewar secular greeting "*dobar dan*" (good day). One day my host told me, with some amusement, that an elderly Muslim woman had come to the conclusion that I must be Russian. I was more surprised than amused: did I look and sound that foreign? But when I deduced her reasoning, I found it comprehensible according to the new nationalistic logic. Since I greeted her with the Serbo-Croatian *dobar dan*, I was not a Muslim, but definitely a Slav. I was not an enemy, but a stranger, just visiting, so I could not have been a Croat or a Serb. Thus, I must be Russian.

The most common greetings before the war conveyed good wishes with no religious connotations or ethnonational references. The two completely neutral and thus most popular greetings during the war, especially when one person was uncertain of the ideological preferences and ethnoreligious identity of the other, became "*kako si*" (how are you?) and "*šta ima*" (what's up?). They sounded awkward because they were very informal and used as friendly questions that would before the war follow an informal greeting. While Sarajevans got used to them as regards, I could not bring myself to say them without first saying "*ćao*" (hi). People who were religious used forms of greeting that were distinctly Catholic, Muslim (derived from Turkish and Arabic), or Orthodox. Before the war, these religious phrases were used privately, within the family, when greeting an elderly person or someone who was a practicing believer. When meeting people on the street or paying a visit during the holidays, however, politeness meant using a greeting appropriate to the other person's religious group. So, when Muslims met during Bairam they said, "Bajram-barčula," short for *Bajram mubareć olsun*, a traditional greeting that continued in spite of the new version printed all over the town reading *Bajram šerif mubarek olsun*, a sign of new Muslim influences coming into the town. But a non-Muslim would use the same greeting to show respect and confirm good social relations with a Muslim. The same courteous practices prevailed among and between Catholic and Orthodox Christians and others.

During the war, choosing the right greeting in official and public situations began to have material consequences. In a hospital, for example, using the appropriate ethnoreligious form would increase a person's chances of getting good medical treatment. Some people were irritated by such blatantly instrumental uses of religious greetings, and others hoped this fashion would pass, but most changed their greeting practices. Often their greetings were incongruous, as for instance a man who came into an office and greeted everyone a bit tensely with *selam*, the Muslim salutation, but after his errand was successfully completed left saying *doviđenja*, the standard secular goodbye. "It happened that someone coming into the room said not only 'merhaba,' but also 'merhaba, dobar dan, as you wish, Allah imanet,'" a young doctor of medicine of secularized Muslim background told me. In situations of need, many made their opportunism completely transparent.

In 1994, I took a walk with a well-known Sarajevan chess player whom I met at the airport in Ancona. As we approached a dark bearded man in camouflage uniform, she greeted him with *selam alejkum* and he answered her in Arabic. I looked at her questioningly since I knew that she had no Muslim roots (though she had previously been married to a nonpracticing Muslim), and only a few days before she had gone into a long explanation to convince a couple of Polish journalists that she was a non-nationalist and an atheist. She explained to me that by using a Muslim greeting, she wanted to show that she respected Muslim soldiers from Arab countries (*muđahedini*) who came to fight for the Bosnian government. When I thought about it later, I realized that this young woman must have accepted the new meanings attached to greetings, while the young woman I quoted earlier was firmly supporting the old ones.

Although still very much aware of the prewar norms of greeting, most Sarajevans adapted to the new circumstances. The traditional prewar respect for people of different religions in the private sphere became complicated during the war since a greeting also implied political positioning in public situations. In this way language became politicized, although there was yet no official rule saying which words and greetings were allowed or recommended and which were not. However, it was understood that everything that could be associated with Serbian was stigmatized, while everything associated with Muslim ethnoreligious identities, especially Turkish words and expressions, was desirable. Greetings became symbols of nationality.

Language

New language rules and recommendations soon followed these changes in practice.[4] With the dismemberment of the Yugoslav state and its institutions, the standard language of Bosnia and Herzegovina, a variant of Serbo-Croatian, needed to be renamed and standardized in accordance with the new nationalist policies. The Bosnian linguist Senahid Halilović, one of the experts behind the new standardization of Bosnian language as distinct from both Serbian and Croatian, was very explicit about the central role that the language has for a people's identity (1995:27–28) and defined the uniqueness of Bosnian language as inseparable from Islamic culture and civilization (1995:32).

The adoption of this language policy in the ethnoreligiously plural milieu of Sarajevo met with divergent political responses. Three publications marking the beginning of a new Bosnian standard, although of a relatively low linguistic quality, were politically significant: *Bosanski jezik* (Bosnian Language) by Senahid Halilović (1991), *Jezik bosanskih Muslimana* (Bosnian Muslims' Language) by Dževad Jahić (1991), and *Rječnik karakteristične leksike u bosanskome jeziku* (Dictionary of the Characteristic Vocabulary in the Bosnian Language) by Alija Isaković (1992). During the war, in 1993, a slim summary of Isaković's dictionary was printed. The language was called Bosnian, and some small alterations had been made. Isaković pointed to vocabulary as the main characteristic differentiating the Croatian, Serbian, and Bosnian languages, giving as an example three variants of the word coffee: Bosnian *kahva*, Eastern or Serbian *kafa*, and Western or Croatian *kava* (1993:3). The recommended vocabulary consisted of words of Turkish or Arabic origin. Although all Serbo-Croatian speakers were familiar with all three synonyms, the standardization of different vocabularies was designed to make these three new languages drift apart.

Another small change was the introduction of the letter "h," a characteristic of some Muslim dialects, which in this way differentiated the new Bosnian standard from the eastern variant of Serbo-Croatian, now Serbian. "It is said: *Words with h have a soul*," suggests Isaković (1993:4, my translation). The letter "h" creates a difference especially between Bosnian Turkism and the same words in Serbian and in Croatian. As this language shift was new and not clearly defined, it caused some discrepancies in practice. Eager Muslim speakers overused the letter "h," putting it into words where it did not belong. People who were more relaxed about their language responded in a joking manner by sticking an extra "h" in every possible word.

As in all of the former Yugoslavia, people living in the same area or town spoke the same dialect regardless of their ethnoreligious tradition. During the war, Serbian Bosnian authorities introduced the Eastern standard whose main characteristic was the pronunciation of the old Slavic sound "ě" (*jat*) as "e." This variant was also called *ekavian*. In Bosnia and Croatia *jat* was pronounced "ije" or "je,"[5] and the variant was consequently called *ijekavian*. The standardization of *ekavian* pronunciation on the Serbian side caused many problems for the speakers on radio and television who were used to the *ijekavian* variant, and because of this Sarajevans used to make fun of them. Some people had used the *ekavian* variant before the war, particularly those who had immigrated to Sarajevo from Serbia and retained their Serbian dialect. My hostess's Serbian pronunciation caused her problems during the war, since the *ekavian* dialect was a synonym for Serbian, and everything Serbian symbolized the enemy for most people in the territory under the Bosnian government's control. One day in the spring, while taking a walk with her husband, she saw a beautiful white blossom on a tree. She proclaimed her joy by saying "*Gle! Beli cvet!*" (Look! A white flower!). The words white and flower gave away her *ekavian* dialect. A man who was passing nearby gave her such a threatening look that she ran to her husband in fright. Using the Serbian variant implied responsibility, even guilt for the war. Nothing concrete or coercive had to be said or done, but fear was planted, and people could be accused without being asked what their position was.

Croats in Sarajevo, similarly, started introducing the new Croatian standard, most obviously on the Croatian radio in Sarajevo. The most ludicrous fact was that this new variant of Croatian was enforced in Croatia during the Tudjman regime and was unfamiliar not only to Croats in Bosnia but also to Croatian Croats. It was paradoxical to watch native Sarajevans sitting in their studio with new Croatian dictionaries, changing their mother dialect with a red pen into new Croatian before reading it on the air. Vocabulary was the most distinctive characteristic by which they could signal that they were speaking not the Bosnian Muslim language but the language of their ethnonational minority. In everyday life, they still spoke the Sarajevan dialect, although some of them tried to use Croatian words instead of Turkisms they would have used before the war.

The consequence of the new language politics was that the speakers of the same Serbo-Croatian language and the same Sarajevan dialect found themselves almost overnight faced with three new and different standards. Serbian and Croatian became minority languages. The obvious inventedness of the standard languages made it difficult for speakers to use them in a natural way. Noticing discrepancies between intentions and their practical results provided Sarajevans with many an occasion for a good laugh.

A person's family background and association with a specific ethnoreligious group was in most cases evident in his or her name. The easiest to recognize were Muslim first names, such as Muhamed, Sulejman, Fatima, Nedžad, or Armin, as well as surnames with Turkisms or prefixes such as Hadži or Kara. Among the generations of Muslim origin that came after the Second World War, quite a few people had foreign names such as Aida, Jamezdin (according to popular etymology, derived from the Serbo-Croatian pronunciation of James Dean), or Alen. Among non-Muslim names, it was much harder to tell whether the bearer was of Catholic or Orthodox background, or perhaps mixed. Many names were common in Croatia and Serbia as well as Bosnia and Herzegovina and were ethnoreligiously unidentifiable. Some names came in slightly different forms—Dinko was non-Muslim, while Dino was Muslim—so that the ethnoreligious background of the bearer was possible to guess. But one could never be really sure, because in many cases these general rules did not apply. "Some Muslim names are different from Serbian and Croatian. But even today I can't tell the difference between Serbian and Croatian names, I really can't. Only the very characteristic ones," a young secularized Muslim woman told me. There was a common rumor that Serbian nationalists (Četnici), when plundering and killing Muslim populations in villages, demanded that men drop their pants because the only way to be sure that a man was a Muslim was to check to see whether he was circumcised. A similar story was told after the Second World War about Croatian nationalists (Ustaše): the only sure way of checking the national identity of civilians was asking people to say a prayer or cross themselves.

During the war, ethnonational identity could have serious consequences. A young man whose parents were both agnostics, the father from a Catholic background and the mother from an Orthodox background, told me how he cleverly escaped suspicions of being a Serb and an enemy by joking about his family:

I needed a document and [the official] asked me: "What's your name?" and I said [it]. "Aha," he said, "You have the name of a Serbian king." I was quiet. He said, "Father's name?" I said [it]. "Aha," he said, "That is a name of a Croatian king." I said, "You know, and my mother's name is [. . .]. She was, if you are familiar with the history, the daughter of Tsar Lazar, who was married to Bajazit." I said, "As you can see, all of us in the family have dynastic names."

Sarajevans joked about others' attempts to categorize them by their names, since the social intermixture of the town was fundamental to its culture. But the politicization of language and personal identities made ethnonationalism a pervasive and unavoidable aspect of daily life and interaction in Sarajevo under siege.

Chapter 7
Mobilizing Religion

How did religion figure into the ethnonational identities that were constructed by nationalist politicians during the war? In the first place, all major political parties utilized religious attachments as a means of popular mobilization, although neither Muslims, nor Serbs, nor Croats sought to erect religiously governed states. Rather, religion became a key marker of group affiliation. The growing salience of religion in daily life met with considerable resistance in Sarajevo. Still, the politicization of religion seemed an inexorable process, as impossible to resist as the war itself. This chapter explores the intricate connections between war, nationalist politics, organized religion, and ethnoreligious identities that were visible in Sarajevo under siege. Over time, as religion became a public matter rather than a private one, religious affiliation mattered most in how people identified one another as friend or foe and became eligible for assistance from religiously based organizations. The existential questions that people had to face in wartime seemed to have a strangely marginal role in the organized religion, yet for many Sarajevans it was precisely the existential threat and fear that pushed them closer to their ethnoreligious roots.

Religious and National Holidays

During the siege, religious holidays became increasingly popular, and celebrations that previously were confined to the privacy of family and friends now became public events. Sometimes it seemed that Sarajevans, who have always been eager to find an excuse for festivities, became even more disposed to observe holidays during the war. Although it was hard to find the materials necessary to create a celebration (or perhaps because of that challenge), holidays from all three religious calendars as well as the "communist holidays" were marked in some way. A young, well-educated non-Muslim man told me in 1996:

It was my birthday [on Christmas day], and neighbors were to come. . . . I didn't have a pack of cigarettes to hand around, let alone coffee. I mean, it was unthinkable. But we celebrated. . . . There were some pine trees near the school, so I broke four or five small branches and we arranged them nicely, tying them together with wire to form a Christmas tree, and then we decorated it with small balls [*kuglice*] that we had from before the war. . . . No holiday passed without a celebration, . . . without anything, but with our spirits, with being there, I mean mentally we celebrated.

It did not look good in the eyes of other people if a person did not celebrate his or her family's own religious holidays. My hosts told me of an episode when some neighbors came to give their best wishes for the Orthodox Easter, upon which my hostess said that she did not celebrate and made them turn around at the door. Her rejection violated the rules of hospitality: you never sent your neighbors away if they came to see you, especially if they came to congratulate you on a holiday. But this was my hostess's way of rebelling against the political atmosphere around them and protesting the use of religion as an instrument of nationalism.

During my fieldwork in the spring of 1996, I was present during five religious holidays: both Muslim Bairams, Ramazanski Bajram (Ramadan), which started on February 20, and Kurban Bajram (Kurban), which began on April 28; the Jewish Pasah (Passover), which started on April 4; the Catholic Easter (Uskrs) on April 7; and the Orthodox Easter (Vaskrs) on April 14. I gathered information from my friends and acquaintances about their activities during those days, and I was grateful to be included in whatever they were planning to do.

During the month of Ramadan, many *iftari* (evening meals after sunset) were organized by Muslim organizations and businesses. Most Sarajevan Muslims did not fast. Some tried to be more observant of the Muslim rules of piety, for instance not drinking alcohol during these days or being kind to others. Many attended at least one *iftar*. The celebrations began with early morning prayers at the mosque (*namaz*), which only men attended, and then Muslim Sarajevans made and received visits. Usually the first day was reserved for relatives, while the following days were for friends, neighbors, and colleagues. My host's family was Muslim, but when I asked whether he would be making holiday visits and whether I could come along, he said that he had no intention of doing so—an expression of his anti-religious sentiments.[1] When Kurban Bajram came, I went to see morning prayers at the central mosque, Begova džamija. I was excited and filled with a sort of solemn respect and joy that I usually feel for collective celebrations: respect because it

Figure 20. A banner with Muslim Bairam greetings in front of the Catholic cathedral. Sarajevo, February 1996. Photo by author.

was not my holiday and I felt ignorant; joyful excitement because I felt that I was a part of something larger than myself and appreciated the sense of belonging. Some men were dressed in traditional Muslim garb; others wore suits and just a small beret. Afterward they shook hands and exchanged best wishes. It was festive but not pretentious, even though the head of state and some top officials participated. The ceremony was held on the common man's level, the style President Izetbegović adopted throughout the war. After the ceremony was over, he walked through the narrow streets of Baščaršija, which were crowded with people.

When I came home, my host joked with me for getting up so early and for my mispronunciation of the word *namaz*: the way I pronounced it, it meant something like jam or butter that can be spread on bread. Eventually he said that if I really wanted to, we could make a round of visits to his family. I think his wife convinced him that I needed to see what it was like. He warned me that it was nothing special and that I would only get overstuffed with sweet baklava and juice (*sok*). He was certainly correct about that! We went round to his sister's, then to the brother who lived in the same house, and finally to a cousin who had other relatives visiting. This cousin had slaughtered a ram, as was the custom among the wealthier families. The original idea was to distribute the meat among those Muslims who were too poor to afford meat. Although the table was filled with food, I already felt full from our earlier visits, so I took only the obligatory baklava and coffee. During the following days, I was invited for baklava in the homes of several friends, which turned out to be the most common way of marking Bairam. Even among people who were not religious and did not know much about Muslim customs, baklava was an obligatory ingredient for the holidays. By the time Bairam was over I could no longer face this sweet pastry, although I used to love it.

My hostess, who knew that I was interested in all sorts of rituals and holidays and wanted to help my research project as much as possible, must have decided that marking all holidays could be as anti-nationalistic as marking none. So, for Passover she boiled a pot of eggs in the Jewish way, for many hours on a very low fire and with onion peel in the water, and made a marzipan cake. There were no Jews in either of my hosts' families or in mine, but she remembered what a dear Jewish friend used to do. In the evening I visited a Muslim family with whom I had become friends, and they informed me that there was no curfew that day. Then they added that I should say "*šalom haver*" to prove that I am Jewish and that this was my holiday in case the police stopped me. The state television was broadcasting a film about Jews in Sarajevo and *Fiddler on the Roof.*

The next day was the Catholic Veliki Petak (Good Friday), commemorated by a mass in the cathedral. The most important mass was the Easter Eve mass, which started an hour before midnight, commemorating the resurrection, which state television transmitted from the Vatican. I went to Easter Eve mass with a young Catholic friend and her family, and we painted Easter eggs together at their home. The painting of eggs was widespread in Yugoslavia before the war, and although it had pagan roots and religious connotations, the majority of the population treated it as a nonreligious custom that was fun for kids. Methods of dyeing and decorating eggs varied; some families used decals and stickers, others more traditional methods.

It was a common Sarajevan opinion that, of all the believers, Catholics were the most pious; they knew their traditions and followed them. So, it was not only coincidence or my Croatian background that led me to Catholics who could explain in detail what they were doing and why and invited me to all their celebrations. Serbs (the Orthodox), in contrast, were commonly thought of as practicing their religious customs more haphazardly.

We visited a Serb relative of my hostess on Orthodox Easter (Vaskrs). In 1996 mass was celebrated in at least two Orthodox churches in Sarajevo, with some Greek UN soldiers in attendance. The main ritual was conducted by the patriarch of the Bosnian Orthodox Church, Vladika Nikolaj, who was in Sarajevo for the first time since the war had begun. State television broadcast the mass, and it was followed by a reception attended by the heads of the Muslim and Catholic communities, as well as leading politicians. While the Catholic and Muslim communities grew because of the war, the Orthodox Church was left without priests, and the community was very small and powerless. A Catholic war friend told me that the only official representative of the Orthodox Church in Sarajevo until 1996, Avakum Rosić, was not a priest (*pop*). "He was like a layman, as an assistant, he couldn't hold a ritual, a liturgy. . . . So their believers, in contrast to Croat believers, were left alone."

After the Second World War, new nonreligious holidays were added to the traditional religious ones. The most important public celebrations were Prvi maj (the First of May, International Labor Day); Dan republike (the Day of the Republic of Yugoslavia, November 29); Dan mladosti (Youth Day and President Tito's official birthday, May 25); and Nova godina (the New Year, sometimes called the communist Christmas). In each of the federal republics Dan oslobođenja (the Day of Liberation), commemorating the victory in 1945, and Dan ustanka (the Day of Insurrection), commemorating the for-

Figure 21. Easter mass with Vladika Nikolaj in the Old Orthodox Church. Sarajevo, April 1996. Photo by author.

mation of the first partisan unit in the republic in 1941, were celebrated on a smaller scale.

The First of May was traditionally celebrated by Sarajevans with a folk festival at Vrelo Bosne, the spring of the river Bosna. During the war it was under the control of Bosnian Serbs, so 1996 was the first time it was possible to go there again. Everyone I talked with waxed lyrical about the fabulous times they had at Vrelo Bosne during the First of May celebrations before the war. But when I asked them whether they were going there in 1996, I could not find a soul to keep me company. So I decided to go alone. In the morning my hosts said that they would come along. I understood that it was very sensitive for Sarajevans to see the place that once symbolized the good life in its postwar condition. The surrounding fields were still sown with landmines; a few people who left the path were killed. Nearby houses had been shelled, plundered, and abandoned. The scene brought back immediate recollections of war and destruction, as well as memories of people and times that were gone forever. Nevertheless, many people gathered at the spring, which was surrounded by beautiful streams, lakes, meadows, and small wooded paths. Here and there rams were grilled on an open fire and barbecued minced meat was sold in special bread (*ćevapi u somunu*). Popular folk music was playing from portable radios, small groups were picnicking on the grass, and some people were dancing a wheel dance (*kolo*). I could picture this place as full of people in the prewar years and I could see that it might be so again, although most of the people there in 1996 were probably strangers or refugees and, like myself, there for the first time.

A young doctor of medicine told me that in 1995 an ethnoreligiously mixed medical staff was on duty in Koševo hospital, celebrating the New Year according to the Orthodox (Serbian) calendar, a previously nonexistent holiday. One of the nurses was of Orthodox family background, so they had baked chickens, potatoes, and cakes, and they were in good spirits. The Serbs from the other side of the town opened heavy fire at twelve o'clock to celebrate. Very few people dared to go out, so there was not much work to do at the hospital. So they passed their time eating, joking, listening to the heavy artillery, and watching television, which was showing a documentary, "Witnesses of Genocide." The whole story was completely absurd, and she told it with a characteristic blend of humorous detachment, survivors' pride, and grief at a shattered world. They were joking about nationalistic holidays at the same time that nationalist warfare was having genocidal consequences for them and their patients, and the television made it all surreal. "You can't find that anywhere. You can find it only here. You know. And when I who am born here cannot put all that together, then for strangers it is terrible," she concluded.

The Imposition of Religious Education

In the autumn of 1994, religion was introduced as an optional subject in primary and secondary schools. The Program of Religious Education (Plan i program vjerskog odgoja i obrazovanja) contained outlines of all the religions found in Bosnia: Islam, Catholic Christianity, Orthodox Christianity, Judaism, and Seventh-Day Adventism. In theory, children and their parents could choose any religion, or not take these classes at all. The responsibility for organizing and financing religious education was left to the respective communities. In practice, Islamic education was introduced in most schools, while Catholic education was offered in one or two. Children who did not wish to be educated in Islam could refuse to attend these classes with their classmates. But Islam was becoming the state religion, and most non-Muslim or nonreligious parents did not want their children to stand out in any way, so they sent them to these classes with the rationale that everyone living in

Bosnia had to know something about Islam. This is a good example of how liberal polices of "free choice" in practice always lead to discrimination against those with less power, in this case the ethnoreligious minorities. The representatives of the Bosnian Catholic Church were displeased with this situation, since the original proposal from the government was that religious education should give children insight into all religions, along the lines of comparative religion or the history of religions, which they supported.

In 1994–95, new textbooks were introduced for most subjects. The curricula in history and language and literature were changed in accordance with the process of Bosnian Muslim identity formation. The following text from the fourth-grade history book is a typical example of how a single nationality—in this case Bosnian Muslims, today called Bosniacs (Bošnjaci)—is constituted as the original and superior people: they were there first, the natives of the land, and they were of higher standing than simple stockbreeders and serfs: "In the Middle Ages Bosnia was populated by a homogenous Bosnian people, called Bošnjani. . . . Turkish authorities populated the desolate parts of the land by Croats and Serbs from the surrounding countries. These were mostly stockbreeders and workers (serfs). . . . So, the Bošnjaci Muslims were left as the only representatives of the Bosnian people—descendants of the medieval Bošnjani" (Imamović and Bošnjak 1994:12, my translation). A Muslim-Croat team of authors legitimizes the contents as nationally neutral and historically true.

Bosnian literature was "cleansed" of Bosnian authors of non-Muslim origin, mostly Bosnian Serbs. The most remarkable example was the winner of the Nobel Prize for Literature, Ivo Andrić, who was expelled from the schoolbooks. Sarajevans feared that the cultural heritage that represented the previous coexistence of three equal ethnonational groups was gradually being replaced by new Bosnian Muslim representations.

Private Catholic primary and secondary schools, which opened in 1995, were well equipped and offered a high-quality education, so even non-Catholic families considered enrolling their children. Similarly, in 1997 a Muslim boarding school opened in Sarajevo that offered education on a high international level. Although all schools had to offer a standard curriculum, there were substantial differences in languages, culture, and religious education between Catholic, Muslim, and state-school programs.

Muslim religious schools (*mektebi*) existed before the war, as did Christian Sunday schools. People could send their children to these schools during their free time, but it was considered a private matter and the majority did not bother with it. During the war, the number of children attending religious education increased. A young secularized Muslim woman living in one of the Sarajevan suburbs told me in 1994 that there was a newly opened *mekteb* in her neighborhood. One day her sister's son came home and asked if he could also go to *mekteb*. Although the family was not religious and the boy's father was from a Serbian family, his mother let him go. Lots of the children he played with were going, and they were happy to get chocolate there. But this trend soon faded away. After some time most stopped attending *mekteb*, including my friend's nephew.

Some Sarajevans were willing to send their children to religious education programs run by faith traditions that were not represented in their own families because they thought that children growing up in a religiously mixed milieu should learn about other religions. This rationale, which nonreligious and non-nationalistic parents seemed to have had when letting their children attend religious classes of various ethnoreligious groups, was in line with traditional norms of mutual respect, as well as of the secularized "brotherhood and unity" ideology: differences in religion, culture, and nationality are a richness, not a reason for mistrust and hatred.

Whatever led people to turn toward mosques and churches, the fact remains that, as a secularized Muslim woman told me in the spring of 1996, "it was very unpopular not to be religious." "Children already have an impression that it is something bad. My son, while playing this summer in the street with other kids, asked them whether they knew what an atheist was. Children didn't know. And then he explained to them that it is a person who doesn't believe in God. All the kids hurried to say, 'I am not an atheist, I am not an atheist.' . . . Then he said, 'My mother is an atheist.' [They responded:] 'Oh, but it doesn't matter, she is nevertheless a good woman.'"

Religious Affiliation and Humanitarian Assistance

The fact that their desperate need for food and money led people to humanitarian organizations that assisted them because of their religious identities and ethnic affiliations seemed ominous to many secularized Sarajevans of various ethnoreligious backgrounds. A young secularized Croat, who worked for a small foreign Catholic NGO, voiced his skepticism about the aid enterprise to me in 1994:

If this war was going on while the people had normal means of existence, I think that they would have turned against the religious communities even more. . . . But of course, the war was coming, poverty was coming, hunger was coming, and suddenly these religious communities appeared . . . as the only ones who had food. Now then, if all of them had some food reserves before the war, . . . no one is going to convince me that [they] didn't know that there was going to be a war, and that they weren't participating in one way or another. . . . And now they are making profits from the war, by moving people closer to their religious communities. Let us wait till the war ends. Already the people are distancing themselves because they can see what is going on. If *hodžas* and priests are buying [German cars and driving them] around the town while people are starving, how, where from?

Even those who did not share this young man's suspicions about corruption and collaboration in wartime were often uncomfortable with the religious strings attached to humanitarian aid.

The Catholic humanitarian organization Caritas distributed aid to people whose names were listed as parishioners and to those who could claim a Catholic connection through a relative, however distant. A Catholic young woman explained that many "were mixed families. It was enough that there was one Croat, a Catholic, a granny, it didn't matter. On account of her, the whole family would get" humanitarian aid. A secularized Muslim woman managed to get help for her family from Caritas because her deceased mother-in-law was Catholic. "She didn't pass on any of her Catholic tradition to my husband, who is a Serb, because they lived in a Serbian village. He didn't know his mother's family, but on account of this mother-in-law I asked if I could enlist myself at Caritas. Because no one was giving food." She contrasted Caritas with Merhamet, the Muslim humanitarian aid organization: "All Muslims will tell you, there is even a joke about Merhamet: 'May HVO defend you, and Merhamet feed you!' ('Da Bog da te HVO branio, a Merhamet hranio!') It is a curse. The HVO was useless as defense, and so was Merhamet as a food supplier. Muslims went to ask Merhamet, but they didn't get anything. . . . Supposedly, Merhamet was supplying the army. . . . Caritas really distributed, and those who had some connection with Catholics, for instance we had their card, but I am not on it. They didn't take me as a Muslim, but they took my husband and children."

Since one of the conditions for receiving aid from Caritas was to have the home blessed by a Catholic priest, some people saw it as forcing people to convert to Catholicism and associated it with the forced Catholicization of the Muslim population by the NDH (Independent State of Croatia) during the Second World War. Others saw it as a formality that could do no harm since a blessing was a blessing, regardless of its source. A secularized Muslim friend who received help from Caritas told me, "Let them Christianize me, and everything I have, it won't harm me. When they came they asked if they could Christianize, my mother who is a Muslim received them and said that they could, that it was all right. That is our Bosnian tolerance." When I asked a young Catholic war friend about the "Christianization" of homes (*pokršta-vanje*), the term I often heard used, she corrected me and pointed out that it was the blessing of homes by sprinkling holy water (*škropljenje*). This distinction was sensitive because Christianization is associated with forcible conversion, while blessing is voluntary. "I know and I stand fully behind the fact that no one was forced!" she declared. I pointed out that the need for food was forcing people. "The need, yes," she conceded, "but that is another matter. But no one said, you have to, you know."

Even Sarajevans of Catholic background did not understand this practice at the beginning. A nonreligious young man from a Croat family who declared himself a Yugoslav before the war recounted his experience:

I told my mother to go and ask for humanitarian aid when they distributed it. She was hesitating—what would the neighborhood say? I told her not to mind that, we were hungry. . . . So, when my mother went to get the humanitarian aid, they asked her whether she wanted a friar to come [and bless the home]. They didn't explain anything. And my mother said, completely sincerely, that there was no need; he never used to come to us, so there was no need for it now. Then the woman crossed out something. When my mother came to fetch the humanitarian aid they told her to go to Dobrotvor, probably figuring from her first name that she was a Serb only married to a Croat. Then I went there and made a big row, without any restraint. I told them to be ashamed, I shouted at them, I told them to look at her birthplace where Serbs never lived. Then I saw two Serbian neighbors in the queue, and I continued shouting, questioning the criterion by which they had more right than my mother. Then a man there told me that my mother said that she didn't want the friar to come to our house. And I told him that he could send three if it's necessary, to write down that three friars could come if they wanted to! I mean, it's absurd, it's dirty.

He was also bitter about new converts who professed to be religious solely for personal gain and the theft of humanitarian aid; supplies were stolen not only when convoys were en route to Sarajevo but also by employees of Caritas, the religious and national brethren who were supposed to be the primary source of safety and solidarity: "There are 50 percent nonbelievers in Caritas, the newcomers, that is. Suddenly they became great believers! They know the 'Our Father' because they learned it in a month in order to get employed by Caritas. These people were dragging loads and loads to their homes. These goods ended up on the [black] markets. Large quantities of goods were coming, and only 60 or 70 percent was distributed. . . . It was a general theft."

This young man thought that food and other necessities should have been distributed to everyone equally. Had this occurred, the division of Sarajevans into distinct ethnonational groups would certainly have been weaker.

The close connections between access to the basic means of existence and matters of ethnoreligious identity politics caused considerable indignation. Survival, religiosity, and nationality became hard to separate. The young man continued:

Everyone is against one common center for distribution, which should be normal if you propagate a "multi" [multinational and plurireligious state]. . . . If you wish to help someone, help him in the right way. . . . Don't create differences. Don't make conditions. It is my spiritual choice whether I should go to church, whether I should sincerely pray. Why force people into doing it? After all, the war has shown the character of people in these territories. . . . A real believer would never take a gun in his hands. And here, the greatest believers were the greatest fighters. So, it is absurd. In all three nations.

People of Muslim background could seek work with foreign Islamic humanitarian organizations, such as the IGASA and the Red Crescent, which like the UN and foreign NGOs paid decent salaries. That required donning Muslim dress, which for women meant covering most of their bodies with long sleeves, long skirts, and headscarves. Muslims were skeptical about how people were recruited to the IGASA. The secularized Muslim woman whose family got aid from Caritas also told me:

Like [Caritas], the IGASA was here for people when they needed it most . . . and in return they probably had some aim. That is, Islamization of Muslims. Now, they say that those who work for them have to wear scarves. Some people don't mind that. Perhaps because they became conscious that they were Muslims, and a woman puts this scarf on and receives a salary of two hundred deutsche marks. In the situation when a hundred marks means a difference between a good life or having nothing . . . that is the price; now why complain if you need help. . . .

The IGASA also provided help to families of fallen Muslim soldiers, *šehidi* (sing. *šehid*), no matter whether they were religious or not.

Aid to the widows and children of fallen partisans in the Second World War, some of whom were also honored as "national heroes" (*narodni heroj*), had been well established and respected in Yugoslavia. The assistance that *šehidi* families received during this war continued an established custom, and most Sarajevans would agree that it was necessary, fair, and moral. The problem was that it was given only to Muslims, and not by Sarajevans' own government but by the IGASA, which demanded that beneficiaries comply with some Muslim rules. Non-Muslim soldiers who lost their lives were placed in the somewhat lesser category of "fallen soldiers" (*pali borci*), and their families were dependent on the Sarajevan government's irregular donations on occasions when it promoted the recognition of religious pluralism.

Sarajevans' attitudes toward Islamic organizations were similar to their attitudes toward the Catholic Caritas: some felt grateful, some had a pragmatic attitude, while others disliked religiously based assistance from foreign countries and saw it as removed from Sarajevan traditions. However conflicting these attitudes were, in wartime most people could actually hold several of them simultaneously. A secularized Muslim woman expressed a mix of gratitude, pragmatism, and discontent when she explained the role of Islamic organizations: "During Ramadan, when there was no bread in Sarajevo, no flour, they distributed *somuni* [round flat bread]. . . . They organized *iftari*, free, for people who fasted. . . . And they really didn't spare the food and help. And this is the price. What can we do? . . . How much you are going to accept it as yours, that is your problem. . . . The more [Europe] leaves us alone to ourselves, the more influence they [Arabs] have." Such a mixture of opinions created cognitive, moral, and emotional confusion that was part and parcel of life during the war. It was the same state that the young doctor of medicine captured with her story of the absurd celebration of the Serbian New Year, and it is the same state that Sarajevans continually dwelt in through their "civilian," "soldier," and "deserter" perceptions of the war.

Most of the people I knew and heard about turned to a religious community at some point during the war, either for help with subsistence or to find a refuge from the destruction that war wrought and the constant fear that accompanied the siege. Religious communities provided not only food and money but also a sense of security, community, and a deeper meaning of life, which gave people peace and the strength to carry on.

The visible presence and vital functions of religious organizations during the war stimulated Sarajevans to reconsider their attitudes toward religion and their own religiosity. The teenage daughter of a secularized Muslim war friend started going to a mosque and then to a Catholic church, which made my friend reflect upon her own Muslim background. Although she never believed in God, she could see that the moral values she held and applied in her daily life were similar to religious morals. She expressed the belief that good shall be returned with good and evil with evil, as well as belief in fate:

This is a story from life, not religious. There are quite a few things that one can't do anything about. I had some tragedies in the family that were sheer destiny. Also, I have helped quite a few people in my life, and for a moment it looked as if when I needed help there was no one to help me, but in the end I see that everything ends well for me. . . . The people whom I perhaps never met before helped me. . . . I don't believe that those who have killed shall receive any good. As it is said, *oteto—prokleto* [taken by force—damned]. In the first place his psyche can't be clean. I understand battle, attacking each other, that is a trauma too, and even these people get crazy. Let alone those who kill without any cause, perhaps someone who is crying, trying to get away, that is [pause], that is terrible. I don't think such persons can ever live normally again.

This woman's perspective was shaped by experiences that had nothing to do with the war—her brother had died young—as well as those she shared with other Sarajevans who lived through the siege—people sometimes altruistically helped one another. What was most meaningful for her was the conviction that perpetrators can never live untroubled lives with a clear conscience; their own deeds condemn them to remorse. But in the existentially fraught climate where nationalistic propaganda was telling her that her family background was essential, this woman, like other Sarajevans, asked herself: How are my Muslim family roots important to me? What in me is essentially Muslim? She frames her experiences with tragedy, altruism, and perpetrators' post-traumatic stress disorder in Muslim terms, as a belief in destiny and faith that good shall yield good and evil be followed by evil. She made sense of her inner life and connected it with the ethnonationalist propaganda that surrounded her. In sum, Sarajevans started to "remember" the ethnoreligious traditions that most of them had lost during the secularization of society following the Second World War.

This woman recalled that even before the war she used to pray in potentially dangerous situations. So the only change that the war brought, she concluded, was that she prayed more and was more aware of the significance of religion: "When I got scared, or when we used to travel on a long journey, I would say a prayer (*proučiti*). I know only one dova: 'Radi esil erat to asri alitemil, haj rami.' Every small child knows that, and others [non-Muslims] know it, too. . . . I don't know [what it means]. Something like, God make it easier, not more difficult. It was only in the war that I found out what it meant."

Similar reflections led many Sarajevans to develop their own personal understanding of religion and their religiosity, which could be related but not easily equated with theological dogma. In this sociocultural and spiritual renaissance of religiosity, faith was filled with meaning by its practitioners, not only by its guardians. A young man of a mixed Christian ethnoreligious background told me in 1996: "I was baptized, but nothing more. During the war I went to church because it was a great relief for me. I went every week, every Sunday, and sometimes even more often. . . . I had a need to go to church and come perhaps an hour before the mass and to be alone and to have a sort of personal adagio with myself, a sort of monologue of my own. . . . I go even now, but of course much more seldom."

A secularized Muslim woman described the increased presence of religion in Sarajevan life as both forced and voluntary:

People have let themselves into some sort of ideological reorientation, they really have, I can see it. I'm not blind. . . . Once I stood in front of the clinic opened by Saudi Arabia. All female doctors were covered while working in the clinic. And since I was there early I saw that all of them came without a scarf. All. But inside, they immediately put the scarf on. . . . What can you do? So, one aspect is economic. They try to buy people in a cheap way, they employ them in this way, on the condition that they should be religious, and in that way they direct people. That is the forced aspect, but there is a voluntary aspect too, why people have passionately turned toward religion. People of all religions are now much more religious. Perhaps it was a way to save oneself from difficulties, poverty, the fear of death, so I mean one had to turn to something, some higher power.

While Sarajevans turned to their religious communities, which demanded an outward display of religiosity, their religious attitudes remained fairly open-minded. With the encouragement of nationalist political leaders, the war brought an increased public presence of religion as well as greater awareness of people's own ethnoreligious roots and reflection on the nature of personal religiosity.

Religion and Nationality in the Army

The connections between coercion and ethnoreligious identity were more direct and powerful on the front lines and in the military, which were never far from the consciousness of Sarajevans. In 1992, Misha Glenny briefly described what later became known as "ethnic cleansing":

The Serbs stormed the urban centers of eastern and then southern Bosnia. Bijeljina, some ten miles from the Serbian border in northeast Bosnia, was the first to fall to a pattern which involved the army eliminating the Territorial Defence before a pack of Arkanovci (Arkan's men) were sent in to "cleanse the territory" (*rasčistiti teren*), just as they have done in eastern Slavonia. The crimes began: the Arkanovci started killing Muslims (men and women) in cold blood, apparently reveling in their demonic work. Zvornik, an industrial town on Drina, was the next to follow. Here the

Arkanovci discovered the local correspondent of *Oslobođenje* and threw him out of the window of the high-rise building where he lived. Bratunac, Srebrenica, Višegrad, and Foča all followed suit quickly. . . . The Serbs left a trail of blood and destruction in their wake as they closed the noose around Sarajevo's neck. (1992:165–66)

Examples of Bijeljina and other towns that met similar fates, macabre scenes of massacres, and the stories of traumatized survivors soon became demonstrations of the character of the enemy and a warning that the same thing might happen to Sarajevo. The message that was thumped into Sarajevans' heads was that the only way to avoid the horrific scenario of "ethnic cleansing" was for Muslims to realize that they were threatened precisely and only because of being Muslims and to join the common cause of their nation. Fear fueled the conviction that the only way to protect oneself and one's family was through the national defense. The reasoning of a soldier's wife shows how the war inscribed national identities that did not previously exist:

There was no other option. It was not because one wanted to fight a war, the situation was imposed, you had to go, to defend your family. If you won't do it, someone will come in, and if they come in, they won't leave you [alive], because that was the first time when some concepts in the war became clear to me. What is hatred, what is a nation, why is someone hating me now. That I am something else [than the enemy is]. I was the same as he [a Serb], I worked in the same firm with him, went to restaurants together, to parties. And now suddenly someone hates you, and I see that it is an irrational hatred, and that anything can happen. If they were to come in here, you've seen, they entered Foča, they entered Bijeljina, and killed unarmed people; they would do the same here.

Being no longer able to differentiate between Serb colleagues and Arkan's men, Muslims began feeling threatened by non-Muslims, in very much the same way that non-Muslims in Sarajevo felt vulnerable.

Soldiers believe that trust between fellow combatants is crucial, even more important than weapons. A young Croat recounted:

You feel fear only the first time at a front line. You wonder whether you are going to be hit or not. You shiver the first time you look through the hole for shooting, and you see the other side 20 meters away. You see a man 20 meters away and you are scared, because if you see him, he sees you. That is the fear that disappears after two or three days. Because the people were with you, you worked, sat and talked, played cards, did your job. . . . But, you know what is the biggest fear of all? Everyone is aware . . . that something can happen. But if I get wounded, will they take me out?

You see, that is the fear. There is no fear in being hit. If you get hit, you have a hole, and it gets fixed. If you don't get hit in the head.

But you need to trust your fellow soldiers to rescue you.

Distrust between soldiers of different ethnonational identities meant that Sarajevan Serbs either served with people who were as much a threat to them as the enemy on the other side or left the town, which many did. The only Serb serving in the ABiH whom I got acquainted with in 1994 was married to a secularized Muslim woman with two small children. While most other men I met had managed to get a civilian job or a transfer to duty in the town, this man was sent to the front outside of Sarajevo. Soldiers felt that fighting for their own town was natural, but fighting for unknown territories of a state that did not exist except as an abstract idea was meaningless. In 1996, when the Dayton Peace Accords were already widely implemented and the army began to demobilize, this man was still held in military service. To me it seemed like discrimination, but many non-Muslim Sarajevans explained that the government needed to keep non-Muslims in the army in order to prove it was composed of multiple nationalities.

The majority of Sarajevan Croats joined their national army, the HVO, which existed in Sarajevo until the end of 1993. As a consequence of the escalation of fighting between Muslim and Croat forces in 1993, the HVO in Sarajevo disintegrated and was transformed into a Croatian brigade, Kralj Tvrtko, which came under Muslim command as part of the ABiH. Many young Croatian soldiers were shocked when their Muslim fellow combatants disarmed them: "The front line we watched was enforced [by Muslim soldiers] with the explanation that an attack was coming. And they all knew that they were going to disarm us. They woke you in the dormitory with the gun aimed at your head, the comrades who were in the trench with you. The army was disarming the HVO, in order to transform it into a new brigade." They perceived this move as a sudden betrayal by people they trusted with their lives.

A young Catholic woman thought that the disintegration of the HVO was followed by distrust of Croatian defenders of Sarajevo, since the new brigade Kralj Tvrtko was not given a "zone of responsibility" (*zona odgovornosti*) to defend. She felt that the distrust was unjust since many young Croats died defending Sarajevo side by side with Muslims: "in proportion to the size of the Croatian population of the town, we have lost the most men. The Croatian youth got killed the most. That means that it [the Croatian youth] saw this town as its own."

Muslim dominance in the ABiH can be traced to its origins; the army was formed out of paramilitary Muslim troops who first fought during the war in Croatia in 1991. Under the control of the government in Sarajevo, the ABiH suffered the same dilemmas and changes as the society at large: ethnonational divisions and the imposition of religion, in spite of officially proclaimed secularism and religious pluralism. Amid the existential threat of combat, a shared ethnoreligious background soon proved to be the main source of safety and trust among soldiers. Non-Muslims felt like a minority, and only when units were composed of men who had grown up together did feelings of safety and trust exist across ethnoreligious boundaries.

Religion did not seem to hold deep relevance for soldiers, however. When life was at stake, religiosity or political opinions were of secondary importance. What soldiers of all ethnonational identities prioritized was to be a good "buddy," to earn the trust of their fellow combatants in order to be able to rely on them. It was characteristic Sarajevan common sense, and Muslim religiosity was met mostly with joking or contempt because it was experienced as not strongly felt by its new practitioners.

Many young men made contact with the Catholic Church in order to avoid armed service, or even to get an accreditation that could allow them to leave the town. Some of them were religious before the war and saw this assistance as a confirmation of their faith in the Catholic community. Others turned to the church for protection without changing their religious views and attended mass in order to be seen, not to pray. The young secularized Sarajevan Croat who eventually left the town during the heavy shelling in the summer of 1995 described his own adaptation to circumstances: "I, who never had anything to do with the church. I was baptized, and everything that one goes through as a child. But after that, in no way. And then, I had to submit to the church in order to save myself from the gun [armed service], and I am very grateful . . . I attended [church services] purely because of the others, but I think that I haven't changed my basic ideas about the religious worldview."

The possibility of becoming a Croatian citizen through conversion to Catholicism was appealing to anyone who wanted to leave Sarajevo. Under the Tudjman regime, the *domovnica* (literally, a certificate of domicile), a certificate that gave the right to Croatian citizenship, was issued to anyone who could prove some connection to Croatia through a parent or even a grandparent, through place of birth, or through longer residence in Croatia. For Sarajevans, obtaining a *domovnica* often conferred a right to leave the town through territories under Bosnian Croats' control. This option was open to everyone regardless of their ethnic background. A secularized Muslim woman told me in 1994: "The double citizenship was attractive. With a *krštenica* [a baptism certificate valid as a birth certificate] you could get double citizenship, which means a Croatian passport with which you could enter Croatia without any problem. . . . [It] meant that you would not be thrown out of Croatia as a Bosnian refugee. A lot of Muslims went over in that way. It is the church that is doing it now, too."

But the process was not as easy as it sounded. A young Croat whom I met hoped to get help to leave the town, but he did not have the nerve to ask for it outright, so he never got a straightforward answer or help with leaving:

I got to know this janitor of the church. A very fine man, nice. . . . He explained to me that they were starting this illegal organization. Illegal [smiling]. To make the long story short, it was to be a humanitarian organization, to help people, with food and other things. . . . I liked the idea because they mentioned going out of Sarajevo. And I forced my friend, who calls himself Orthodox, to come along. He argued that he is a Serb, but I told him not to worry. The first time we went there, we were ninety people in a corridor. . . . A man explained what it was about and then they distributed tin cans to everyone. I don't remember what was in the cans, but I was hungry and we were so happy. But when the talking was over, we had to pray. . . . I looked at the people around me. I had no idea what to do. I stood up, but I didn't know how to pray. To begin with I didn't know how to hold my hands. So I followed with one eye what others did and mumbled something. I turned around and I saw that my friend also mumbled something. A man standing beside us was so loud that he covered us. Afterward we agreed that it was embarrassing so we decided to say that we didn't know what to do, because they said that they were going to teach those who didn't know. So we did it, and I even got a rosary (*krunica*) because the janitor liked me. And I liked him. I told him that I was an atheist. . . . I wanted to be honest. But it simply didn't work. . . . Everywhere I found some peace, but here I was always tense.

The Catholic Church faced a dilemma between gaining more members and losing people by letting them leave the town.

The changes that ethnonational politics wrought in public space also had consequences for Sarajevans' daily interactions. We now turn to how social relations changed because of growing ethnonational and ethnoreligious divisions.

Chapter 8
Reorienting Social Relationships

The most significant shift in the ways Sarajevans related to one another was their war-induced concern with national affiliation. Before the war, whatever concern they had with identifying others' ethnoreligious background and ethnonational identity was aimed mainly at being respectful of differences. During the war, however, it became vital for people to identify one another's position—their ethnonational identity, their feelings about other groups, and their opinions about nationalism itself and who was responsible for the war—in order to know whether a reliable relationship could be established or maintained. In this painful and contradictory process, Sarajevans both assumed and resisted the creation of new meanings for their national identities. They tended to generalize about ethnonational groups, but they also realized that individuals varied. When relating to people they knew well, Sarajevans did not generally let national animosities take over their interactions. At the same time, they held general ideas about members of their own and other national groups that assumed or asserted such marked differences among them that mutual understanding and respect often seemed inconceivable.

The experience of victimization by the war, which Sarajevans as well as other people throughout Bosnia felt acutely, opened the ideological space for identification and condemnation of the enemy "other" in nationalist terms. Nationalistic elites were able to use this sense of victimization to propagate a degree of national differentiation that otherwise would not have gained so much ground. Biases against other national groups, especially when generalizing about "others," were not a result of existing or "primordial" animosities among Bosnian nationalities, but were strongly influenced by the war itself. The national enemy that was condemned depended on the military situation at a given time. Muslims who felt like victims of Serbian aggression condemned Serbs, while Serbs and Croats who felt like victims of the Muslim-dominated Sarajevan regime condemned Muslims. Muslim ambivalence toward Croats in Sarajevo reflected the fact that Croats were both allies and enemies during different periods of the war. Muslim-Croat relations were good until late 1992, when fighting began between the two national armies, and improved again after the Bosnian Federation was established in 1994. Relations between Serbs and Croats in Sarajevo were relatively good, as Serb and Croat military forces never fought in a significant way in this part of Bosnia and Herzegovina.[1] In this way, national identification positioned people morally and politically during the war.

A joke that circulated in Sarajevo commented on the relative importance of national belonging: How do people manage to leave Sarajevo? When they pass Croatian snipers they raise two fingers (which is the Catholic way to cross oneself), when they pass Serbian snipers they raise three fingers (the Orthodox way to cross oneself), when they pass Muslim snipers they raise five fingers, the whole hand (the Muslim way of praying), and when they finally get out they raise one finger, the middle one (an expletive gesture). In practice, the attention that had to be paid to various armed groups was mostly a matter of paying money and making sure that they had received it. The joke made a poignant connection between national identities, religion, and war profiteering, while celebrating the primacy of life.

Over the course of the war, Sarajevans started to interpret some of their everyday experiences and social relations in terms of ethnonational identities. This process of national identification was by no means a one-way street to a homogenous nationalism, however. Some people struggled to resist the rising tide of nationalist feelings, even as they had to cope with the world that was shifting around them.

One evening in September 1994, my hosts watched an old serial about the life of Vuk Karadžić, the nineteenth-century Serbian linguist who reformed South Slavic writing rules[2] after participating in a failed uprising against the Ottoman Empire. In this program, shown on Serbian television, the Turks were the bad guys and the Serbs the good guys. When the program was made several decades earlier, "Turks" were the Ottomans, the invaders who ruled over the South Slavs—the people whose rebellions led eventually to the formation of Yugoslavia. In the context of the ongoing war, however, "Turk" took on different meanings. Serbian media often called Bosnian Muslims "Turks," positioning them as the enemy and picturing them as villains. Showing this old serial on television was surely no coincidence; its implicit purpose was to support the historical truth of the current Serbian nationalist ideology. In the popular imagery, "Turks" were seen as foreigners, with lesser rights to the land, or as Slavs who had converted and were of lesser moral standing because of their disloyalty to their Slavic roots and brethren. "Turks" were portrayed as a brutal people, but also as spineless opportunists.

The Muslim-dominated Bosnian government reversed the imagery: the enemy and villains were Serbs, who were often called Chetniks (Četnici, sing. Četnik). A Chetnik was imagined as primitive, untidy, long-haired, and bearded. Serbian troops in this war referred to themselves as Chetniks, making a historical connection to the Serbian royalist soldiers who fought for the Serbian and Yugoslav king and the former kingdom of Yugoslavia, as well as to the Chetniks of the Second World War who fought against both the Nazis and Tito's partisans. In Sarajevo the term Chetnik was increasingly used as a synonym for "the enemy soldier" in order to distinguish between "Serbs," who could also be good, decent, normal people, *raja*, and those who joined the other side in the war. The word was loaded with moral condemnation. Chetniks fought unfairly, their behavior was inhuman, they slaughtered women and children, and they destroyed everything people had. In short, a Chetnik was an immoral, bad person. This shorthand could occasionally take paradoxical turns as national terms in daily use lost their national meaning and assumed a purely moral one. A friend of mine told me that he once saw a *bula*—a woman who taught in an Islamic school and always dressed in Muslim clothes with a veil—hit her son in the backyard of a multistoried house. The neighbors thought that she was too brutal, so one of them started screaming: "Stop the Chetnik woman (*četnikuša*)! She'll kill the child!" To call a *bula* a Chetnik could be seen as a contradiction in terms, but in Sarajevo during the war it made perfect sense.

In socialist Yugoslavia Chetniks, along with other nationalist military forces such as Croatian Ustashas (Ustaše, sing. Ustaša), were condemned as nationalists and traitors to the People's Liberation Struggle (*Narodnooslobodilačka borba* [NOB]) and the "brotherhood and unity" (*bratstvo i jedinstvo*) of Yugoslav peoples, because they were allies of the German invaders and fought against partisans during the Second World War. The extreme Croat nationalists implied continuity with the Second World War by referring to themselves as Ustashas. A person judged to be a Croatian nationalist could also be called Ustasha, while the nationally most neutral and thus most moral label for Croats during the war was Katolik (Catholic), probably because it referred only to ethnoreligious identity and not to a politicized national identity.

Because of my Croatian background, I heard mostly derogatory terms used by Muslims referring to Serbs, and by Croats referring to Muslims. The old derogatory labels for Croats, Šokac or Latin,[3] were never used in front of me, and I only heard a variant of Latin once in 1995, when a secularized Muslim woman with whom I developed a war friendship was irritated with Croats who obstructed the Croat-Muslim Federation and exclaimed: "I'm sick and tired of this *latinluk*!" An older derogatory term for a Serb was Vlah,[4] while a relatively positive label was Pravoslavac (Orthodox), probably for the same reasons as Katolik (Catholic) was the most positive label for Croats. The older derogatory word for a Muslim was Balija. These older derogatory names for members of different religious groups in Bosnia and Herzegovina were revived during the war and sometimes acquired new meanings.

Because of the changes in the political and ideological situation during the war, people from the same ethnoreligious background perceived changes in different ways, and labels appeared that marked the heterogeneity within each national group. The most important distinction that Sarajevans made, even when talking about national identities, was between good and bad members of a national group.

For example, Sarajevans distinguished between various types of Muslims. "Real Muslims" were the old believers, and "April Muslims" were those who discovered their Muslim identity at the beginning of the war (in April 1992) and became newly committed to religion or converted to nationalist ideology. While everyone respected the "old Muslims," opinions about "April Muslims" were mixed. Some looked upon them with contempt and also called them "newly composed" (*novokomponovani*) Muslims, alluding to the kitschy folk music that was popular among "less cultivated people." Others saw the popularization of religiosity as a natural consequence of war and Serbian aggression. Croats could be classified as Catholic believers (Katolici), nonbelievers, Sarajevan and Central Bosnian Croats (who were seen as loyal to Bosnia), and Herzegovinian Croats (Hercegovci), who were seen as more extreme nationalists and separatists. Sarajevans also divided Serbs into "good Serbs" and "bad Serbs" or just "Serbs." The "good Serbs" were the "Orthodox," who often did not want to be associated with Serbian nationalism, but also included the Serbs who stayed in the town and showed their loyalty to the Bosnian government either by openly condemning Serbian politics or by joining the ABiH. "Good Serbs" could also be prewar friends, colleagues, and neighbors who said that they were leaving and somehow kept in touch during the war. "Bad Serbs" were those suspected of knowing that the war was coming, and who suddenly left the town without telling anybody and without making contact afterward. Those who stayed in the town but never openly condemned the Serbian side were also suspected of knowing about the war and just waiting for the Serbian troops to enter the town, and were thus perceived as "bad Serbs."

People of all nationalities, although most often those who before the war had identified themselves nationally as Yugoslavs, who held to the pre-war ideology of "brotherhood and unity" and criticized the government for dismantling it, were now labeled *jugonostalgičari* (Yugonostalgists). Like many other concepts, nostalgia in this context had a double meaning: on the one hand, it implied a sentimental attachment to political ideals that were already irrecoverably lost, and a denial of or refusal to come to terms with present reality; on the other hand, it was understood as the only way of preserving a thread of connection to the political organization of society that was good and viable. In this sense, Yugonostalgia was a part of the Sarajevan "imitation of life."

The ascription of these national labels to individuals depended on the situation. National identification was a process that happened over time, and the same person could be classified differently in different situations. Similarly, with time and experience, a person could change his or her own notion of belonging to a certain national category.

Muslim Perspectives on Ethnonational Identity

In the early 1980s, Ernest Gellner perceptively observed that "nowadays, to be a Bosnian Muslim you need not believe that there is no God but God and that Mohamed is his Prophet, but you do need to have lost that faith" (1992:72). During the siege of Sarajevo, being a Muslim meant that you rediscovered that faith and were forced to see for yourself what it meant in the new situation. Would you start going to the mosque regularly, pray five times a day, observe the Ramadan fast, attend *iftari* in the evenings, and celebrate Bairams? Or was it enough if you simply continued to take off your shoes when you came inside, drank your coffee out of a *fildžan*, and ate *pita* or baklava? Were you a Muslim if you blamed Karadžić and Mladić for the war and cursed the soldiers' "Chetnik mother" when the shells exploded? What did it mean if you covered your head with a shawl, or wore a dark beret, and went to Merhamet and IGASA for help with food and work? Did the ABiH under the Sarajevo government's control protect your interests? Were these the military forces you should join? While for some people being a Muslim meant being religiously observant and identifying with Bosnian nationalism politically, other Muslims did not perceive these as characteristic of themselves. But Sarajevan Muslims had this predicament in common: throughout the processes of national division and homogenization that started with the breakup of the former Yugoslavia, were intensified by the war, and continued after the peace agreement, everyone had to come to terms with the revival of all of these aspects of their ethnoreligious and national identity. To be a Muslim in Sarajevo meant remembering that faith and reconsidering what it meant in everyday life, where its meaning never was only religious, but increasingly political.

Sarajevan Muslims generally saw themselves as mild, tolerant, and politically naive people, different from the Muslims who moved from rural villages to Sarajevo during the war. Ideas about their specifically Bosnian variant of Islam and the lifestyle characterized as being between East and West became central issues of identity. What it meant to be Muslim was defined in political terms by nationalist leaders and figured in political debates among ordinary Sarajevans.

The late Alija Izetbegović, who served as the first president of Bosnia and Herzegovina, articulated the idea of a distinctly "European Muslim" identity: "I personally feel most comfortable when I say that I am a European Muslim, because that's what I am. When I go to the East, some things there disturb me; some things disturb me also when I go to the West. I feel best here, in Bosnia. Probably because it is East and West, and the good that exists on both sides" (Izetbegović 1996:43–44, my translation). While characterizing Bosnian Muslims as combining the best of two worlds along the "Great Border" between the Ottoman Empire and Europe, his formulation acknowledges some tensions and contradictions: "By our faith we are Easterners, by our education Europeans. With our heart we belong to one world, with our brain to the other. . . . Each of us who is honest has to admit that he asks himself often: who is he, to which world does he belong" (Izetbegović 1995:137, my translation).

Izetbegović characterized the Bosnian spirit in terms similar to many Sarajevans: "The line of friction between two worlds, East and West, moved across Bosnia over several hundreds of years and it created what we call Bosnian spirit. The basic characteristic of that spirit is tolerance, the capability of living with someone different from you" (Izetbegović 1996:125, my translation). Most Sarajevans could probably identify with being the people of the Great Border (an idea that also figured in prewar Yugoslav ideology[5]): tolerant, used to living with differences, forgiving, and morally good. But when East was defined as Islamic faith and West as education, the identification as Bosnians of the Great Border became problematic for those who neither were religious Muslims nor came from a Muslim family. As a result, the feeling of genuine Bosnian belonging was evoked only in people of Muslim ancestry, and the identification as people of the Great Border became an essential characteristic of the newly defined Muslim identity. Making ethnoreligious identification into an essential characteristic of the border identity was a process that many people found troubling.

Even more controversially, Izetbegović promoted the merger of faith and politics, which was one of the cornerstones of Islam, in an Islamic state. When he had first expressed this opinion in his (in)famous *Islamska Deklaracija* (The Islamic Declaration, 1970), he was convicted of "associating with intention of hostile activity" and making a "counter-revolutionary threat to the social order of SFRY [the Socialist Federative Republic of Yugoslavia]" (Okružni sud u Sarajevu K.212/83 od 20.8.1983 godine [The District Court in Sarajevo K.212/83 of August 20, 1983]).[6] At the same time, he was aware that this agenda might lead to factional strife within the SDA and conflict with other Bosnians (1996:125) When translated into political terms, Izetbegović's notion of balancing between East and West became problematic and self-contradictory, which did not pass unnoticed by Sarajevans.

Secularized Sarajevan Muslims, contrary to their president, stressed their weak religiosity and European way of living. As a well-educated woman put it: "Most of the Muslims were not so religious; even today when many fast and bow in prayer (*klanjati*), they don't know how to say a prayer (*učiti*). Me, too. . . . I have never said that I was anything else but Muslim. I can be Yugoslav and Muslim . . . but, I didn't go to the mosque, or pray to Allah (*klanjati*)." In Sarajevo, the expression "European Muslim" meant anything between a wish to merge politics with religion in an Islamic state to a longing for a Western capitalist, prosperous, and democratic society enriched by Eastern customs and the centuries-old Bosnian ethos of coexistence. Those who identified themselves, or were identified by others, as Muslims chose those meanings of their new identity that they perceived as relevant to themselves.

Muslims' Attitudes Toward Serbs and Croats

As Muslims and Serbs were the largest national groups in Bosnia and Herzegovina, members of these groups were in frequent, close contact and often intermarried. Muslims recognized a shared historical destiny with Serbs.

Izetbegović put it succinctly: "If we talk about the Bosnian mentality, we could say that it is closer to the Serbian. Because we lived for a long time together under the Turks" (1996:126, my translation). Some Sarajevan Muslims continued to believe that ethnonational identity was not an important characteristic of individuals and to affirm family bonds with Serbs. A young secularized Muslim woman thought that the prevailing enthusiasm for national divisions had been carried too far. "Everyone is tired of it. . . . Especially in Sarajevo, it is impossible to carry out such a division. . . . My sister's husband is a Serb. My mother's sister is married to a Serb. My father's brother is married to a Serbian woman. So we are mixed. We get along well. . . . I can't imagine living in a homogeneous national milieu and it seems to me that, if I had to live in such a milieu, I would rather go to another country. . . ." Even mentioning leaving Sarajevo for a place where ethnically mixed families would be welcome bespeaks deep alienation from the current climate.

Other Muslims tried to explain the inexplicable event of war between Serbs and Muslims by seeking to find some difference between these two groups that might have gone unnoticed earlier. One secularized woman observed that the Serbs had a more collectivist mentality: "The mass psychology is slightly stronger in a Serb than in a Muslim. We have never felt a strong national or group belonging." This abstraction projected nationalist sentiments on the other and defined Muslims as the more tolerant people. It was probably adopted from current Muslim nationalist propaganda. But when it came to individual Serbs, the woman thought that their personalities were more important; her notion of collectivism either did not apply or was forgotten. On the concrete level, Serbs became a heterogeneous group, and being able to establish that a Serb in question was not among those who shelled and shot at the town was essential for the Muslims who were hypothetically willing to reestablish relations with Serbs. This woman explained that there were no problems with "the Serbs who were here the whole war, and we know what they were doing and that they suffered the same as we did." But "a Serb who returns, you don't know where he has been, whether he was up on Trebević and shot at you."

The guilt of shelling Sarajevo could also be generalized to apply to all Serbs. I remember once talking in a café to two sisters in their forties, both secularized Muslims. Both had been married to Serbs, and each had one child. One of the women had divorced long before the war and now lived with a secularized Muslim, while her sister had been widowed long before the war and remained single. Neither had cared much about the national identity of her husband before the war. During the war, both women worked for the ABiH. The widowed sister suddenly said that she could never again fall in love with a Serb. She was very categorical and slightly chauvinistic, and I anticipated an explanation that presumed Serbs were immoral and inferior to Muslims. I wondered how she could know that a man she was falling in love with was a Serb or not. Would it show? But her answer was not what I expected. Rather, it was very rational; I perceived it as somewhat cold-blooded and almost macabre. All right, she admitted, she might fall in love with a man not knowing that he was a Serb, but as soon as she found out it would be impossible to continue. I asked why. Because you could never know whether he was up there shooting at your child, wounding and killing so many others, she answered. She worked as a nurse on the front line, so she knew what she was talking about. Chills went up my spine. And even if he himself had not been a shooter, she continued, she could never be sure about someone from his family, his blood.

A secularized Muslim woman who divorced her Serb husband during the war expressed general notions about the contrast between militantly nationalistic Serbs and tolerant, non-nationalistic Muslims. Serbs were to blame for the war; they were obsessed with a dream of Greater Serbia and by an irrational hatred and desire for vengeance fueled by the centuries under Turkish rule:

Yugoslavia suited them because they were the majority national group (*nacija*). . . .[7] Serbs left the town, ran away, at the beginning of the war in April; they thought they would come back after fifteen days. [Serbian extremists] would attack, scare us, slaughter, kill everyone they could. . . . They thought that the mild Muslims would get quiet. The army [JNA] would . . . come in between to settle the conflict, and there would again be Yugoslavia as they wanted it. But we all knew that it was no longer Yugoslavia, that it was Greater Serbia. Because with those *četnik* signs, it was clear that there was nothing good awaiting the Muslims. They slaughtered earlier too, and from the stories and what happened in the territories that they conquered they killed people just because they were Muslims. . . . They could have got Muslims on their side if only they had not slaughtered and killed. The majority of Muslims in Sarajevo thought that the army [JNA] had good intentions. . . . I never realized that they have in fact always hated us so much, secretly, that it is their vengeance, from the Turkish times when they probably suffered because they were oppressed. . . . But I don't understand why they mixed so much. Why marry a Muslim woman?

This woman's own experience contradicted her general viewpoint enough to raise this final question, yet she could not see that the hatred she projected onto the past had arisen during the war.

Another common attitude was that the Serbs believed in the "lies" on their radio station (SRNA). According to the same woman, at the beginning of the war, the Serbian radio was "lying so that the hair rose on your head . . . almost as if we were throwing shells on ourselves.[8] What soldier would leave his house and go to the front line to shell the town? If he doesn't kill his child he'll kill some relative. But, no. The majority of them believed in it." Any Serb who did not condemn the other side was suspected of sympathizing with the enemy and condemned as sharing responsibility for the siege of Sarajevo. "Naturally, we also have nationalism," this woman conceded, but she did not seem to think that this was the major reason why Serbs who stayed in Sarajevo "felt under pressure" and were not trusted.

In the spring of 1996, the exodus of Serbs from the parts of Sarajevo that were to be reintegrated with the main body of the town under the Bosnian government's control could be seen on the television daily. Sarajevans were stunned by this evidence that the enemy also had its tragedies and share of suffering. Those who had the generosity to feel sorry for Serbs in endless refugee queues on the roads out of town often said that they pitied Serbs for being so easily seduced by inhuman leaders like Karadžić, Milošević, and Mladić.

The Serbs who were perceived as good were those who demonstrated, as well as repeatedly stated, that they were ashamed of their people and leaders because of what they were doing. The same woman described one "good Serb": "There is for instance a man who is married to a Muslim woman, he has a son here. He was expelled from Trebinje. He works with us as a judge. He was supposed to be a federal judge. . . . And he says, 'I weighed eighty-six kilograms and I fell to sixtyish. I have been eaten away, I have melted because of the shame. But people are treating me like a drop of water in their palm.' I am really happy that there are people like him; that means that not all of them are like that [the nationalists]."

The process of ethnonational identification of oneself and others and the reevaluation of mutual relations across ethnonational lines is ongoing in Sarajevo. The woman whose views I have explored had started to identify herself as a Muslim and her husband as a Serb, and because they had two children she was forced to make sense of relations between Serbs and Muslims. Such people, with personal bonds and interests, had a special need to understand each other. In this case, contact with her former husband was maintained through their children, who were in contact with both. Direct information about the "other" was the ground for a constant revaluation of political discourse and about people's own ideas and actions.

I met some Sarajevan Croats through my Muslim friends and acquaintances who seemed to be eager that I meet "good, normal" Croats who had stayed and had no nationalistic tendencies. The same secularized Muslim friend who uttered her irritation over *latinluk* wanted me to talk to her colleague: "I have introduced you to him on purpose, because he is a Croat, and because he is Sarajevan *raja*." It was March 1995, and the three of us were sitting in her office. During the conversation it turned out that he ranked as Sarajevan *raja* because he did not leave Sarajevo, because he had a sense of humor, and, in spite of being born in Herzegovina, was not harsh and nationalistic as Herzegovinians supposedly were. So, a "good Croat" was equal to a "good person," *raja*; it did not matter where you were born as long as you showed your loyalty to Sarajevo.

When it came to more general ideas, Croats were perceived as more religious than other ethnonational groups. Croats were regarded as more inclined toward the West; they had ties to Croatia, through Catholicism to Rome, and were through history and culture influenced by the Austro-Hungarian Empire. Their European orientation meant that they were seen as snobbish people who thought themselves superior to Muslims. This stereotype mirrored the Croats' attitudes toward Muslims: slightly arrogant questioning of Muslims' religiosity and their claim of a separate national identity.

During my work in Sarajevo, I often heard people who identified as Muslims say: "We can forgive, but we shan't forget." I found this outlook disturbing. First, it identified Muslims as the victims and Serbs as the perpetrators, the Muslims as those who were morally entitled to confer forgiveness and the Serbs as those who had to repent. The second part was equally disturbing because it said that the Serbs would never again be trusted, even if they were to share life with Muslims in the future. Some men in refugee families I became acquainted with, who previously had no special interest in weapons, declared that after the experience of Serbs coming into their villages and destroying everything Muslim, carrying out "ethnic cleansing," they were going to make sure that their sons knew who they were—Muslims—and knew how to handle a weapon.

The doubleness of this formulation reflects the ambivalence of Muslims' interpretation of their relations to Serbs: on the one hand, a wish to be tolerant, peaceful, and forgiving, as opposed to Serbian selfishness and aggressiveness; and on the other hand, putting all of the blame on the Serbs and being unable to trust them ever again. This view fitted perfectly with the contemporary image of Muslims as naive innocents and Serbs as violent aggressors and with the lesson that Muslims have learned in the war: they never should have trusted the Serbs in the first place. Despite its pretensions, this sentiment has nothing to do with a possible solution or a better future. Perhaps, for Muslims, it was also a way of forgiving themselves: the Serbs forced them to kill and destroy, committing acts that they always found unacceptable, against their nature. Perhaps, too, it was a way of making sense of their experiences in the war and an attempt to ensure that war would not happen again, or at least to protect their children from similar experiences.

Although this attitude was not often openly expressed by people who had lived in Sarajevo before the war, such statements arouse concern about the fragile state of social relations between the town's Serbs and Muslims, which were painful for all of them. The hope lay in Sarajevans' capacity to reevaluate their opinions of each other, which I witnessed so often during my fieldwork.

Serb Perspectives on Ethnonational Identity

While Sarajevan Muslims felt like the victims of Serbian aggression, Sarajevan Serbs felt victimized by the newly established Muslim regime and what they perceived as its anti-Serbian ideology. It was difficult to tell how many Serbs stayed in Sarajevo, but Sarajevans thought that many had left at the beginning of the war. Sooner or later it turned out that most of my friends and acquaintances knew some Serbs who had remained. I was seldom introduced to them, in part because I am Croat but primarily because Serbs in Sarajevo kept a low profile, which their non-Serb friends respected. Although I respected their discretion, I wanted to hear about their experiences and attitudes. In the end, I had to ask to be introduced to a Serb, which felt awkward. One of the Serbs with whom I could talk was the caretaker of the Old Orthodox Church (Stara Crkva), whom I contacted at work in April 1996. We had several friendly and fairly open conversations before we recorded a loosely structured interview, but I did not get to know him better. From what I have heard from other Sarajevan Serbs whom I met, his experiences and opinions were shared by others, which is why I discuss his way of describing these common issues.

The caretaker was a widower in his sixties, with two grown daughters who each had a son. They fled at the beginning of the war to Spain, but he decided to stay to take care of his sick sister. He lived alone near Marindvor in an apartment house that had been abandoned by Serbs and taken over by

Muslims who held high positions. His home was searched twelve times, and he felt the pressure of being a Serb and Orthodox believer. His family was old Sarajevan Orthodox and he felt strongly rooted in Bosnia. He suffered greatly from the loss of social networks and security that the war created, but he found a refuge in the remains of the Orthodox Church and his faith, as did many other religious Sarajevans. He was supportive of the city's religious pluralism and multiethnic society but was disillusioned as to the possibility of reestablishing it.

The caretaker and many Sarajevan Serbs felt ostracized by the treatment they received from the authorities, at their workplaces, in their neighborhoods, and from their friends. As the caretaker related:

My brother was fired, for example. He was an engineer. . . . He was told, "You have an ugly name and surname. We shall pension you." . . . Then in the municipality where I live, when they were distributing the little food they had—biscuits, milk—I was not on the list. When they gave shoes, I was not on the list. Then they gave winter jackets; I was not on the list. So as a result, you started to feel uneasy. But what offended me the most was this. I am a generous man, I like people, I like to joke, laugh. Muslims were 90 percent of my friends, really, and I honestly liked and loved them. I had many girlfriends who were Muslims, because I really loved them. I was never nationally indoctrinated. . . . But now, do you know what happened? For a long time my best friends turned their heads away from me. Now as peace comes closer some of them say, "How are you?" . . . I said, "Now I don't know you. Why did you turn away your heads from me? Please, what did I do to you?"

When I suggested that his former friends might have avoided him because they were afraid to be seen with him, or perhaps even suspected him, he replied that they wanted to humiliate him.

I have heard several cases of Sarajevan Serbs being forced into early retirement, and they were all convinced that it was done in order to cleanse the workplace of Serbs and employ Muslims instead. Sarajevan Serbs generally depended on the civil courage of their prewar colleagues, neighbors, and friends. I had met non-Serbs who retained their personal bonds to Serbs they knew and did not ostracize them, but the very fact that it took a lot of courage to do so bears witness to the general anti-Serbian atmosphere.

The caretaker believed that the ostracism he and people close to him experienced during the war was entirely because of their Serb nationality. As a result, this national identification became important to him in a way that it had not been earlier: "Now they are taking away our right to say that we are Serbs; instead they insist that we should say that we are Bosnians." Being Bosnian "is one thing, but my choice of national belonging (*opredelenje*) is

Serbian and it will never be possible to wipe it out, in the same way that the Orthodox religion shall never be possible to wipe out."

Fear of Muslim Newcomers

Most Sarajevans had problems with their new Muslim neighbors. These "internally displaced persons" from villages in rural Bosnia were seen as a threat to the secularized urban culture of Sarajevo. From my observations, Sarajevan Muslims established neighborly relations with refugee Muslims, while "mixed" families and non-Muslims had almost no contact with the newcomers. The gap between native Sarajevans and newcomers was widest for Serbs, especially in neighborhoods that had been predominantly Serbian; after most of the Serbs left the town, many newcomers settled there, a circumstance that only exacerbated divisions. Serbs, and non-Muslims generally, who remained in neighborhoods where most of the people stayed had support from their longtime Muslim neighbors. The remaining Serbs often made a very clear distinction between old Sarajevan Muslims, with whom they shared the notion of Sarajevanness, and the newcomers, whom they saw as a threat. The caretaker clearly identified the Muslim newcomers as responsible for the changes that were taking place, especially the disappearance of the pluralist, non-nationalistic Sarajevan milieu that he identified with:

You have the native Muslims, who were born here. They didn't change a lot. . . . But, the strangers came, terribly many Šiptari [Yugoslav Albanians], terribly many of those from Sandžak, that is horrible. I think that they make 60 percent now in Sarajevo.[9] They have completely taken over everything. And they are a very rough folk, very difficult folk, who also committed crimes against the Serbian folk.[10] And now we have this kind of folk. Here, we had a nice culture; this was the crossroads between West and East. People lived here. Whoever came to Sarajevo before the war could live here; he could find his place.

The caretaker described the tolerant culture of Sarajevo as at the crossroads between East and West, similarly to the description of President Izetbegović. Although Izetbegović defined this culture as a part of Bosnian Muslim identity, making it easy for Muslim Sarajevans to accept his definition of their identity, Sarajevan Serbs did not give up the notion that this culture was theirs as well and that it had thrived in multiethnic Sarajevo. However, the caretaker did not identify the Muslim newcomers with this same culture. He described his old neighborhood in positive terms and lamented the sudden departure of his neighbors:

I lived in a new apartment house. It just so happened that we were all Serbs.[11] The others were not believers but atheists. The house had eight apartments, a wonderful house, it felt like one's own home. Now there are no Serbs except me in this house. Seven have left. The apartments were beautiful. But they left over night. They left such fortunes that I was simply surprised. . . . They just said, "Tomorrow we shall not be here." One family is in the Czech Republic, one in Germany, one in Belgrade, and one even in Canada. They left; they couldn't live here any longer. They were insulted.

He regarded his new Muslim neighbors as illegitimate residents and feared their apparent monopoly of political and social power: "I hear them in the evenings saying: 'We should get rid of this one too, so that we can be alone.' Imagine when you hear that. And from a university professor, but he is from Sandžak. In the apartment above is the police chief of one part of the town. [In] two [other apartments there are] Muslim officers."

Because of the war in Croatia, where Tudjman's regime effectively "ethnically cleansed" most Serbs, it could be expected that Serbs' general feelings toward Croats were not especially positive. However, I never heard any such comment. After the Muslim-Croat conflict in 1992–94, Sarajevan Serbs described Sarajevan Croats primarily as fellow victims of the Muslim authorities. "Croats have also felt it here in Sarajevo. I have many friends who are Croats. They fired two of them without any reason," the caretaker told me. The idea that the only way to live normal lives in future was within a religiously and ethnonationally pluralist society where all citizens enjoyed equal status was common among Sarajevan Serbs.

It is interesting to compare Muslim accusations against Serbs with the Serbian point of view. The facts about the war were seldom disputed, but interpretations of those facts became informed by nationalist viewpoints. Muslims generally accused Serbs of wanting to integrate Bosnia and Herzegovina into Greater Serbia, a state with a Serbian majority in which Serbian culture and religion would be dominant. One of the phrases that was taken as a sign of Greater Serbian ideology was the Serbian claim that wherever there was a Serbian grave, it was Serbian land. In that respect, the caretaker could be classified as a Serbian nationalist: "We thought that we would live in Bosnia and Herzegovina where we were born, where our graves are. I have over thirty-six graves of my own. Do you know what that means? That is a bond." But from his perspective, by naming the graves that tied him to the Sarajevan soil, he was just affirming his right to remain in his home as a rightful citizen. At the same time, he blamed Muslims for wanting to make a greater Muslim state: "If this continues here in Sarajevo, it won't be good. Then it is not the multinational state, not the multireligious, multiethnic state. No, that is a multi-Muslim state, to tell you the truth. Alija Izetbegović is not leading us the good way. He took us the wrong way. . . . We imagined [something else], that is why we stayed here." By calling it a "multi-Muslim" state he was ironic about Muslim politicians' frequent use of the prefix "multi," as they characterized Bosnia as a multireligious, multiethnic, and multinational state. He regarded their talk about pluralism as a cover for their actual intentions—to establish a Muslim state.

Some Serbian Sarajevans shared the caretaker's opinion that non-Muslims were left alive only because of the government's interests in maintaining its image in the West: "Muslims need us here. To support their position of a multireligious, multiethnic [state] . . . we are practically in service to the Muslim authorities. . . . So that they can say that Serbs are free, they live well, do they lack anything? But we lack everything, absolutely everything." Others took it as a sign from the authorities that it was still possible for people of all ethnonational identities to live in Sarajevo, continuing the prewar Sarajevan spirit.

People who perceived the former Yugoslavia as a home of all ethnonational groups where each group was represented on equal terms, and who regarded the federal Republic of Bosnia and Herzegovina as the republic in which this principle was most important and functioned best, took the fall of this state by a war waged among these ethnonational groups as an evidence that it was impossible to live together in the future. They saw an administrative division between nationalities as the only way to prevent the same war from recurring. The caretaker explained:

I would say that we got along, and we got along very well. But on some levels they invented stupidities. And here is what we got. A bloody war never before seen in history. And it will last for a long time. So long as the questions are not solved. One people cannot command the others. . . . Here Muslims want to command the Croats and Serbs. It won't work; it won't work. The blood shall run until we extinguish each other. Make entities, so that no one can interfere. . . . To travel, to walk freely [is all right], but here is the Croatian authority and it shall be so as long as there is history. Here is Muslim authority, and here is Serbian. And that is Bosnia and Herzegovina, there you are, live there. Whoever doesn't like it can go somewhere else.

This type of solution appealed to non-Muslims because it was a way of escaping the Muslim dominance that many feared.

Croat Perspectives on Ethnonational Identity

Croats had always been a national minority in Sarajevo. During the war, the Croatian community had a strong center in the Catholic Church and its humanitarian organization, Caritas. As non-Croats were attracted by the help the Catholic community was providing for Sarajevans, the community grew in numbers and importance. Many of the newly recruited Catholics were not religious, and they came from families with mixed ethnoreligious backgrounds, which enabled them to adapt to the shifting political situation. A young Croat described this practice as opportunistic: "I don't know if you can find anyone who can honestly say that he is pure Croat. Because people who are half-Croats are going to say that they are Croats, although their mother is Serb, on the account of their father being Croat. . . . People always choose what is better. If your mother is Muslim, when [there are tensions between Croats and Muslims] you'll stress that. Now, when the relations are okay, then he is a big Croat."

Croats, like Serbs, felt threatened by the increasing presence of Islam in public life, because they interpreted it as a threat to the ethnonationally blended nature of their hometown. They felt ostracized by Muslim authorities who showed little trust, especially at the beginning of the war when Croats suddenly were forbidden to go to their prewar jobs, their apartments were searched, and some were even interrogated. Sarajevan Croats kept the notion of being Sarajevans in the first place, and the fact that many young Croat men joined the defense forces at the beginning of the war was often pointed out as evidence of Croatian loyalty and love for Sarajevo. As they were an obvious national minority, Sarajevan Croats often interpreted the events of the war as supporting the picture of Sarajevo as an ethnonational melting pot: "You know," a young woman told me, "people say that multicultural, multireligious Sarajevo is just an empty phrase. But, for us who live here, it is not an empty phrase."

Some resolved to stay and believed that such a society was going to prevail in the end, because that was the only choice they seemed to have. They were strongly opposed to Croatian nationalist politics, especially coming from Herzegovina's Croatian leadership, which sought to separate Herzegovina from Bosnia and make it ethnically pure. A young Croat declared his allegiance to Sarajevo as his hometown and his ideal: "Don't you have your apartment here [in Sarajevo]? So how can you support those who want to drag you there [to Herzegovina]? . . . I don't know what is hidden behind the words, but if it is said that the town is shared, that it is multi, as Divić said, I am going to support it as long it is that way. . . . That is what we have to fight for. To stay here, on these territories. Be here! Live here! Save this!"

Other Sarajevan Croats lost their belief in the possibility of a society free from the domination of one nationality over others. They saw the national division of Bosnia and Herzegovina as the only solution, and consequently they left the town. A young man explained that this trend affected everyone: "There is not a single person today whose national feelings are not at least a bit awakened, and who is not moving closer toward her or his national group. Absolutely none." For some people, identifying themselves as Croat and/or Catholic was not important, while others felt this was their basic identity. However, in both cases the importance of being a Sarajevan was crucial, because it gave them the legitimacy to stay in their homes and live with full civil rights.

At the beginning of the war, Croats held Serbs responsible for starting a war based on national separatism. They accused Serbs of knowing that the war was coming and for the unnecessary and provocative expressions of Serbian national belonging. The animosity was congruent with the political and military situation between Croatia and Serbia, which had been at war since 1991. In Sarajevo, however, as the war went on, Serbs and Croats did not feel threatened by the other nation's troops or politics, but rather by the local pro-Muslim regime. As Sarajevan Serbs became a minority during the war, Sarajevan Croats began to feel greater compassion toward them. Even the Serbs who had left during the war, and who were generally seen as traitors to pluralistic Sarajevo, were seen by Sarajevan Croats as a necessary part of the town if the life they were used to was to be reestablished. Portraying Serbs as decent and moral people unjustly ostracized by their Muslim neighbors was understandable because this was how Croats themselves increasingly felt. This perception of Serbs said more about the identification of Croats with their threatened existence than about their actual relations with Serbs.

Sarajevan Croats often reacted to the threat they felt from Muslims' increasing power by expressing their contempt for and superiority over Muslims. Most of the examples focused not on Sarajevan Muslims, but rather on Muslim influences from outside: the Arab world, and the Muslim newcomers who had been displaced from eastern Bosnian villages.

However often they portrayed Muslim newcomers as "primitive," Croats kept up their private contacts with Muslim neighbors and friends, which made them realize that even Muslims were having a hard time because of the increased importance of Islam and ethnonational identities. Croats were aware that Muslims did not like the visible presence of Islam in public life either, and that its growing power over their private lives was a humiliating experience. They also knew that, although it was generally easier to live in Sarajevo if a person had a Muslim name and origin, it took much more courage for a Muslim to express his or her discontent with the regime.

But in general terms, Croats arrogantly regarded Muslims as not genuinely religious and not a legitimate nationality because the group had emerged later in history than the Croatian Catholics and the Serbian Orthodox. A typically Croat narrative sounded like this: "Four generations ago, there were no Muslims. . . . They were either Serbs or Croats who during the Turkish Empire in these territories changed their religion for some reason or the other. Some in order to survive, others in order to live in comfort. . . . Actually, they are the only people who acquired their nationality because of their religion." When I objected that Muslims nevertheless existed for many centuries and had many old traditions, the answer was: "They don't really feel it. And I understand them; it is hard to pray to God in an unintelligible language."

Croatian arrogance toward Muslims included a component of pity because of the isolation from the Western world that Muslims were forced into by their government's pro-Islamic politics. A young man drew some interesting conclusions:

It is obvious that only Muslims are interested in this abortion of the federation [between Muslims and Croats]. Because without the federation they will be isolated from the rest of the world, which is against them having some kind of a state here. . . . I am really irritated by the United States because as soon as some sort of agreement is in sight they say that they will remove the embargo [on selling weapons to the Bosnian government]. . . . This gives them [Muslims] a reason to start military offensives and get killed. It seems to me that the interest of the West here is to exterminate as many of them as possible.

In this view, Muslims were acting under the delusion that the West would sympathize with them as the victims of genocide and the proponents of a multinational state.

Croats had a different picture of the war from Muslims, and their national identification was also political and moral. While Croats felt that this was a civil war between the peoples of one and the same country, and often saw it as a war waged by the rural population against the townspeople, Muslims stressed the nature of the war as a Serbian "aggression" of which they were the prime victims. A young Croatian man told me that this was the reason why Sarajevans increasingly socialized with people of the same nationality during the war. One evening he invited me to dinner with a young Muslim man who became his friend at the university. "We can talk to each other," he said, "but we don't agree. We don't have similar opinions, but that is probably normal. No, no, it *is* normal!" He acknowledged that this difference influenced their relationship: "I don't keep anything to myself. Perhaps I should. While he keeps quite a lot to himself. But we have a different view of this war. He thinks that it is exclusively an aggression, and I think that it is a civil war." When we discussed what a civil war meant, he concluded that this was not a typical civil war, since three nations were involved. "It is definitely a national war," he concluded. This sentiment struck me as yet another demonstration that the opinions expressed during the war were grounded in the speaker's affiliation and the moral stance he or she was taking. These two friends could probably agree that the war was a "national war," but they were using different national terminology and ascribed the guilt and suffering in different ways, which made any discussion morally sensitive and difficult.

From Yugoslavs to Sarajevans

In the political atmosphere that forced everyone to declare their national identity as Muslim, Serb, or Croat, many Sarajevans found themselves at a loss. These people had either declared themselves nationally as Yugoslavs before the war—according to the last prewar census, this group comprised approximately 10 percent of the city's residents—and lost that option with the breakup of Yugoslavia or refused to strengthen the division of people along national lines. Many Sarajevans accepted the idea of Yugoslav nationality as a way of marking that they belonged together with the members of their families, friends, colleagues, and neighbors who happened to have different ethnoreligious backgrounds.

During the war this ideology was still strongly held and expressed. When they spoke in general terms, Sarajevans identified differences between national groups in fairly essentialist ways. But when it came to Sarajevans and people they knew personally, the tendency was to stress their common Sarajevan culture, where differences in national identity and ethnoreligious

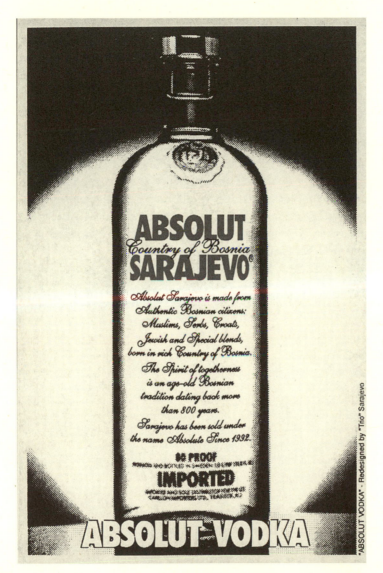

Figure 22. An "Absolut Vodka" ad redesigned by Trio stands as a symbol of the ideology of the "fourth nation." The label reads: "Absolute Sarajevo is made from Authentic Bosnian citizens: Muslims, Serbs, Croats, Jewish and Special blends, born in rich Country of Bosnia. The Spirit of togetherness in an age-old Bosnian tradition dating back more than 800 years. Sarajevo has been sold under the name Absolute Since 1992." Bought in Sarajevo, March 1995; reproduced courtesy of Trio.

background were not important. Moreover, this shared culture valued the experience of living in a religiously, ethnically, and nationally blended milieu and knowing how to negotiate differences in a sociable manner. A Sarajevan journalist called the people who did not identify with one of the three major national groups the "'fourth nation,' the people who simply experience life in Bosnia, the real and multiethnic one, not used for the perfidious purposes of the ruling clique in federation, in their minds and hearts" (Karlaš 1998:31, my translation).

Sarajevans who could be identified as "the fourth nation" stressed that they still did not care about the nationality of a person, but rather about other human qualities. Even those who began to reevaluate their sense of national belonging and would describe essential differences between ethnonational groups still reasoned that it was hard to find a person who could claim a homogenous background. They stressed the importance of the Bosnian tradition of respecting, learning about, and socializing across ethnoreligious differences, which they considered their normal way of life. A secularized Muslim woman articulated how she developed this perspective through her own experiences:

I have lived in a mixed marriage, and I think that I grew by seeing their [Serb Orthodox] customs, going to their family patron saint feasts (*slave*). . . . God is one for all, but some call him in the Arabic language, while others call him differently. And I know that each of these religions supports the basic human values. . . . We want to live normally, to mix; after all, the whole world is mixing. I don't understand what religion and nation have to do with it. And if love exists in the world, if there is humanity, are you going to look to see whether someone is a Croat or a Muslim if you like him, if he is nice toward you, if he is a man, educated, everything that you look for and are attracted by?

In the former Yugoslavia people could signal that they belonged together despite their different ethnoreligious backgrounds by identifying nationally as Yugoslav, and during the war identifying as a Sarajevan filled the same function. But as this notion was threatened by war and the promotion of nationalistic politics, in order to protect their identity Sarajevans soon assumed an arrogant, superior stance toward non-Sarajevans. They often blamed the Muslim newcomers to Sarajevo, whom they considered primitive and condemned for supporting nationalist parties before and during the war. "This is the conflict between rural and urban. . . . This is not a war. This is the Peasant Rebellion (Seljačka Buna). . . . We Sarajevans, no matter who and what we are, Muslims, Serbs, or Croats, feel a need to organize because we are Sarajevans," a young woman told me.

The resentment that secularized Sarajevan citizens felt toward the newcomers is epitomized by a story I was told in 1995 by another highly educated woman from Sarajevo. A refugee who occupied a deserted apartment in one of the skyscrapers noticed a strange door on his floor of the building one day. When he opened it he saw that there was a small room, completely empty. He was very happy because he could store all his reserves of wood and food there. But one day recently, when the electricity came back to Sarajevo, his storeroom disappeared. There was only a hole left. He was desperate and ran to the police, shouting that his storeroom was stolen. The policeman smiled at him and asked understandingly, trying to calm the refugee down, "You mean, your storeroom was plundered?" "No! Not plundered! The whole room is stolen," cried the refugee. It turned out that the empty room the refugee had found was the elevator, which, when the electricity came on, was called to another floor in the building.

Being Sarajevan was considered to be morally and culturally superior to being Bosnian, so many non-Muslims, as this young man from a mixed Christian background, preferred to define themselves as Sarajevans (Sarajlije): "I lost the state to which I belonged where I always wrote: citizenship SFRY, nationality Yugoslav. Now, when this happened I went by my father's nationality. Of course, I would never renounce my mother's origin either. . . . I was born in Sarajevo, but I wouldn't say that I am a Bosnian. Although I am. I would say that I am a Sarajevan (Sarajlija), of Croatian nationality, but I would never say that I am a Bosnian." When I asked him why not, he smiled uncomfortably and said, "I cannot say that I don't love Bosnia. But I think that by my education and my upbringing I am above Bosnia. Above what has always been a general notion here."

Even native Sarajevans and good friends were becoming nationalists during the war, a trend that was much more threatening than the nationalism of the "primitive, rural" other. Perhaps Sarajevans projected the responsibility for nationalism outside of the city in order to cope with the bitter fact that longtime residents were also changing. For Sarajevans who were strongly committed to the former Yugoslav ideology of "brotherhood and unity" as the only moral way of relating between people of different Bosnian and Herzegovinian national identities, the shock of discovering that a friend had become a nationalist was much more disturbing than their shared indignation with "newcomers."

A middle-aged man told me a sad story:

I lost one friend, a real friend from childhood who simply went mad. . . . When I meet him on the street, I run away to another street. . . . We hadn't seen each other for four months when the war had started, and when there was heavy shelling I hurried to his place. So I went to him, and he opened the door, and we hugged and kissed heartily, how are you, where are you, and so on. And then he started to talk. That was no longer the man who had been my friend. These were not his opinions. . . . He began to hate one nation [*narod*] to the degree that he would kill them. Just because they are members of that nation. I can't understand that. I mean, I can't socialize with such people. . . . I was telling my story, trying to bring him to some sense, and I cried as I bid him farewell, mourning that friendship with these tears that poured in front of him, which could have been because of my story, but these tears were only meant for this farewell; at that moment I lost a friend. I like to say that I have lost two teeth and one friend in the war. I haven't been able to mend either the teeth or the friendship. That is a terrible feeling. To lose a friend you had known for a long time.

While most Sarajevans who began to identify with their ethnonational group saw the political solution to the atrocities as dividing the country into three nationally homogenous entities, the "fourth nation" was eager to promote a heterogeneous, multinational, and multireligious state where all citizens would be treated equally. As the possibility of a pluralistic state became more and more unrealistic, they reoriented their hopes toward local life in Sarajevo. But, if the Sarajevan prewar identity of an urban ethnoreligiously and nationally blended milieu is to survive in its full richness, it has to be recognized and promoted politically. Sarajevo still lives in the power struggle between nationalistic politics and local traditions of national blending, which has now been intensified by the exigencies of war-induced trauma and poverty.

Chapter 9
Reconceptualizing War

Government wars aren't my wars; they've got nowt to do with me, because my own war's all that I'll ever be bothered about.
—The protagonist in Alan Sillitoe's *The Loneliness of the Long Distance Runner* (1959)

Conventional European ideas of war as an ordered, potentially just means of pursuing national ends simply do not hold when confronted with a real situation on the ground. Our concepts of soldiers fighting on the front lines while civilians work to sustain the war effort are of little use, as I found out during the siege of Sarajevo. The distinction between civilians and soldiers dissolved when civilians were constantly shelled and shot at by snipers and soldiers spent two-thirds of their time at home doing civilian chores. The concept of enemy was equally elusive. In Bosnia, the identity of the enemy shifted over time as alliances and antipathies among national groups and military forces changed; the enemy was produced by the war, not the other way round. In just war theory, the legitimate cause for state violence is defense against actual or imminent attack. But who was defending what against whom, when the war in the former Yugoslavia created the differences between national groups and the conflicts between their interests, rather than being caused by them? Nationalist solidarities and oppositions were generated by war itself, not vice versa; this war was a means of creating new states with exclusive ethnonational claims.

In this situation, people who did not share the nationalist views of political elites and military leaders might refuse to fight without being regarded as traitors. The negative connotations of desertion were turned to general acceptance, or even approval, when men left combat units not because they were afraid or disloyal to their countrymen but rather when they gathered enough courage to be loyal to them and stop carrying out acts of violence against those they did not see as their enemies. Many Sarajevans thought of nationalistic politicians as dishonest, pursuing their own power by pitting former friends against one another, and they realized that the war led only to mutual destruction rather than to victory or national security. The futility of war itself became as apparent to Sarajevan soldiers as to civilians under siege. Sarajevans were forced to make personal choices during the war. In deciding whether to go to or remain at the front lines, and in choosing to maintain or sever their relationships with people who might be seen as belonging to the enemy group, they were forced to take a personal stand. The ways in which they legitimated these choices by nationalist discourse is the key to understanding how the personal was intertwined with the collective, in this case nationalistic political ideologies and power relations.

The choices people made in specific situations were often contradictory, and the effort to rationalize his or her decisions made each individual in Sarajevo express divergent and contradictory opinions based on his or her experiences. Situations of war tend to cause this type of cognitive dissonance because of the profoundly disruptive changes that involvement in armed conflict inflicts on people's lives.[1] This psychological condition, which arises from the unavoidable conflicts between people's expectations and norms and the conduct they observe and in which they participate, is intolerable for very long. The disorientation and discomfort it creates must be resolved in order to sustain any sense of personal identity, much less integrity. What I have described as the process of changes of normality is one way of capturing people's struggle to restore a modicum of cognitive consistency.

How did Sarajevans attempt to make sense of the contradictory positions in which they found themselves in relation to the war? Sarajevans held three different conceptualizations of war that they struggled to integrate, which represent divergent stances in relation to the siege and the nationalist conflict that any individual could occupy simultaneously, depending on his or her choices and thoughts in specific situations. I call these three different modes civilian, soldier, and deserter, but in the Sarajevan situation they do not carry the common meanings and connotations of these terms. Rather, these are understandings of what was at stake in the war, ways of positioning the self in relation to the conflict, and ultimately modes of rationalizing what people themselves did. The profound lack of clarity within this framework about what power of choice people had and what responsibility they bear for their actions is inherent in the wartime situation as Sarajevans experienced it. Yet careful analysis reveals some patterns in Sarajevans' changing perceptions of war. After defining these three stances, this chapter traces them through time, places them in relation to people's understandings of social order, and scrutinizes the ways they legitimated their actions through political ideology that transformed their personal sense of national identity during wartime.

The civilian mode of thinking about war is characterized by a perception of war as opposed to peace. Peace is considered normal, a civilized, moral way of living with juridical routines for dealing with manslaughter and material destruction in such a way that criminals are punished and violence is contained. War is a disruption, an interval of time that is abnormal and generally impossible for "us" to experience. War is something that "others" experience, whether it is "others" in time, such as our predecessors, or "others" in space, people somewhere else around the globe. Sarajevans themselves began with this view: they often recounted how they watched the war going on in neighboring Croatia, yet were still taken aback when Sarajevo was hit (Softić 1994:6). A young woman told me in 1994: "War in Dubrovnik. We watched it on the television; they said that there was no water for seven days. That was incomprehensible to us, that you could live without water. Or, that there was nothing to be bought in the stores. I couldn't understand that. But, when the war started here, when I experienced it, . . . then you understood what you had been watching on the television."

When civilians are subjected to war-related violence, the civilian mode becomes impossible to maintain, but it does not disappear. People feel so helpless in the face of an incomprehensible situation that they are at a loss for how to sustain their existence, much less act effectively. So a new mode is added, the soldier mode. The power of this way of understanding lies in its cognitive organization of war: it makes war comprehensible as a social phenomenon that can be controlled by human beings and thus renders it acceptable. War has a legitimate cause and aims, and it presumes clearly differentiated political entities that are engaged in armed conflict. In this mode, warfare has its own set of rules that differ from peacetime norms. These rules legitimate what would otherwise be socially and morally unacceptable, such as killing other humans and wreaking havoc on a city. In the soldier mode, these actions are clearly differentiated from what would have happened in normal circumstances, so the murderous or destructive actions a person takes do not make him or her into a different person. It is understood that this abnormal mode of living will end when the war does.

However, what we do in wartime and the choices we must make under abnormal circumstances do change us and our perceptions of ourselves, or at least make us constantly reconsider what is acceptable and what is not.

Even though political ideologies that legitimate those actions help us come to terms with many changes, for most people killing or ostracizing those who yesterday were their friends and neighbors and taking or destroying their homes are discomfiting acts, and in the long run they are difficult to rationalize through any political ideology. At some point, people realize that these violent circumstances are an unavoidable part of daily existence and that they must come to terms with the changes that have transformed their lives, from their means of subsistence through their relationships with others to their political ideology, in this case involving mainly their sense of ethnoreligious and national identities. This cognitive change does not substitute for the civilian and soldier modes of perceiving war, as it does not take away the civilian's feelings of helplessness or the soldier's need for moral impunity. Rather, it adds to them a new deserter mode, in which people feel personally and morally responsible for their own deeds, despite their powerlessness in conditions of war, and increasingly strive to make their own choices regardless of the military and political forces that previously had determined their actions. What is more, in this mode of thinking, the differences between war and peace become blurred; the two states increasingly resemble each other.

As I sought to explore what Sarajevans thought about these issues, I found that those who were or had been soldiers kept a low profile. Even those Muslims who had been involved in the military defense of Sarajevo on the side of the Bosnian government were reluctant to be identified as soldiers. In this respect, they resembled the Serbs who had remained in the besieged city but worried that their loyalties might be suspect. Being or having been a soldier was not an identity that people wanted to affirm publicly. Although looking for soldiers or ex-soldiers to interview felt uncomfortable, I was determined to talk with some of them because I realized that their voices and viewpoints were an essential dimension of the wartime experience. All Sarajevans had to make choices in relation to the war, and the extremity of their situation was best captured in the situation of those who had chosen to bear arms. People did not point out that someone was or had been a soldier, however. It seemed to be something that men had to do, which many tried to avoid, and some managed to evade or escape, but not many seemed proud of their time in the military. I had a feeling that some soldiers were haunted by frontline trauma, such as watching the deaths of their comrades in arms, while a sense of shame hovered over the whole group, as if they had been complicit in extending a conflict from which Sarajevans suffered. They knew that they had shot at people, and even if some were not sure, most knew that they probably also wounded and killed people. Things they did and experienced were best forgotten, because these things were at the same time traumatic and shameful.[2] None of these subtle hints of discomfort was explicitly acknowledged. Rather, the whole subject was surrounded with an implicit "Do not unravel" sign. The fear that I might be identified as a sensation-seeker also inhibited my inquiries.

Eventually, I had to ask one of my war friends, whom I call Emir, for an interview. Emir was a man in his forties from a Muslim ethnoreligious background with whom I became acquainted in the spring of 1995. Since he and his wife were fairly young and modern, with two teenage children, we found many common interests; I especially appreciated their sense of humor and their sense of the absurd. I spent quite a few late evenings at their apartment, eating, drinking, and chatting. Although they knew about my research, in this private, social setting, we never really discussed it, just as we never discussed Emir's attitudes, choices, and experiences as a soldier. I only knew that he voluntarily joined the ABiH at the beginning of the war but was no longer at the front. When I asked him if he was willing to talk to me about his experiences and thoughts about the war, he agreed. He described the choices he made: from a civilian, turning into a soldier, and then finding ways of avoiding the armed service. In the analysis that follows, I situate Emir's first-person account as much as possible in the context of situations and experiences that Sarajevans shared.

The Official Story and Individual Views of War

When the electricity started coming back in 1996 and Sarajevans spent more time watching television, a series of programs about the beginnings of war caught my attention. Suddenly I realized that people's chaotic and opaque experiences were being formed into a coherent story. These were no longer private experiences and opinions, with each person's views as valid as any other's. The story was now becoming official and shared. While we all recognized its components, it failed to capture many of our own experiences and it posited some "facts" that we did not recognize. A schoolbook presented what became a generally accepted account:

After the independence of Slovenia and Croatia, following the logic of political events Bosnia and Herzegovina also had to go the same way. At the referendum held on

February 29, 1992, the citizens of Bosnia and Herzegovina opted for a self-sustained, independent, and sovereign state. The European Community recognized the national and legal existence of the Republic of Bosnia and Herzegovina exactly on the date of the beginning of the Serbian-Montenegrin aggression against Bosnia and Herzegovina, April 6, 1992. Finally, on May 21, 1992, the Republic of Bosnia and Herzegovina was accepted as a member of the United Nations. (Imamović and Pelešić 1994:121, my translation)

April 6, 1992, was identified as the official beginning of the war in Sarajevan media, as well as in Western accounts. On that day snipers on the roof of the Holiday Inn opened fire on thousands of people demonstrating in front of Bosnia and Herzegovina's Parliament in Sarajevo, in a direct reaction to the recognition by the European Union and the United States of Bosnia and Herzegovina as an independent state. The referendum on independence, held some weeks earlier, was boycotted by the Serbian population, while most of the Muslim and Croat population participated. The leading Serbian party, the Srpska demokratska stranka (Serb Democratic Party, SDS), which stood behind the Serbian boycott of the referendum, took international recognition as a threat to Serbian people and initiated an armed conflict by shooting at the demonstrators. Such an account is given by Gutman (1993:xxvii), Imamović and Bošnjak (1994:17), Imamović and Pelešić (1994:121), Vulliamy (1994:73ff), Gjelten (1995:24), and Ramet (1996:246f). Other authors pick different events (Glenny 1992:167) or are less specific (Owen 1996:2; Rieff 1996:17; Woodward 1995a:1; Zimmermann 1996:186), but they still try to link the beginning of the war to some violent event filled with political significance. The problem with this effort to establish the onset of violence and thus the political significance of war is that the choice of events depends entirely on the author, and authors chose dates and events that correspond to their overall political interpretation of the war.[3] Consequently, the more political power behind an account, the more valid it is assumed to be and the more generally accepted it becomes, so the official story of the war will of necessity be the story of the politically empowered.

From the very start, political leaders interpreted events in terms of conflict between national groups. Consider, for example, the Bosnian government's identification of the first victim of the war: Suada Dilberović, a twenty-four-year-old student. In 1996, Vrbanja Bridge, where she was killed on April 6, 1992, was renamed Suada Dilberović's Bridge, and her death was commemorated with a plaque and flowers. By then, when the siege of Sarajevo was being lifted, it became clear that this young woman symbolized all the losses that occurred during the war, especially the civilians who had been

Figure 23. A plaque and flowers on Suada Dilberović's Bridge, commemorating her death as the first victim of war. Sarajevo, April 1996. Photo by author.

killed by random shelling or sniper fire. That the first official victim of the war was a young female student with a Muslim name was hardly coincidental. A man would have been a potential soldier, and an old person would not have represented the destruction of the future so poignantly. A student was a symbol of education, the cultivation of intelligence, something that was good for the prosperity of every nation-state. In the simplified division of the world into good and evil, which is characteristic of wars seen in the soldier mode, a student represents the ideal good and is opposed to the primitive, uneducated, uncivilized other—Serbs, IDPs, and the war itself. Muslims were positioned as *the* victims in this war, especially by the official interpretation of the Sarajevan government, although it was generally accepted that other groups also had their share of suffering and losses.[4] Only a week after her death, Suada Dilberović was referred to as "the first heroine of Sarajevo's defense" (*Preporod* 1992). According to Hedetoft, a "hero" represents a "cluster of national meanings" (1993, quoted in Jabri 1996:140). The transformation of a participant in an anti-nationalist protest demonstration into a nationalist hero is an ironic indication of the construction of a Muslim national consciousness that took place during the war.

Most of the Western accounts of the war (which sometimes refer to it in the plural) organize it into major phases: the war in Slovenia, "the Serb-Croat war," and the "war between Bosnia-Herzegovina government forces and the Bosnian Serbs in Bosnia-Herzegovina" (for example, Owen 1996:2). Even those who concentrate on Bosnia and Herzegovina divide it into phases. For example, Magnusson (1993:23–24) defines three phases: a Serbian "blitzkrieg" from May until July 1992; the consolidation of Serbian and Croatian positions during the autumn and winter of 1992; and the war between Muslims and Croats that escalated starting in the summer of 1993. These periods had only indirect significance for people in Sarajevo. Still operating in the civilian mode, they perceived the wars in Slovenia and Croatia as unbelievable or as happening to someone else. The Serbian offensive in eastern Bosnia was felt only afterward, when Sarajevo came under siege and the town was flooded by refugees and residents heard dreadful stories of what could happen if the Bosnian Serbs' troops were to enter Sarajevo.

The periodizations imposed by historians are not useful for comprehending what war was like for the people who lived it. Sarajevans had heterogeneous understandings of when war began, and their views were place specific and context dependent. Indeed, the official account is counterproductive, since it implies that only one viewpoint is valid. What these generalizations demonstrate, rather, is the drive to provide clarity and structure to war itself, typical of the soldier mode. The "thickness" of concrete experiences, by contrast, leaves space for different ways of remembering war—a fact that becomes strikingly obvious in the versions that the conflicting parties usually promote. Over time, the opaque reality of war as experienced by individuals becomes organized into a narrative with fixed and symbolically pregnant dates and events. Finally, the social memory of war becomes politically biased by those who have the power of turning it into history.

For Sarajevans, the war began on whatever day they were first subjected to heavy shelling. A letter written by a young woman in Sarajevo to her sister in Zagreb on April 6, 1994, recalls these disparate moments of realization.[5]

Do you remember how nonplussed the neighbors in Radićeva were when, immediately after we arrived, we asked them to tell us what their cellar was like and even to show it to us? Funny, on that April 7, '92 the war had not yet seriously started for them, because no shell had yet fallen in their courtyard. But we, who lived only twenty or so minutes further away, had already had the experience of spending forty hours in a cold cellar crowded with neighbors, from babies to seventy-year-olds. (Softić 1994:11–12, my translation)

The disruptions of peacetime life occurred one after another, but so insidiously that people did not add them up. Emir described interruptions in transportation that interfered with his work, but at that time, he said, "I had no idea (pause), I couldn't even imagine this sort of war happening. . . . I continued going to my firm, but you didn't really know whether to go or not. Trams were not working, and some people came while others didn't. You came to work, but you didn't have anything to do. Total chaos." Then, suddenly, a moment came when people realized that circumstances had changed so drastically that the situation could no longer be perceived as peace. Only then was it possible to look back at the previous disruptions of normal life and decide which of them was most significant. In this sense, war arrived only in retrospect, as people made sense of the past in relation to recent events.[6] At that point the civilian mode characteristic of peacetime existence lost its power and the soldier mode became dominant.

Many Sarajevans experienced the course of the war as a flow of time filled with a constant struggle for survival and a helpless waiting for the siege to end. During the first year, the dates for the next negotiations, both hoped for and dreaded, were temporal points that organized life into bearable periods. Whenever a negotiation and a ceasefire failed, a new date was set. People hoped that if they only endured the intervening weeks or months everything would return to normal. By the time I arrived in Sarajevo in 1994, people were aware of this little time-trick that they played and invariably found themselves cheated by. In September 1994, a ceasefire that had lasted over six months was being brought to an end by the gradual escalation of random shelling and sniper activity.[7] By that time few people cared about negotiation dates, because after the tenth or twentieth projected or actual negotiation date passed and whatever talks were or were not held failed to change the situation, the prospect of the war ending became unreal. Sarajevans organized their lives in accordance with the state of war in the way that is characteristic of the deserter mode. As people left behind any notion of victory or defeat, the date that hostilities began, too, lost its significance. Time itself acquired a fluid character. Sarajevans' orientation in time became distorted as a part of the general derangement of any predictable order and the futility of their own actions. Tone Bringa encountered a similar distortion of time when she talked to villagers among whom she had done anthropological fieldwork before the war, but who were now refugees.[8] Her informants mixed tenses after they had been expelled from their village by violent means. "They were living in a time, a dramatically and constantly changing time, which was neither in the past, the present, nor the future," she explained (1995:xvii).

While Sarajevans looked toward possible negotiations to restore the peace, the international media and authorities in Bosnia and Herzegovina singled out particular instances of violence as especially significant. The events that received the most exposure, even political exploitation, were the two shellings of the central Markale market and the shelling of a bread line in the shopping street Vaso Miskin on May 27, 1992. The chronicler of *Sarajevan War Drama* wrote:

Shock! Stress! Swallow fastened in the throat! Stupor. Television cameras informed the civilized world about the massacre in Vaso Miskin Street. Serbian medieval forest-people aimed at and hit the people waiting in the queue for their daily bread. Body parts thrown around, blood, dead, wounded, tears, cries. God, is there a proper punishment for these crimes? Shelling the innocent people. . . . "Serbian people show by their conduct that they do not belong to civilization," proclaimed the American statesman John Baker. (Miličević 1993:15–16, my translation)

A Sarajevan chronicler and an American statesman express here attitudes that exemplify the simplistic bifurcation characteristic of the soldier point of view, in this case into good, innocent, civilized Sarajevans and evil, "savage" Serbs. The ascription of responsibility indiscriminately to all of the "Serbian people" by a representative of the most powerful military force in the world was especially unfortunate because it fueled the imposed ethnonational divisions and attitudes hostile to reconciliation. Sadly, this type of statement is characteristic of diplomatic interventions that supposedly aim at achieving peace.

Eventually, the dramatic nature of events forced those who observed them from afar to feel compelled to act. While in 1992 an international diplomatic statement was an achievement, the shelling of the Markale market on February 5, 1994, led to an international intervention that forced the Bosnian Serbs' Army to withdraw heavy artillery twenty kilometers from the center of the town and marked the start of the first long ceasefire. The second massacre at the Markale market on August 28, 1995, triggered the long-awaited NATO bombing of Bosnian Serbs' artillery positions on the mountains surrounding the town and eventually led to the signing of the Dayton Peace Accords.

For the vast majority of Sarajevans, the massacres that outsiders found so appalling that they changed the course of political, diplomatic, and military activity were not the most significant events they experienced during the war. People pointed out that there were so many violent acts against civilians in Sarajevo during the war that it was ironic that the international community needed the media's overexposure of an event where between twenty and seventy people lost their lives in order to decide to do something effective.[9] The shelling of civilians standing in line to buy bread aroused public outrage because the civilians represented the essence of innocents struggling for bare subsistence. Indeed, the last two massacres were so effective in provoking intervention that many people felt a certain doubt as to whether the Bosnian Serbs had been the ones who fired. Perhaps the shelling came from the Bosnian government's side in a calculated effort to draw international attention to the unsustainable character of the situation, as the Bosnian Serbs suggested (cf. Owen 1996:274, 357; Zimmermann 1996:156). The fact that international and UN observers must have been able to locate the positions from which the shells were fired but never announced it made the shelling seem like a political ploy. These massacres became a powerful public symbol for the character of the siege of Sarajevo: Serbian savages' war against the civilized world. Sarajevans' skepticism about the official version of these events paralleled the divergence between their own experiences and public representations of the conflict. The darkest days were those on which people suffered personal losses, which were often not accompanied by massive casualties but occurred with an incomprehensible randomness. For the people I met in Sarajevo, the massacres became important mostly as points of orientation in remembering the character of the preceding and following phases of the war. More important were the cold and foodless winter that followed the shelling of 1992, which marked the hardening of the siege, and the reopening of the tram traffic in March 1994 after the February massacre, which gave the first hope that the war might really end.

During the spring of 1995 most of the people dreaded May 1, when the 1994 ceasefire was to end. Nothing happened in Sarajevo that month; instead, "ethnic cleansing" took place in Srpska Krajina in Croatia. The much-feared shelling of Sarajevo came in June and continued almost unabated until NATO bombed Bosnian Serbs' positions around Sarajevo in August 1995. Sarajevans welcomed the bombings and perceived this intervention as a turning point that signaled the West's decision to stop the war. Although the "peace process" that followed can be divided into stages, Sarajevans took nothing for granted until it produced concrete results: the Dayton Peace Accords, the lifting of the siege of Sarajevo, the gradual reintegration of the sections of the city held by Bosnian Serbs throughout the war, postwar elections monitored by the international community, international aid for restoration of the town, and a return to the peacetime routines of life. The signing of the Dayton Peace Accords in December 1995 brought a sense of relief, but significant change occurred only when people could walk in the streets knowing that there were no more snipers aiming at them almost a half a year later. The first time they walked through the reintegrated parts of the town, it was hard to believe that only a few days before it had seemed the most impossible thing in the world. The cognitive gap between immediate threat to life and its absence was so wide as to preclude building conceptual bridges between them.

The terrible disappointment with peace came later, when people realized that, although they were not being shot at any more, which was by no means a small thing, no other major changes had taken place in their lives. Apartments were damaged; gas and electricity were not always available. People were out of work and still had to depend on humanitarian relief. Along with the physical and economic fabric of their lives, their social networks had been destroyed. Although some people were coming back from their places of refuge abroad, those closest to them often did not. One woman voiced a common sentiment: "The worst thing that happened in this war is the peace. There is no enthusiasm. After the Second World War we all went and built the country with our bare hands, volunteering. But now, people are so disillusioned." Through the imitation of life, people had kept an idea of peace in the back of their minds. But the war did not stop in a clear-cut way, and the ending of the war was marked by same type of fluidity as its beginning and its course. Peace, when it came, did not restore the prewar life people remembered but required them to continue struggling with many of the aspects of war they had found most distressing.

The conventional idea of war held by civilians, as an anomalous situation confined to a limited period of time, arises from a need to impose some order on the otherwise confusing phenomenon of war, where even the linear organization of time is unattainable. For Sarajevans, as for many people in the aftermath of war, the need to put the events of war behind them without forgetting what happened laid the groundwork for a retrospective simplification of the war's complexities and the eventual ritualizing of events, which is typical of the soldier mode. Shared memories of war generate social cohesion. They are ritualized around specific dates and events that have collective significance, but these events are chosen and their meanings inscribed by those in power in order to validate their position in the new, nationalistic social order.[10] Because of this, the individual experience and perception of war always differs from the politically empowered, official version. The victorious side enshrines its soldier viewpoint, while the deserter mode in which increasing numbers of people operated through the duration of the war is set aside.[11]

Ordering War

Many accounts describe this war as "unimaginable" (Morokvasić 1998:66) and unprecedented in its cruelty (Vuković 1992:14–15; Imamović and Bošnjak 1994:17; Kubert 1996:141). As Isaković put it: "I do not know whether this is war. The word war does not encompass everything that is happening. War has some rules. This is something unprecedented. Unprecedented and not previously experienced forms of evildoings and dirtiness of these evildoings" (Isaković 1994:13, my translation). Such extreme characterizations bespeak the writers' inability to assimilate the appalling facts of this war to their idealized conceptions of European history. The supposed uniqueness of the experience of this particular war points to a common characteristic in these accounts: people's inability to let go of their perceptions of the normal peacetime order of things. Similar accounts exist also for other wars and genocides.[12] It is as if a refusal to realize the possible consequences of what is happening around them can protect people from what they fear.

In Sarajevo, people continued to go to work even though everything was collapsing around them. Information about what was going on was indirect and unclear, and signs of divisions and groupings along ethnonational lines began to appear. Nationalist politics and national interests started to take over the joint Parliament of Bosnia and Herzegovina, leading to the SDS boycott and eventually the demise of civilian political institutions. In March the town was blocked by barricades, set up by masked people who later were identified as Serbs, especially Serbs from outside of Sarajevo, the villagers, the uncivilized, primitive "others." A Serbian wedding party was shot at, apparently for an aggressive display of Serbian symbols in the city center. Some thought that national signs were unnecessary and silly, while others tried to do something to stop the division of society. But not many thought that these disruptions were significant or going to last. Even when they started referring to "the war," people thought that it would not last long and that the prewar order would soon be reestablished. Those who felt that life was not sustainable in these conditions fled the town with their families, as Emir's Serbian neighbor did: "That man was scared. He was terrified. Of what would happen to him. He came to our apartment once, casually, to have coffee. Afterward, when I replayed the scene in my mind I had the feeling that he came to investigate the situation, to feel the terrain, whether he was in danger, and to see what mood the neighbors were in. But he was a totally scared man. So I wasn't at all surprised when he left." Only in retrospect, though, could Emir understand how endangered his Serbian neighbor felt.

Most Sarajevans applied the term "war" to the situation after they had been shelled. Experiencing life-threatening circumstances on an unprecedented and unimaginable scale made it imperative for them to find some way of understanding and dealing with the situation and stimulated their adoption of the soldier mode. The schoolbooks used in areas under the control of the Bosnian government illustrate the conceptual organization of war by identifying opposing sides. In 1994, in the midst of the conflict, new books offered a sweeping account of Serbian aggression:

Their intent was to . . . accomplish the ancient dream of the Serbian nationalists to make a so-called Greater Serbia. . . . The attack started on April 6, 1992. The former Yugoslav People's Army and domestic Chetniks armed to the teeth started to attack the unprotected settlements and the unarmed people with the most lethal weapons. . . . [The people] showed a fierce resistance. With hunting guns and hand-made weapons Bosnian and Herzegovinian fighters confronted the tanks, cannons, and airplanes of the aggressor. . . . Then the Army of Bosnia and Herzegovina was formed. In a short time it became an organized power that took a stand before its people in order to protect them from the crimes of Serbo-Montenegrin aggressors and domestic Chetniks. . . . The intention of the aggressor was to clear the Bosnian and Herzegovinian territories of the non-Serbian people, in the first place of Bosniacs, in order to create an ethnically cleansed Serbian territory. . . . The unprecedented crimes followed. Women, children and old people were slaughtered, there were rapes, plundering, and burning. Villages, schools, factories, mosques, old monuments, all that was Bosniac and Muslim, was disappearing in flames. (Imamović and Bošnjak 1994:17–18, my translation)

The narrative of unarmed civilians ruthlessly attacked by a powerful enemy army, the victims whose valiant resistance becomes embodied in their own army, is well known from narratives of the Second World War and the partisan resistance against Nazi Germany and Fascist Italy. The difference here is that "the people," Bosnian Muslims, are called Bosniacs.[13]

What Emir called "the centers of power" framed the war in the nationalist idiom from the very start. The identification and consolidation of the enemy, united in its assumed interests and goals, assigned responsibility for causing the war as well as guilt for whatever happened during its prosecution. It turned the otherwise appalling immorality of destruction into an organized and understandable phenomenon, an acceptable reality. It is more reassuring to perceive war as a continuation of politics by other means, as Clausewitz's (in)famous definition put it in 1832, than to face its chaotic and horrific nature (see Clausewitz 1997). The legitimate nationalist explanation characteristic of the soldier mode of thinking eased the helpless desperation of the civilian mode of thinking when people were confronted with the atrocities of war.

The organization of war into sides with political aims is the mode of thinking characteristic of states. It is often strongly infused with moral judgments, because from the perspective of each side in the war, the enemy is the evil, self-interested aggressor while "our guys" are the defenders of basic human rights and universal values. This dynamic produces conflicting interpretations of war, and the "winner" usually gets to establish its interpretation as the sole true one, making war understandable and coherent. During the war in Bosnia and Herzegovina, moral positioning permeated all aspects of life, starting with the label used for the violence occurring there. By choosing one of the existing labels—war, civil war, aggression, or genocide—you automatically positioned yourself as supporting either the Croat, the Serb, or the Muslim side. Generally speaking, the Serbian side wanted to define the war as a civil war in order to prevent international intervention. For the same reason, the term also suited international observers. "Aggression" was used mostly by the Bosnian government to blame the Serbs for the war. The Bosnian government used "genocide" to assert that Muslims were being slaughtered solely because of their ethnoreligious identity and to characterize ethnic cleansing as among the worst crimes in human history. Some foreign journalists and intellectuals used "genocide" to point to the unacceptable conduct of the war: that innocent civilians were being murdered in violation of international law. I have chosen to use the term "war" to describe these events and situations because that was the term most commonly used internationally as well as locally. It also admits of multiple sides and does not assign blame automatically. However, it is important to be aware that anthropological research in such a politically sensitive field is by necessity positioned.

Sooner or later, the experiences of war create situations in which the disruption of life can no longer be justified or understood by any rules or logic of war. Emir recounted one incident that for him emptied the war of meaning:

In my old unit there was a boy from the orphanage near our headquarters. In the orphanage he had a younger brother and sister. A fine boy. Good person. Scared and young. He had just turned eighteen years of age. After I changed units I heard that he got killed, somewhere in Vogošća.[14] They were going, naively, over a field, and an anti-aircraft cannon was shooting at them. He got hit in the groin. They couldn't evacuate him so they hid for some time, and he bled to death. There was a comrade with him who tried to help him; they had bread with them so the comrade tried to stop the bleeding by pressing the bread against the wound. But he died. What hurts is that the brother and sister he was taking care of—he was their mother and father—they lost him.

The crucial point with this account is that Emir sees the young man in the first place as a person in relationship to others, not as a soldier. He identifies with the siblings' loss, not with the national cause. The young man's death felt so unjust that no cause could be seen as worth it (see Morokvasić 1998:66). The longer a war goes on, the m.ore likely people are to have experiences that make the war seem senseless; the soldier mode of thinking does not hold. At this point, when nationalist justifications fail, the deserter mode begins to emerge.

As the war continued, the distinction between civilians and soldiers faded for men in the hills as well as for the dwellers in the town below. Emir found surviving in Sarajevo more of a challenge than serving in the military:

We went to the lines of separation [front lines] in shifts, five days on the line and ten days rest [at home]. . . . Coming home was chaos. You came from terrible hygienic conditions, sleeping for five days in a half-destroyed, deserted, and filthy house, making fire in ovens that were falling apart, digging trenches but not being able to wash yourself. . . . So, when you came home your first thought was to take a bath. [But] there was no electricity, and no gas to warm the water. You had a bit of wood. . . . I always took off all my clothes immediately in the hall, and went into the bathroom, which was freezing in wintertime. You washed yourself quickly. Then all the domestic activities were waiting for you. . . . The first thing I would do after coming from the front was to fetch water. I needed a whole day for this. And the same before leaving for the front. . . . There was always a crowd waiting for water. People were nervous, there was shelling. It was interesting when a shell would fall, you didn't leave the queue, because if you had already waited for two hours, what then? You had to have water. . . . That was really the worst, bringing the water.

In Emir's account, the distinction between soldiers' and civilians' experiences of war is blurred. His life was threatened in both places, but being shelled while fetching water as a civilian was worse. He found more sociability as a soldier, as men found ways of passing the time together. At home, he did not go to neighborhood gatherings, where mostly women went. "In five days [on the front lines] you had time to talk enough, to change the flow of thoughts in your head," he explained. "So I'd stay at home and listen to the news, meditate in the dark, pointlessly."

Moral Choices and Political Legitimation

Nationalist accounts of April 6, 1992 avoid mentioning the fact that the demonstration in front of the Parliament in Sarajevo that day was civilians' last attempt to resist the violent imposition of national separatism. The anti-nationalist demonstration gathered at least twenty thousand participants on the streets.[15] In the former Yugoslavia, all demonstrations were organized by the state. Now, the people were answering the dissolving state with the same message that had been imposed on them for so many years: brotherhood and unity. One speaker said, "Let all the Serb chauvinists go to Serbia and let the Croat chauvinists go to Croatia. We want to remain here together. We want to keep Bosnia as one" (report by Michael Montgomery, *Daily Telegraph*, April 7, 1992, quoted in Malcolm 1994:235). Officials of the government of Bosnia and Herzegovina came in for criticism when they advanced the idea of separation. Many Sarajevans resisted national divisions wherever they appeared. In his firm, Emir heard "a rumor that a Serb branch had been formed" and was upset that others seemed to be going along: "How could they be destroying" what existed in Sarajevo? "In the beginning we had even secret meetings, younger people, we wanted to pursue our own line, we wouldn't allow the division, we were against national firms."

Even after the protests failed and national separation increased, many Sarajevans refused to believe that further escalation of violence was possible and that war would be fought between Bosnian nations. When Emir joined the defense forces, he explained, "I still didn't understand the situation. I asked whether all [nationalities] were represented in these units. They showed me the list and I saw that there were Croats, Serbs, and Muslims on it. Naturally, since we lived in a mixed part of the town. So I volunteered." This mixed group met in a public building in May 1992. The defense forces were as chaotic as the situation in the town. "Shells were already falling, bullets whistling, front lines were established. It was more or less already known which territory belonged to whom. . . . Sometimes we went to the lines of separation [front lines], although these lines were protected in the first place by the people living there. They protected their hearths. There was still no consciousness formed in people." In this account, Emir retrospectively described the initial civilian ways of acting and emphasized the powerlessness of that position. When Emir referred to his naiveté and lack of consciousness, he was speaking from a soldier stance: it was naive not to realize that there was a war going on, that the antagonistic sides were different national groups, and that he belonged to the Muslim side represented by the Bosnian government. He regarded his attempts to maintain unity at work in much the same way: "Today you see how all that was naive. You thought you could do something, but you could do absolutely nothing. The centers of power where decisions were made were detached from our institution, and we were totally out of touch with those centers."

In peacetime, citizens have power; in war, they are powerless. Emir's civilian mode of thinking became overtaken by the soldier mode. The decision to shift from a mixed military unit to an almost purely Muslim one, which consisted of men from the quarter of town where he had spent his childhood, followed logically. The fact that he was personally acquainted with everyone, including the Serbs, who served in this unit made them worthy of trust. At the time that Emir gave me this soldierly explanation, he knew that the decision involved deserter logic: you go where you feel most safe, and that is with people you know well. But his explanation was still in the soldier mode, which is why he needed to explain why he could trust the Serbs in this unit. In this way of thinking, fellow Muslims were by definition trustworthy.

In *The Body in Pain*, Elaine Scarry describes the process of polarization that takes place in wartime:

In the opening moments of war [there are] no longer the diffuse . . . persons, projects, and concerns that existed immediately prior to war's opening, because those . . . separate identities have suddenly crystallized into two discrete identities. . . . The distinction between "friend" and "enemy"—identified by Carl Schmitt as the fundamental distinction in politics equivalent to good and evil in moral philosophy and beautiful and ugly in aesthetics[16]—is in war converted to an absolute polarity . . . registered in some version of us-them idiom. (Scarry 1985:88)

War has a propensity to enforce both an antagonistic division between groups and homogeneity within groups. As Vivienne Jabri has observed, nationalism legitimizes war, while "war is a constitutive element of collective identity" (1996:139–40). In Sarajevo, the war was indeed the constitutive element of ethnonational groups, and nationalism indeed legitimized the war. War enforced both division and homogenization along ethnonational lines, and thus *created* antagonistic national groups, contrary to a widespread misconception that the war was *caused by* nationalistic antagonisms.[17]

Accepting the war entailed accepting its aim: the division of the population into national groups and territories. For Emir, seeing the situation in the soldier mode meant choosing to identify with the Muslim side. Emir's wife articulated this process concisely, using an argument strikingly similar to that promoted by the government in Sarajevo:

Serbs made a mistake when they went into Bijeljina and made a bloody fight, because it was the Arkanovci[18] who found the unprepared, unarmed folk. And they made bloody slaughters. Tremendous obstinacy, defiance, and the wish to survive were awakened in the people, and they realized on the basis of this event that we were something different. There, I never knew that I was a Muslim, but now I know that I am something different [from the Serbs] because somebody is slaughtering me. . . . And then the people . . . arrayed themselves without weapons; without anything they defended themselves.

The reciprocal logic of war—discovering difference in the process of conflict—is audible in this account. In this logic lies the power of war to define false truths: discovering difference becomes a way of explaining the violence.

Identification with the national cause was implicit in war terminology. Thus far Emir had referred to the front lines as "lines of separation" marking the divisions between the three Bosnian nations. Further on in his account Emir used another term, "the line of responsibility." Each military unit was assigned responsibility for a specific part of the front line that surrounded the city. Using "responsibility" to denominate what soldiers were doing at the front line—bearing weapons and shooting at the enemy—turned the abstract and collective nature of soldiers' tasks into an individual moral act. For an adult male in Sarajevo, it was easy to associate this responsibility for the front line with his responsibility for his own family. Both the family and the front line needed to be "protected," and when acts of war are defined as defense, this identification works even more easily. As duty to the nation was translated into responsibility for the family, the social roles of soldier and father, brother, or son became interchangeable.

By the fall of 1994, Emir and many other Sarajevans had realized that the unity and defense of the nation in whose name they were fighting were just words in the mouths of politicians who were not sacrificing themselves for the cause but benefiting from the conflict. They began to understand people who were not willing to fight for any cause and to see that the enemy soldiers were probably in a situation similar to their own. Emir questioned the neat division into a Serbian and a Muslim side and the guilt of all Serbs; being a soldier lost its meaning. In his account, he identified the initial cause of the war as the split along national lines for which the Serbs were to blame, reflecting the official interpretation of the government he lived under. When he described the defense of his own hearth as the reason for joining the army and his fear of unreliable Serbs in the mixed military unit, he was operating within the same explanatory framework. But when it came to his neighbors and his fellow combatants, his account was full of understanding for the reasons behind their fear, their refusal to take up weapons, and their decision to leave the town. Here, the war stopped making sense, and the soldier mode did not apply. Emir explained the situation of a Serbian neighbor:

The man simply didn't want to go to the army, so they said, very well, you won't carry a gun but then you'll dig trenches. He probably didn't like it so he left. . . . The digging of trenches was worse for people who were not soldiers. . . . When I was on the line of responsibility I knew when I was sheltered and when I was visible. . . . But these people came from outside and they didn't know the terrain. The ones guarding the line didn't tell them what they needed to know. You know, they exposed themselves, and got hit by a sniper or a grenade. . . . There were these units of Civilian Defense . . . they came for one day to dig. . . . When an antitank shell hit my apartment, this Serb neighbor was the first one to come and help, to clean it up. A fine man. Not because he helped me; I also thought highly of him before. He knew how to fix many things. . . . He had tools, so when I needed something I went to him, and if I didn't know how to do it he would show me. And he was always ready to help.

Another man who served in a trench-digging unit explained why soldiers on the line did not help those who dug: most of them were Serbs. In his unit, the soldiers provoked the trench diggers by saying that the Serbs on the other side were their own people, so they would not hurt them and they had nothing to fear. Trench diggers often felt that they were exposed to the fire from both sides.

In his account of another Serb neighbor, Emir not only showed human understanding of the man's decision to leave but also acknowledged for a moment that his own decision to join the ABiH was wrong:

They left by the end of the summer of 1992, so they were here for some time. It is strange, but he wasn't mobilized anywhere. But I don't know, these were the subjects that you couldn't openly ask people about, because there were many people hiding from the army, not only Serbs but also Muslims. Smart people, really. Smart, not smart, I don't know. Yes, they are smart, now. From today's perspective, when you add all things up, when you see that most of the politicians talk about one thing and do something else. All the politicians hid their sons or placed them abroad, or had them

Figure 24. The holes in the ground are entrances into a system of trenches and tunnels on the front line in Dobrinja that was dug by people who did not want to bear weapons. This task was more hazardous than fighting; enemy soldiers could hide in the buildings just across the street. Dobrinja, spring 1996. Photo by author.

employed somewhere where they were far away from, from [pause] dangers. So it was not only characteristic of Serbs. The majority, well, not a majority but a large number of people, tried to avoid the gun [armed service], of course, in order to protect themselves. Especially in the beginning, because they couldn't grasp the whole of the situation. Because what happens if you wait, rely on someone else? Who is that "someone"? I mean, if you don't join the forces and resist, your destiny is clear. He'll come to your house, into your apartment. Besides all the moral dilemmas.

Here Emir wrestled with his moral dilemmas and the burden of his own choices. After describing the impossibility of sustaining the national cause and the righteousness of the decision to avoid military service, he once again used the soldier mode of thinking in order to justify having become a soldier. This moral pendulum, swinging back and forth between the deserter and soldier viewpoints, is characteristic of accounts by people existentially involved in war.

Personal choices in war are perceived to be of existential importance: any decision can be a decision between life and death, although amid the chaos of war it is most often impossible to predict which act might be the one that will save you. Collective ideology legitimates individual choices, endowing them with a sense of moral righteousness, while the collective depends on the loyalty of individuals. The historian Eric Hobsbawm elucidates this characteristic of nation-states: "As modern war illustrates, state interests now depended on the participation of the ordinary citizen to an extent not previously envisaged. . . . The degree of sacrifice which could be imposed on civilians had to enter the plans of strategists. . . . The question of the 'nation', and the citizen's feelings towards whatever he regarded as his 'nation,' 'nationality' or other centre of loyalty, [was placed] at the top of [the] political agenda" (Hobsbawm 1990:83). War depends on the mobilization of public opinion and of citizen-soldiers.[19]

In adopting the soldier mentality, Emir identified as a Muslim and supported the Muslim cause and the government in Sarajevo. But the inconsistencies between the national doctrine and his experiences led him to conclude that those who avoided military service did the right thing. At that point Emir had deserted the soldier cause. Eventually he managed to act in accordance with this realization: "Until 1994 I was on these lines of separation. After that I continued in the same unit but not in the fighting formation. I went over to the command, to finances, as an accountant; I did some programming. Basically I saved my ass. I got myself out of the way." Emir's disappointment in the national cause meant giving up making moral judgments of people around him based exclusively on their nationality. Serbs could be good, trustworthy people, while Muslims could be bad and cheat others. Emir's departure from the armed service was the consequence of his dissent from the national cause and its soldier mentality.

The inconsistencies in accounts of war appeared when the conversation came to the personal level of experiences and relationships, in much the same way that consistencies in ideas about another group's national character disappeared when it came to other people whom Sarajevans knew personally and stayed in contact with. On the concrete, experiential level, uncertainty about what was right or wrong and why all this was happening prevailed, and people attempted to understand others' choices even though they were different from their own. It is possible that nationalist explanations lost their power over people in Sarajevo as the war went on because people got used to danger and were not terrified any more. In the beginning of the war, nationalism helped to quiet people's existential fear about what was going to happen. It offered a solution and made it possible for people to act, even in a situation that made them feel completely powerless. As people learned how to survive in the midst of war, nationalism lost its soothing power. Fear receded into the background as something that people had to live with.

Nationalism also lost its power because the choices people made no longer needed moral legitimation. When Emir decided to depart from the armed forces in 1994, any action that offered a prospect of making a person's life better was seen as natural and moral. Just as some soldiers shifted into the deserter mode, Sarajevans no longer judged others by the soldier standard. In both Sarajevo and Croatia, I noticed that the fiercest nationalists were those who avoided military service and those who gained economic and/or political power while the majority of the population lost it. Those who benefited from war needed to legitimize their position, and nationalism was the perfect way of doing it in these political circumstances. The men who served at the front lines, who were exposed to the dangers of war, were often the least nationalistic. They had the courage, as well as the moral capital, to question the righteousness of the grand national cause. So, contrary to the common assumption that personal experiences of violence and loss make people into nationalists, in the beginning of the war in the former Yugoslavia fear and the threat of violence and loss made people incline toward nationalistic ideology and, over time, personal experiences of war tended to move them away from it. Many people who suffered personal losses because of the war used nationalist rhetoric to make some sense of their loss. Nationalism has profited from mourning, as people seek some redeeming value in what would otherwise be random personal tragedies. The rationalizing power of nationalism and soldier logic should not be underestimated, for people living in the war as well as for the observers.

The Transformation of Trust

Changes in people's attitudes toward war began with the shocking realization that war was possible. The normal order of civilian life was shaken. Daily shelling was a constant threat to life. The media continuously reported on massacres of entire families in villages and small towns across Bosnia. Every day the incidents were closer and closer to Sarajevo. The encompassing existential threat that informed Sarajevans' lives made people doubt that their prewar sociocultural and political norms were still valid. Gradually, more and more segments of the old society ceased to function, and new normalities had to be established.

In this situation, the political call for national solidarity based on the distinction between "them" and "us" was answered. The group to be protected expanded from the family to the nation. The bewilderment characteristic of the civilian mode of thought was replaced by an acceptance of the war and nationalist explanations for its causes. In the soldier mode of thought, the dominant model for explaining the war was the nationalist paradigm of the ruling political-military elites, and every Sarajevan found her- or himself testing it in everyday situations. Emir described the process by which he adopted a nationalist viewpoint after he joined the armed forces:

They took us to a location, the first encounter, with a real front. You came and saw bloody uniforms thrown around. The people you met were retelling the stories, how someone was wounded, how someone got killed. . . . Only then did you understand the situation and what was going on. And you saw yourself in a situation of real danger. Danger to life. . . . But you didn't have any other choice. My decision to join was not in the first place because of national feelings. . . . It was difficult and risky to leave the town, so what next? Your own decision became simply imposed on you, the decision to defend yourself, and nothing else.

As time went by, more and more Serbs were leaving. Suddenly someone would not come for several days. When you sent men to see what was going on, it turned out that he had left. You know, it was war. You went with them [Serbs] to the front line and you asked yourself with whom were you actually serving? How safe were you from that same fellow soldier? So I went over to a unit with mostly people from Vratnik,[20] where I was born. . . . These were the guys whom I more or less knew, and here were our [local] Serbs from the Muslim quarters of town (*mahale*) also. It is interesting that there were no cases of someone turning his back on you or running away. It might be because they knew who they were with and were not feeling threatened or afraid. Because those who ran away must have been as scared of me as I was scared of them. It was because we didn't know each other. But here [in the new unit] the situation was different. If you had a Serb with you, you knew for sure who he was.

While mistrust on the grounds of national identity disrupts relationships when people move from the civilian mode to the soldier mode, trust can be restored among familiar friends when they move toward the deserter mode.

Emir realized that in a war he had to join the collective defense. Perceiving the war in the soldier mode, he lost his individuality and started to identify himself as interchangeable with any other person in the same uniform, fighting for the same government and for the same national cause. He was no longer personally responsible for the consequences. His choice was imposed on him by the situation.

The vital importance of group solidarity is apparent in Emir's decision to change units in order to feel safe among men he knew, Muslims and a few Serbs from the neighborhood where he spent his childhood, not the anonymous Serbs who, he felt, could have betrayed him at any time. The exception he made for Serbs he knew personally is one indication of his modification of the nationalist ideology. After the war became a way of living, Sarajevans began to notice more discrepancies in the nationalist ideology. All Serbs were not the same. Moreover, Emir knew that the unreliable Serbs felt the same mistrust he did; he perceived them as similar to himself rather than as members of the other group. The soldier logic of homogenous and mutually exclusive groups endowed with opposite moral and immoral characteristics was called into question when people realized that not all members of the enemy nation were bad and immoral and that not all of their own national brethren could be trusted. The deserter mode began when people were no longer willing to offer their lives for the sake of a national cause. Those who experienced war atrocities most directly were most aware of the shallowness of its legitimation. As people shifted out of the solider mode, they reaffirmed their identification as Sarajevans.

Although the process of developing civilian, soldier, and deserter perceptions of war had a chronological dimension, after some time people in Sarajevo incorporated all three modes of thought and switched between them, depending on the social occasion, the point they were making, and the complexity of their experience. Generally, the more public the occasion, the more ideological the statement. During the war in Sarajevo people publicly expressed the necessity of defending themselves, their fellow citizens, and their country by using weapons against the aggressor. They legitimized violence from their side and found evidence to lay guilt on and often demonize the other side. They talked about the rules of war to show how the other side was breaking them. Privately, it was harder to maintain clear definitions of national causes; categorizations of friends, neighbors, and family members into "us" and antagonistic "others", notions of just and unjust violence; and concepts that neatly divided war and peace. War experience blurred borders into a continuum of social relationships that shifted over time and depended upon context.

This interpretation of experiences of war in Sarajevo is applicable more generally. The actors and discourses on the official political and diplomatic level, international as well as national, generally adopt the soldier mode of thinking. In wartime, this military mode tends to monopolize public discourse through the media. Without firsthand war experience, most people tend to combine the civilian and soldier modes of thinking. Faced with the horrors of war, some struggle to retain the civilian mode, which positions them ideologically as pacifists, as was the case with some journalists who wrote about the war in Bosnia and Herzegovina. While the civilian mode might seem naive and even dangerous, the soldier mode of reasoning and its extension beyond the boundaries between civilians and the armed forces makes genocides possible. In situations of socioeconomic crisis, the division into moral "us" and immoral "them" together with rationalizations that remove the moral responsibility for violence and promise a utopian future for "our" purified nation—especially if the world does not seem eager to intervene[21]—make people able to commit atrocities that we normally find unacceptable and would never have been able to commit without the emotional tricks of legitimation.

Only firsthand experience of war seems to give rise to the deserter perspective. Coming to terms with the utter insecurity of existence, accepting war as a part of life without approving of it, and blurring such basic categories as war and peace, civilians and soldiers, justice and inhumanity, winners and losers makes talking and writing about war as an experience extremely difficult. It is often impossible, or at least risks sounding illogical to the peace-minded listener. Most of the people with firsthand experience mix all three modes, either in speaking, as in Emir's account and other examples from Sarajevo, or in text, as in many a story collection or diary published by Sarajevans during the war.[22]

This analysis, which is by its nature a reflection on war experiences, faces the same problem of communicating the incommunicable. The most difficult challenge in writing about the siege of Sarajevo is explaining the deserter perception of war to people who have no personal experience of organized violence on a massive scale. The prevailing modes of thought among observers are the stances of civilian and soldier. In Sarajevo, as in other instances in which armed conflict erases the distinctions between civilians and soldiers and undermines the neat nationalist explanations that justify systematic violence, the deserter mode may arise, not as a means of evading moral responsibility for individual actions or as a refusal of social solidarity, but precisely as a form of dissent from rationalizations that excuse atrocities and as an affirmation of the multifarious connections among people on which civil societies are based.

Epilogue

Today, on the twelfth anniversary of the Dayton Peace Accords, I sit at home in Uppsala and talk on the phone with my hosts' daughter, who is visiting Sarajevo. She tells me about a graffito that appeared on the central post office some years after the war: "Tito, come back!" Under this, someone had written: "I am not crazy!" and signed it, "Tito." With characteristically Sarajevan humor, this graffito summarizes the core of the social and political problems before, during, and after the war: the tensions between ethnonationalism and pluralism and between neoliberal capitalism and socialism.

The dream of democracy remains but a dream. The new multiparty system did not diminish the power of patron-client relationships and the state's almost complete subordination to foreign powers and interests, both political and economic. The civil society that took shape with the escalation of armed conflict in the early 1990s is still too weak to be able to make a significant difference in this despotic political scene.

In postwar Bosnia and Herzegovina, international diplomacy as well as national politics must grapple with the duplicity that lies in the tensions between forces working toward pluralistic socialism and those working toward ethnonational capitalism. The Office of the High Representative (OHR) operates under the Peace Implementation Council (PIC), consisting of representatives from Canada, France, Germany, Italy, Japan, Russia, Turkey, the United States, the European Commission, the European Union, the Organization for Security and Cooperation in Europe, and the United Nations. The paradoxes of Dayton have continued to plague the OHR: promoting ethnonational pluralism through constituting Bosnia and Herzegovina as one state, and at the same time accepting ethnonationalistic politics and consequences of war waged in its name by recognizing the territorial division into Republika Srpska and the Bosniac-Croat Federation. In 1997 the OHR was given a mandate to dismiss nationalist politicians and civil servants obstructing the functioning of the state of Bosnia and Herzegovina and to make necessary legislative changes in order to promote effective implementation of the Dayton Peace Accords (so-called Bonn powers). This hegemonic politics promoted parties and politicians who were less nationalistic, and in 2000, when the Alliance for Change won the elections in the Bosniac-Croat Federation, it looked for a moment as if an alternative to nationalism had been found. Within a year, however, nationalistic politicians were again gaining power, state institutions continued to be paralyzed, and the OHR again dismissed several nationalistic politicians. The elections of 2002 were not so harshly controlled by the OHR, voter participation was barely over 50 percent, and the three major nationalistic parties—the SDA (Stranka demokratske akcije, Party of Democratic Action), the SDS (Srpska demokratska stranka, Serb Democratic Party), and the HDZ (Hrvatska demokratska zajednica, Croat Democratic Union)—won once again. The OHR decided to work together with them toward the admission of Bosnia and Herzegovina to the European Union and NATO. The OHR's mandate, which was supposed to end in the summer of 2007, has been extended for a year because of the unstable situation in the country, and a new high representative, Miroslav Lajčak, has been appointed.

The situation regarding the army and police forces of Bosnia and Herzegovina is as paradoxical as the whole constitution of the state. Since 2002 there have been three constitutive peoples throughout Bosnia and Herzegovina: Bosniacs, Serbs, and Croats. The state has a joint army, but it consists of three ethnonationally based brigades wearing symbols of both their ethnonational group and of the supposedly unified state of Bosnia and Herzegovina. The joint ministry of the interior operates in separate ethnonational regions (called "entities" in the Dayton Peace Accords), each with its own police force.

The climate in which Sarajevans must negotiate their postwar situation swings back and forth between ethnonational homogenization and building social solidarity along other lines. The emergent grounds of shared interests and divisions along non-national lines include political ideology: advocating social democracy, opposing neoliberalism, and seeking to alleviate poverty and diminish economic inequality. Interest groups have been formed by disappointed war veterans, returnees, and those who stayed. Local interests matter to everyone, regardless of their ethnoreligious background.

The economy has been from the start in the hands of the IMF and the World Bank. The OHR's so-called Bulldozer Commission, consisting of both local businessmen and international experts, imposed major economic reforms in 2003–4 in order to make Bosnia and Herzegovina more attractive to investors. The exploitation of those without power that had

Figure 25. A statue of President Tito in front of the former JNA barracks Maršal Tito in the center of the town after the JNA's departure. Sarajevo, March 1996. Photo by author.

come to full bloom during the war and was supported by national politicians continued.

I continue talking with my hosts' daughter. Late November is gray and rainy both here and there. She is not sure what this visit to Sarajevo means. She has been traveling back and forth between her home in exile and her home in Sarajevo for a decade now and, like many refugees and emigrants, has discovered that she does not completely belong to either of these homes. In exile, she is too Bosnian; in Sarajevo, she is too Western. She belongs to two cultures and to neither. She faces the dilemma of whether or not to return, as do most Bosnians in exile. Although her parents miss her, they do not wish her to return. They encourage her to pursue her career in exile, where they know she also has a good social network. Other of my war friends have become parents and grandparents. Some children have returned from exile, some have not. Bosnians whom I know in Sweden have mostly not returned because their children have grown up in Sweden, and although their social circles and status are worse than they were in Bosnia and Herzegovina, they still see better possibilities for the family to thrive. They have gone back and tried to reclaim their property, most often to sell the apartments and houses to their current occupants.

In Sarajevo, my hosts' daughter tell me that she loves chitchatting with a shop assistant in a small store around the corner, but she feels that the shop assistant is too nosy when she asks her all about her family and exile: she invents lies about her work, about having children and being married, and about her ethnoreligious background. Her Sarajevan friends think that she has become closed, lonely, and worn out, while she sees their efforts to convince her that they are spontaneous, socially open, free, and satisfied with their lives as a way of coping with their envy of her higher living standards. Sarajevans' famous openness to socializing at any time, for any reason or no reason at all, seems to her increasingly a myth to be repeated rather than put into practice. Time flexibility and social spontaneity depend on widespread unemployment, which has remained between 40 and 50 percent throughout the postwar period.

Since this summer, the prices of milk, bread, and oil have risen drastically, by as much as 50 percent. Perhaps people are increasingly worried about the possibility of a new war, as Miroslav Lajčak has suggested, or maybe it is just a habit to store reserves of flour, sugar, and oil. My hosts' monthly pensions are around three hundred *konvertibilna marka* (convertible marks, which the OHR invented in 1997 together with the Central Bank of Bosnia and Herzegovina), now worth 0.51 Euros. Their daughter, who lives fairly modestly, needs one thousand convertible marks per month.

Amusedly, she tells me a story about the postal carriers. Postmen are still delivering pensions door to door, she says almost unbelievingly. They go around with their bags full of cash. She asked her cousin and his friend, two young Sarajevan men she called young *raja*, and whom I had known as children during the war, how it is possible that the postman does not get robbed in an environment so full of poverty, injustice, and weapons. They answered, "He has a pistol." "But someone can shoot him in his back," she argued. "No, you don't understand," says one of the young men. "The pensioners would tear into bits anyone who'd try to hurt the postman. They would attack him like piranhas from all the sides and tear him apart. Not a hair-straw would be left of anyone who would attack the postman." Everyone follows the postman, she explained. Some wait for him in front of the post office; others crouch on their windowsills like flowerpots.

The employed are somewhat better off. A female secondary school teacher earns one thousand convertible marks a month, plus lunch coupons (two hundred convertible marks) and transportation. Compared to the shop assistant who works from 7 AM to 5 PM, the salary is decent. My hosts' daughter feels sorry for the middle-aged shop assistant. Although they do not talk about salaries, the shop assistant tells her that she works all seven days of the week, and every year has only one day off for Bairam (officially a three-day holiday) and only seven holidays.

The appeal of the Tito graffito resonates with its wartime predecessor: "Serbs, come back! You are forgiven for everything." But, more significantly, it could just as well be used in the huge advertising campaigns launched at young Bosnians and Hezegovinians abroad to lure them back with promises of job opportunities and prosperity. The latest joke from Sarajevo illuminates local ambivalence toward this campaign.

Two beggars sit under the statue of Ban Jelačić [on the main square in Zagreb, Croatia]. One has a sign hanging around his neck saying "demobilized Croatian defender," and the other's sign says "demobilized Serbian fighter." In the box of the first one there is a lot of money; the other's box is empty. An old man comes and throws ten kuna in the box of the first one. Then he goes to the other and asks, "Why do you beg here? Go to Belgrade [Serbia] and beg there. You fought for them." Then the old man turns again toward the first box and out of sheer protest throws ten more kunas in it. When the old man was gone the Serb says to the Croat, "Fuck, Mujo, who was he to advise us on how to do the marketing?"

Ironically, Bosnians today are fairly well adapted to their countries of exile.

While the nostalgia exiles feel makes them yearn to return, they know that their civilian souls long for a country that no longer exists. Their more patriotic impulses may make them wish to return to their ethnonational territories and their people, in good soldiery spirit. Yet, the deserter-like spirit within them is bound to shout back: "I am not crazy!" In this cacophony of inner voices, emotions, and ethical stands, which is characteristic of all exiles, my hosts' daughter found the most soothing position: In her favorite little café, on a hill overlooking the town, hangs a photograph of Tito on the wall, under which it is written, "I am just watching you." In the situation that continues to prevent Sarajevans from feeling recognizable to themselves, the questions of normality and craziness are probably best grappled with by simply watching—for those who have the opportunity. It is a sign of not really being able to live the "normal" life. As they no longer feel quite like themselves, Sarajevans watch to see: Who can I be today? Do I wish to be that? But "I am watching you" is also a humorous way of taking a step out of this situation, dis-identifying from the present, without being forced to find an alternative. Instead of feeling desperate about the lack of an alternative identity, "I am just watching." But this lack of identity also means having no sense of a fullness and completion in life. Imitation of life has taken its postwar turn: Watching life is a position of potential negotiation and change, hopeful, yet destructive in the long run because of its emptiness of meaning.

Notes

Chapter 1. Civilian, Soldier, Deserter

1. The classic formulation of this notion is Clausewitz 1997:22. Jabri (1996:98–99) critically considers both conventional and current perspectives on war. In the case of Bosnia and Herzegovina, for the conventional view of the war, see Rieff 1996:17. For other critiques of this notion of war, see Scarry 1985:81–139, and Nordstrom and Martin 1992a:13.

2. For critical analyses, see Scarry 1985:67; Taussig 1992:22.

3. My approach is similar to that of an increasing number of anthropologists doing fieldwork in the midst of mass political violence; see especially Nordstrom and Robben 1995; Daniel 1996; Nordstrom 1997; Aretxaga 1997; Kleinman et al. 1997; Zur 1998; Ben-Ari 1998; Port 1998; Green 1999; Allen and Seaton 1999; Nelson 1999; Sluka 2000; Robben and Suárez-Orozco 2000; Löfving and Maček 2000; Das et al. 2000; Das et al. 2001; Schmidt and Schröder 2001; Löfving 2002; Finnström 2003; Utas 2003; Kolind 2004; Nordstrom 2004; Richards 2005; Bougarel et al. 2007.

4. A student of mine, who fled from Sarajevo as a boy, recently wrote about Ahmadou Kourouma's position in *Allah Is Not Obliged* (2006), a novel about child soldiers in West Africa: "Kourouma is brutally honest and not afraid of anything. He hits us exactly in our most vulnerable spot. He makes you feel shame and discomfort, but at the same time he is not bitter towards us. He simply understands everything too well to be bitter. Nothing can any longer surprise him or make him resigned." This statement is a perfect description of the deserter perception of war.

5. I first heard the word *prolupati* during the war in Croatia in 1991. Its two components, when conjoined, meant that someone went crazy because of the war. The verb *biti lupnut* (to be slightly hit) is a euphemism for being slightly crazy, and *pro* is a prefix that signifies going through something physically or cognitively. Thus, *prolupati* can be translated as going crazy beyond the bounds of what is considered normal.

6. The concept of a "limit situation" was developed in studies of the Holocaust, which emphasized the incomprehensibility of their predicament to those who were caught up by it and asked how much of their experience could actually be communicated to those who had not experienced it themselves. The concept was first articulated by Primo Levi in his book of 1947, *Se questo é un uomo* (*If This Is a Man*, published in the United States under the title *Survival in Auschwitz*). Elie Wiesel and the historian Raul Hilberg are among the many intellectuals who have grappled with this problem.

7. Other anthropologists have adopted this approach to writing. For example, Linda Green (1994:230) decided to include her own experiences of fear and violence in her account.

8. In this book I use several terms as synonyms for *narod*: people, nation,

nationality, and ethnonational group. All of these terms have been used by different authors in this sense.

9. The Republic of Bosnia and Herzegovina, as its name indicates, consists of two regions but in literature, political discourse, and everyday speech, Herzegovina is often subsumed under Bosnia. The label for inhabitants of Herzegovina is "Herzegovinians" (Hercegovci).

10. Jasenovac was the largest concentration and extermination camp in Croatia during World War II, which almost no one survived. Prisoners there included Jews, Serbs, Gypsies (Roma), and communists or their sympathizers, as my grandfather was.

11. I use quotation marks around the UN categories "refugees" and "internally displaced persons" because they presume stable, recognized national boundaries that did not yet exist in the territories of the former Yugoslavia. Indeed, they were being forced upon most of the population and forged in a gruesome war. "Displacement" is also a gross understatement for intentional destruction, murder, and scaring people away with lethal weapons.

12. Branko Đurić, one of the "Surrealists," works as an actor in Slovenia and has become internationally famous as one of the main protagonists in Danis Tanović's *No Man's Land*, which won an Oscar for the best foreign language film in 2002.

13. For more about Bosnian jokes, see Vucetic 2004.

14. While in Zagreb in 1993 I got acquainted with two women from Zenica who had already boarded the airplane when somebody with an "international" card came to the UN's check-in and they were obliged to get off. After some days of unsuccessful waiting at the airport they decided to travel back to Zenica by bus. Everyone in the humanitarian organization they worked for was worried, but the women were firm. Days of tense waiting passed before they sent a message from Zenica that they had arrived safely. As we had feared, they were stopped at a Serbian checkpoint and interrogated, but they managed to joke about the Serbian surname that one of them had and the soldiers let them pass without hurting them.

Chapter 2. Death and Creativity in Wartime

1. See, for example, Karl Jaspers on "boundary situations" (1970:177–222), Elisabeth Kübler-Ross 2003, Heidegger 1996, and Kierkegaard on "angst" (1981).

2. In Bosnian, the word *kako* means both "what" and "how." In Bosnian the joke goes: "Kako zove pametan Bosanac glupoga?—Telefonom iz inozemstva!"

3. Many authors have noted the circulation of macabre humor in situations of despair; see, for example, Taussig 1992:18.

4. It is common to compare the Olympic Games with war, which is sometimes perceived as a form of competition between nations, with demonstrations of power, winners, losers, and prizes in common.

5. See Carolyn Nordstrom's fine contrast of "Lobster Boy's" maturity with his audience's reactions and her comparison between "Lobster Boy" and war-affected people in Mozambique. She concludes by saying that "it is time we begin to understand those whom we write about at least as well as they understand us" (1997:18–19).

Not everyone manages to survive mass political violence psychologically. Among Holocaust survivors and contemporary refugees are many who continue living without being fully present emotionally (see Kaplan 2002). They remind me of people in Sarajevo who were said to have *prolupati*, gone emotionally numb while continuing to function outwardly.

Chapter 3. Struggling for Subsistence

1. The Croatian military forces played a role only during their conflict with the Bosnian government in 1993. The rest of the time, they functioned as allies of the Bosnian government. Hereafter, I speak mostly of the Serbian and Bosnian sides.

2. For example, the humanitarian aid sent by the "blue ways" had to pass various control posts where between 30 and 50 percent had to be left to the controllers. These costs are probably the reason why approximately 80 percent of humanitarian aid delivered to Sarajevo through the UNHCR entered the town by air and only 20 percent by road (UNHCR 1994:14).

3. Patron-client networks, locally called connections (*veze*), existed in the former Yugoslavia and explain why politicians were distrusted even before the war. During the war in Sarajevo politicians and "internally displaced persons" (IDPs) from eastern Bosnia were suspected of getting benefits through connections. For a good introduction and examples, see Bougarel et al. 2007. For the prewar period, see Allcock 2000, Sekelj 1993, and Woodward 1995a, 1995b.

Chapter 4. Tests of Trust

1. In Bosnia and Herzegovina as a whole, a quarter of the original 4.3 million citizens became "refugees" (crossing recognized national boundaries) and half were "internally displaced" (to other parts of Bosnia and Herzegovina). Three-fourths of Bosnians and Herzegovinians, totaling over 3 million people, left their homes during the war. See UNHCR 1994.

2. In Bosnia and Herzegovina there were two major types of godparenthood: to a baby at christening, and to an adult at his or her wedding. While the godmother mentioned first was this young man's godmother from the time of his christening, his mother's godfather was from his parents' wedding.

3. See, for example, Philip J. Hallie's account (1979) of the mostly Protestant villagers of Le Chambon in the French Alps who saved many Jewish children.

4. "Cleansing," like "displacement," is an understatement characteristic of war terminology used to obscure otherwise morally unacceptable acts of murder and destruction. Thus the quotation marks for what has become known as "ethnic cleansing."

5. The best-known and best-documented instances of survivors' guilt are from Holocaust survivors; see Des Pres 1976 and Nutkiewicz 2003. On bystanders, see Hilberg 1992; Barnett 1999; Staub 1989; and Cesarani and Levine 2002. It is interesting to compare survivor's guilt with the internalized guilt that constitutes

some psychological personality types, which, according to McWilliams (1984, 1994), are more prone to altruistic work such as in social and humanitarian engagement.

6. The phenomenon of feeling safer if another person is present, especially if one person is the caretaker with responsibility for the other, is a common psychological fact not specific to wars.

7. This interview was conducted in March 1995. NATO's bombing of Serbian positions around Sarajevo in August and the Dayton Peace Accords in November proved this woman's intuition to be correct.

8. For examples, see Thomas and Znaniecki 1984. Another well-known example of children being sent away from parents that caused many personal tragedies is the Finnish children sent to neutral Sweden during the Second World War. Today Sweden has large numbers of child refugees coming without adult company, whom the country has no adequate system for taking care of.

9. The term "mixed marriage" suggests that ethnoreligious and national identities create bounded groups and that associations within the group differ from associations with members of other groups. I use the quotation marks to mark that this was not the case in Sarajevo, and people in "mixed marriages" were mostly offended by this categorization.

10. The notion that the chronic fear produced by war kills emotions and makes people behave more by instinct is widely held. When it comes to reproduction, two reactions are connected to war and genocide: the wish to continue the species may disappear, or the urge to re-create life may strengthen. Both responses arise from the awareness that something existentially threatening to the species is occurring, and they coexisted in Sarajevo.

11. Both words mean neighbor and were part of Sarajevan vocabulary. *Susjed* is of Slavic origin, while *komšija* is of Turkish origin, but most people would use them synonymously. In everyday usage, the word *komšija* was more usual in Sarajevo and other parts of the former Yugoslavia that had been under Ottoman rule, while *susjed* was used more in the parts of the former Yugoslavia that had been under Austro-Hungarian rule. During the war, I was under the impression that non-Muslims preferred the non-Turkish word, *susjed*. What my host did in this interview is fairly common in the regions rich in synonyms: he ascribed a slightly different meaning to two words that originally meant the same thing. The more languages and cultures are impregnated by various influences, the richer possibilities of expression they offer. This phenomenon is easily forgotten in the climate of national purification and homogenization processes.

12. It is likely that she was interrogated during the night and detained for twenty-four hours, but the fact that time does not add up registers the disorientation induced by war.

13. These adjustments occurred not only in the process of industrialization, but also in the depopulation of the countryside after the Second World War.

14. The influx of the Muslim rural population from eastern Bosnia had begun during the 1980s, as government policy granted them advantageous conditions if they settled in the outskirts of Sarajevo, for instance, in Velešići, Buča Potok, and Boljakov Potok.

15. *Raja* is colloquially used for ordinary simple people, and it comes via Turkish from the Arabic word for servants and flock. *Papci* (sing., *papak*) means literally pig feet, i.e., something primitive and dirty.

16. Jovo is a typical Serbian name, and Mustafa a typical Muslim name.

Chapter 5. Political and Economic Transformation

1. This situation changed after the Dayton Peace Accords, and efforts have been made to constitute a Bosnian and Herzegovinian administration on the republic level with all three national groups represented in proportion to the population. Bosnians and Herzegovinians were accustomed to this system from the national quota system in the former Yugoslavia, which was originally introduced in 1910 under Austro-Hungarian rule.

2. Goražde was a small town in eastern Bosnia that had been partly evacuated; the remaining Muslims (both soldiers and civilians) were surrounded by Serbian troops. There were three "Muslim enclaves" in the territory controlled by Bosnian Serbs—Žepa, Srebrenica, and Goražde—that the UN had declared "safe havens." The UN stationed peacekeeping troops there to observe and report any military violations. Bosnian Serbs' troops attacked and occupied Žepa and Srebrenica in June and July 1995, resulting in a notorious massacre and a mass exodus of fifty thousand Muslims (see Owen 1996:387).

Chapter 6. Language and Symbols

1. For example, the streets named after Muhamed Gandura, Fuad Midžić, Mesud Džemidžić, Omer Maslić, Refik Šećibović, Muzafer Sadović, Mehmed Jakubović, Alija Hodžić, Ahmet Fetahagić, Sadik Kadrušić, Nusret Pašić, Muhamed Kadić, Zehra Muidović, Alija Alijagić, Muhamed Džudža, Mehmed Zvona, Semsudin Karkin, Muhamed Repovac, Remzija Omanović, Avdo Karabegović, Husein Brkić, and Mustafa Golubić.

2. As the popular story goes, when the Ottoman Turks conquered the Serbian kingdom in the fourteenth century, some of the Serbs fled to the mountains, which are today in Montenegro but were at that time part of the Kingdom of Serbia, and they remained the only pure-blooded Serbs throughout the four centuries of Turkish rule.

3. Other streets named after non-Muslims that were not renamed include the streets of Branisalv Nušić (a Serbian playwright), Branko Mikulić (a prewar Bosnian politician), Gavrilo Princip (a Bosnian Serb activist who assassinated the Austro-Hungarian archduke Ferdinand in Sarajevo in 1914), Ivan Cankar (a Slovene writer), Ivan Goran Kovačić (a Croatian Serb poet and national hero who was killed in the Second World War), Ivo Andrić (a Bosnian winner of the Nobel Prize), Marko Marulić (a Croatian renaissance playwright), Oton Župančić (a Slovene poet), Radoje Domanović (a Serbian writer), Rudi Čajavec (a national hero of the Second World War), and Tin Ujević (a Croatian poet).

4. For a more detailed linguistic analysis of the new political and nation-building

processes in Bosnia, Serbia, and Croatia, see Sito-Sucic 1996; J.Trtak 1999; Levinger 1998; Magner and Marić 2002; Greenberg 2004; Škiljan 2005.

5. Some dialects pronounce it as "i" and are called *ikavian*.

Chapter 7. Mobilizing Religion

1. He used to joke: "Hodža je ubio Boga u meni," which means that the *hodža* beat him, but literally means "The *hodža* killed God in me." The point was that the *hodža* who taught him Islam when he was a child used harsh physical punishment, which spoiled religion for him.

Chapter 8. Reorienting Social Relationships

1. Croatia and Serbia had been at war since 1991, when Serbian troops had taken control of parts of Croatia with a Serbian majority, called them Srpska Krajina, and "cleansed" them of Croats. Croatia ostracized its Serbs from the start, and in 1995, through the military operations "Storm" (Oluja) and "Lightning" (Bljesak), it "ethnically cleansed" Croatian Serbs from Srpska Krajina. The offensive was sanctioned by the international community and, according to popular opinion, was planned by American strategists. Even if this allegation is not true, the name of the violent campaign clearly shows the inspiration: the 1991 U.S. offensive in Iraq called Desert Storm.

2 Vuk Karadžić made the written language more phonetic, more distinct from Russian, and closer to Serbian vernacular speech. Like many nationalists, he also collected folklore. As his reforms simplified and distinguished all South Slavic languages, he was celebrated in all of Yugoslavia.

3. "Šokac" comes from the name for Catholic inhabitants of some northern Croatian provinces that originate from Bosnia, Herzegovina, and Dalmatia and speak the *ikavian* dialect. "Latin" is based on the fact that most Croats are Roman Catholics.

4. "Vlah" is Vlach or Walach, a label for people scattered throughout territories of the former Yugoslavia during the early Middle Ages who spoke a Romance dialect. The label was used by all Serbo-Croat speakers for persons of different faith, foreigners, strangers.

5. In the former Yugoslavia, though, the character of the Great Border was not religious. It was variously described as the historical border between two parts of the Roman Empire that ran right through the country; the imperial border between the Austro-Hungarian Empire, the Venetian republic, and the Ottoman Empire; as the geographical border between continental and Mediterranean climate zones; or as the contemporary political and military border between Soviet communism in the East and European and American capitalism and NATO in the West. The important thing though, was that the notion of being the people used to living on the Great Border, knowing how to contain the best of all these worlds, was well known and easy to identify with.

6. He was sentenced to fourteen years in prison. On appeal, in 1985 this conviction was changed from "hostile activity" to "hostile propaganda" and the sentence was

reduced to eleven years. He was released from the prison in Foča in 1989, after five years and eight months.

7. Even some of the Western accounts of Yugoslavia described it as a state with a balanced relationship between one nation-building group (Serbs) and a number of smaller ethnic minority groups (e.g., Hettne 1989), while the political ideology of Yugoslavs was that it was a federal state in which all the major nations had equal rights and power.

8. The speaker was referring to the accusations from the Serbian side that the deaths from shelling in Sarajevo were caused by Muslim troops in order to draw attention to the war and make Muslims appear the victims while placing blame on Serbs.

9. According to UN statistics, "displaced persons" composed about one-third of the wartime population, so this 60 percent figure vastly overestimated their numbers.

10. My impression was that most of those who came from eastern Bosnia and the Sandžak region were driven away from their homes by Serbian troops, either experiencing "ethnic cleansing" directly, or leaving their homes in order to avoid it. Of course, the history of eastern Bosnia is burdened by massacres from the Second World War and earlier times, and probably every Serb and Muslim can reach for a story of mutual atrocities if he wants. I have also heard stories of mutual help from these parts of Bosnia, but in the climate of dividing Bosnians into three nations these experiences were easily forgotten.

11. Later in the interview I discovered that most of these couples were "mixed" and that only one spouse in each of the couples was a Serb.

Chapter 9. Reconceptualizing War

1. For another case of cognitive dissonance caused by mass political violence, see Hinton's description of Cambodia during the Khmer Rouge regime (1996). On cognitive dissonance generally, see Cooper 2007, Harmon-Jones and Mills 1997; the classic work is Festinger 1976.

2. This is a typical feature of trauma: it causes the victim to be ashamed, to take responsibility for what has happened as if, had he or she been a better person, stronger and more moral, this event would not have happened to him or her. Typical examples are victims of rape and incest. The psychological logic behind this illogic is that by taking responsibility one also maintains a sense of control over the threatening reality. This sense of control over the incontrollable reality was something that Sarajevans tried hard to recreate.

3. For example, Glenny (1992:167) places the beginning of the war on March 22, 1992, when heavy fighting followed the referendum and Izetbegović's rejection of the Lisbon maps. But why was this fighting more significant than, for example, the fighting between Croats and Serbs of Herzegovina that began in the autumn of 1991 (see Lucić 1992)? The answer is probably that this fighting took place only in Herzegovina, as a part of the war Croats and Serbs were waging in the region surrounding Dubrovnik. This answer implies that Bosnia and Herzegovina did not exist as a state with defined boundaries before the alleged beginning of the war in 1992, which calls into question the legitimacy of diplomatic events that followed (such as the recognition of the sovereignty of a state that was actually already at war

and dissolving in April 1992), as well as of the histories that place the beginning of the war on April 6.

4. The plaque was changed in 2001, in accordance with the 1999 decision that the name of Olga Sučić should be added to the name of Suada Dilberović (*Službene novine Kantona Sarajevo* [Official Newsletter of Sarajevan Canton] 19/1999), so that the bridge is now called Suada Dilberović's and Olga Sučić's Bridge. The addition of a woman with a name recognizable as Serbian signals a shift in official policy to recognize Serbs among the victims.

5. See also Bringa (1995:xvi) and Lagumdžija (1995:11).

6. For example, the account written in 1993 by Zlata Filipović, who is described as Sarajevo's Anne Frank, is not an authentic diary. The entry for April 6, 1992, reads: ". . . .war is here!" But that fact was not yet established at the moment she was supposedly writing it. Although retrospective, her writings are representative of attitudes toward events in Sarajevo during the war.

7. As everything in war was relative, so were the ceasefires. The 1994 ceasefire meant that no heavy shelling of the town was allowed, but snipers and occasional shelling did not cease.

8. They were Muslims expelled by the HVO.

9. For example, if we look only at the numbers of people killed, Gjelten (1995:128) reports that in the week of September 13–20, 1992, 925 people died, compared to the sixteen killed in the bread line massacre.

10. See also Connerton's discussion of the cohesive character of social memory and how it legitimates the contemporary social order and power elites (1989:1–3).

11. For a fine account of how memories of war are individually negotiated by three Sarajevans in the postwar period, see Sorabji 2006.

12. See the characterization of the Holocaust in Bruchfeld and Levine 1998:77.

13. At the time when this schoolbook was written, the label Bosniac had not yet officially replaced the label Muslim for this nationality, but it was already well established within Muslim nationalist discourse.

14. Vogošća is a Sarajevan municipality some distance out of town that was held by Bosnian Serbs through the war and reintegrated in March 1996.

15. The reported number of demonstrators varies between twenty thousand (Magnusson 1993:23; Gjelten 1995:2) and fifty thousand to one hundred thousand (Malcolm 1994:235).

16. Schmitt 1976:26.

17. The misleading presentation of war as caused by nationalistic antagonisms was manifest not only in the nationalistic propaganda of Bosnian political elites but also in all the reports, especially during the first years of the war, that explained war in Bosnia and Herzegovina as a continuation or consequence of violence during the Second World War. Even worse, some reports suggested that bloodshed was in the nature of the people living in the Balkans: "The strongest motivating factor involved in the Balkan wars [of 1913] was . . . aggressive nationalism . . . [that] drew on deeper traits of character inherited, presumably, from a distant tribal past. . . . And so it remains today. . . . It is the undue prominence among the Balkan peoples of these particular qualities . . . that seems to be decisive as a determinant of the troublesome, baffling, and dangerous situation that marks that part of the world today" (Kennan

1993:6). For a work that refutes the idea of the Balkans as "endemically violent" and points to the decisive role of politics and nationalism, see Carmichael 2002. Gagnon (2004) goes even further, and argues convincingly that the Yugoslav wars of the 1990s were initiated by the elites in order to preserve their political and economic power.

18. These paramilitary troops from Serbia were known for their extreme brutality and nationalism. The leader, Željko Ražnjatović, alias Arkan, was wanted by international police for his criminal activities even before the war. He was killed in Belgrade in early 2000, in what seemed to be a gang attack.

19. Some Western nations, though, use professional soldiers in military operations outside their own territory.

20. Vratnik is an old part of Sarajevo with a predominately Muslim population and character.

21. Several analysts of genocide have come to the conclusion that these are the general circumstances that make genocides possible: socioeconomic crisis, exclusion of a group from the moral community, a utopian ideology, and nonintervention from outside. For comparative examples, see Fein 1993; Mazian 1990; and Porter 1982. Some of the largest genocides of the last hundred years—for example, the Holocaust, Cambodia, and Rwanda—confirm this analysis.

22. For example, Softić 1994; Vuković 1992; Miličević 1993; Filipović 1993; Lagumdžija 1995; Veličković 1996; Halilbegović 1994; Štraus 1995; Karahasan 1993; Isaković 1994; Kebo 1996.

Glossary

Akashi, Yasushi. UN secretary-general's special representative and head of the United
Nations Protection Force (UNPROFOR) in 1994–95, after Thorvald Stoltenberg.

Alipašino polje. Suburb of Sarajevo.

Ancona. Town in Italy.

Andrić, Ivo. Nobel Prize-winning novelist.

Arap. Arab.

Arkanovci. Arkan's men, that is, Serbs involved in "ethnic cleansing" in Bosnia.

Armija Bosne i Hercegovine (ABiH). Army of Bosnia and Herzegovina.

baklava. Sweet pastry.

Bašeskija, Mula Mustafa. Eighteenth-century Sarajevan chronicler.

Begova Džamija. Main mosque in Sarajevo.

Bijeljina. Bosnian town near Serbian border.

Bosniacs (Bošnjaci). Muslims as a specific national group within Bosnia.

Bosnians (Bosanci). All residents of Bosnia.

bratstvo i jedinstvo. Brotherhood and unity.

Buča Potok and Boljakov Potok. Village-like suburbs on the slopes of Sarajevo.

bula. Female teacher of Islam.

Careva Džamija. Mosque in Sarajevo.

Caritas. Catholic aid organization.

Čengić Vila. Suburb of Sarajevo.

Četnici (Chetniks). Term initially used by Serbian military forces that fought against
Yugoslav partisans during the Second World War, then applied to Serbian soldiers fighting against the ABiH. In Sarajevo, the epithet was applied to all the
"jerks" who besieged the city.

Crni Marko ("Black Marko"). Troop leader in the Croatian Army in 1991.

danak u krvi (tribute in blood). Kidnapping of Bosnian boys to serve in the Ottoman
army.

Dayton Peace Accords. "The General Framework Agreement for Peace in Bosnia and
Herzegovina" negotiated by former Yugoslavian and international representa-
tives, initiated in Dayton, Ohio on November 26, 1995 and signed in Paris on
December 14, 1995.

Dilberović, Suada. Young woman of Muslim family background honored as the first
victim of war in Sarajevo.

Dobrinja. Suburb of Sarajevo.

Dobrotvor. Orthodox aid organization.

domovnica. Certificate of domicile (citizenship) in Croatia.

Dubrovnik. Town in Croatia.

džamahirija. An Islamic state.

"Fata" (Fatima). Female character identified as Muslim.

fildžan. Small coffee cup without a handle (Turkish).

Glenny, Misha. British journalist posted in the former Yugoslavia.

Goražde. Town in southeastern Bosnia.

Grbavica. One of the oldest and most central suburbs of Sarajevo; it was held by Serbs during the siege.

Halilović, Senahid. Bosnian linguist involved in the differentiation of the Bosnian language from Croatian and Serbian.

HDZ (Hrvatska demokratska zajednica). Croat Democratic Union.

Herzegovina. Part of Bosnia and Herzegovina.

Herzegovinians (Hercegovci). All inhabitants of Herzegovina.

Hrasno. Suburb of Sarajevo.

HVO (Hrvatsko vijeće obrane). Croat Defense Council.

IDP. Internally displaced person.

iftar. Evening meal during Ramadan.

IGASA. International Islamic relief organization.

IMF. International Monetary Fund.

Izetbegović, Alija. Former president of Bosnia and Herzegovina (Muslim) who died in 2003.

janjičari. Ottoman soldiers in units composed of Christian children.

JNA (Jugoslavenska narodna armija). Yugoslav People's Army of the former Yugoslavia.

Karadžić, Radovan. Former Bosnian Serb (SDS) politician and president of Republika Srpska, now under international indictment for ordering genocide in Srebrenica and war crimes in the shelling of Sarajevo.

Karadžić, Vuk S. Nineteenth-century Serbian linguist and language reformer.

Karić, Enes. Bosnian Muslim scholar and minister of education in the Republic of Bosnia and Herzegovina during the war.

komšijski odnosi. Neighborly relations.

konvertibilna marka. Convertible mark.

Kovači. Cemetery and a part of town close to the center of Sarajevo.

Kralj Tvrtko. Croatian brigade in the ABiH.

krštenica. Baptism certificate.

kumstvo. Godparenthood: *kršteno kumstvo,* christening godparenthood; *vjenčano kumstvo,* wedding godparenthood; *šišano kumstvo,* haircut godparenthood (Muslim in origin).

Kurban Bajram. Muslim festival.

Lajčak, Miroslav. Slovak diplomat serving as the sixth international high representative for Bosnia and Herzegovina.

Ljubljana. Capital of Slovenia.

Löfving, Staffan. Swedish scholar and journalist.

mahale. Quarters or districts of a city (Turkish).

Mannerfelt, Karine. Swedish journalist.

medresa. Islamic school (for religious education only).

mekteb. Muslim school (offering comprehensive education).

Merhamet. Muslim aid organization.

Miljacka. River in Sarajevo.

Mladić, Ratko. Chief of staff for the Army of Republika Srpska, now under international indictment for genocide in Srebrenica and war crimes in the siege of Sarajevo.

Milošević, Slobodan. Former president of Serbia and Yugoslavia who died in 2006 during his international trial for genocide, war crimes, and crimes against humanity.

Mostar. City in Herzegovina now inhabited mostly by Muslims and Croats.

mujezin. Muezzin.

"Mujo" (Muhamed). Male character identified as Muslim.

namaz. Early morning Muslim prayers at a mosque.

narod. The people.

NDH (Nezavisna država Hrvatska). Independent State of Croatia during the Second World War.

Nedžarići. Suburb of Sarajevo.

Nikolaj, Vladika. Serbian Orthodox church leader.

NGO. Nongovernmental organization.

NOB (Narodnooslobodilačka borba). People's Liberation Struggle, led by Tito's partisans during the Second World War.

Nova Gradiška. Town on the front lines in Slavonia (Eastern Croatia).

OHR. Office of the High Representative for Bosnia and Herzegovina.

Oslobođenje. Newspaper published in Sarajevo.

opasna zona. Dangerous zone.

pali borci. Fallen non-Muslim soldiers, in contrast to *šehidi.*

papci. Jerks.

pazi snajper. Watch out, sniper.

PIC. Peace Implementation Council, an international body guiding and legitimizing the OHR.

podrumaši. Cellar people.

pokrštavanje. Christianization.

pravna država. Juridical state, rule of law.

prolupati. Go crazy.

PTT (Pošta, telegram, telefon). Post, Telegram, and Telephone Company.

rahatluk. Peaceful relaxation.

raja. Group of youthful associates, or decent people.

Ramazanski Bajram. Ramadan, Muslim festival.

rasčistiti teren. To "cleanse" the territory ethnically.

Ravno. Village in Herzegovina.

Ražnjatović, Željko. Alias Arkan, leader of the Arkanovci.

Republika Srpska (the [Bosnian] Serb Republic). Separate entity for Bosnian Serbs that unilaterally broke away from Bosnia in 1992.

Rosić, Avakum. Sarajevo's only Orthodox priest during the war.

šamija. Headscarf worn by religiously observant Muslim women.

Sandžak. Region in Serbia with a relatively large Muslim population before the war.

Sarajevans (Sarajlije). All residents of Sarajevo.

SDA (Stranka demokratske akcije). Party for Democratic Action (Muslim).

SDS (Srpska demokratska stranka). Serb Democratic Party.

šehidi. Muslim soldiers killed in the war and honored in burial.

Selimović, Meša. Novelist.

SFRY (Socijalistička federativna republika Jugoslavija). Socialist Federative Republic of Yugoslavia (1945–92), encompassing present-day Bosnia and Herzegovina, Croatia, Macedonia, Montenegro, Serbia, and Slovenia.

sijela. Social gatherings.

Silajdžić, Haris. Bosnian politician (Muslim).

škropljenje. Blessing of homes by Catholic priests by sprinkling holy water.

Slavonia. Eastern Croatia.

Slovenia. Former republic of the former Yugoslavia, today a member state of the European Union.

šoljica. Small coffee cup with a handle (Fr. *demitasse*).

Split. Harbor town in Croatia.

Srebrenica. Small town in Bosnia where Muslims were victims of genocide.

Srpska Krajina. Serbian-dominated region in Croatia.

Srpsko gradjansko vijeće. Organization for the protection of the civil rights of Serbs who stayed on the Bosnian government's side in Sarajevo.

"Suljo" (Sulejman). Male character identified as Muslim.

Titova Road. Road in Sarajevo named for Tito.

Trebević. Mountain outside Sarajevo where artillery and snipers lodged.

Tudjman, Franjo. Former president of Croatia who died in 1999.

UNHCR. United Nations High Commission for Refugees.

Uskrs. Roman Catholic Easter.

Vaskrs. Orthodox Easter.

Velešići. Village near Sarajevo.

Vrbanja Bridge. Bridge across the river Miljacka in central Sarajevo that was often targeted by snipers.

Zadar. Coastal town in Croatia.

Zagreb. Capital of Croatia.

zona odgovornosti. Specific zone of responsibility defended by a military unit.

Zvornik. Industrial town on the river Drina, now under Serbian control.

References

Allcock, John B. 2000. *Explaining Yugoslavia*. London: Hurst; New York: Columbia University Press.

Allen, Tim, and Jean Seaton, eds. 1999. *The Media of Conflict: War Reporting and Representations of Ethnic Violence*. London: Zed Books.

Anderson, Benedict. 1992 [1983]. *Imagined Communities: Reflections on the Origin and Spread of Nationalism*. London: Verso.

Andrić, Ivo. 2005 [1946]. "Pismo iz 1920." In *Priča o vezirovom slonu i druge, odabrao i priredio Kruno Pranjić* [Vezir's Elephant and Other Stories], ed. Kruno Pranjić, 37–51. Zagreb: Konzor.

"Anthropologists Against Ethnic Violence—A Statement." 1993. *Anthropology Today* 9(6):28.

Aretxaga, Begoña. 1997. *Shattering Silence: Women, Nationalism, and Political Subjectivity in Northern Ireland*. Princeton, N.J.: Princeton University Press.

Barnett, Victoria J. 1999. *Bystanders: Conscience and Complicity during the Holocaust*. Westport, Conn.: Greenwood Press.

Bauman, Zygmunt. 1991. *Modernity and Ambivalence*. Cambridge: Polity Press.

———. 1992. *Mortality, Immortality, and Other Life Strategies*. Cambridge: Polity Press.

———. 1993. *Postmodern Ethics*. Oxford: Blackwell.

Ben-Ari, Eyal. 1998. *Mastering Soldiers: Conflict, Emotions, and the Enemy in an Israeli Military Unit*. Oxford: Berghahn Books.

Bougarel, Xavier, Elsa Hjelms, and Ger Duijzings, eds. 2007. *The New Bosnian Mosaic*. Aldershot: Ashgate.

Bowman, Glen. 1994. "Xenophobia, Fantasy, and the Nation: The Logic of Ethnic Violence in Former Yugoslavia." In *The Anthropology of Europe: Identities and Boundaries in Conflict*, ed. Victoria A. Goddard, Josep R. Llobera, and Cris Shore, 143–71. London: Berg.

Bringa, Tone. 1993. "Nationality Categories, National Identification, and Identity Formation in 'Multinational' Bosnia." Special issue, *Anthropology of East Europe Review* 11(1–2):69–76.

———. 1995. *Being Muslim the Bosnian Way: Identity and Community in a Central Bosnian Village*. Princeton, N.J.: Princeton University Press.

Bringa, Tone and Debbie Christie (director). 1993. *We Are All Neighbours*. (film). The Royal Anthropological Institute (distributor).

Bringa, Tone and Peter Loizos. 2001. *Returning Home: Revival of a Bosnian Village* (film). Tone Bringa (director). The Royal Anthropological Institute (distributor).

Bruchfeld, Stéphane, and Paul A. Levine. 1998. "*Om detta må ni berätta*": *En bok om*

Förintelsen i Europa 1933–1945 ["Tell Ye Your Children": A Book about the Holocaust in Europe, 1933–1945]. Stockholm: Regeringskansliet.

Carmichael, Cathie. 2002. *Ethic Cleansing in the Balkans: Nationalism and the destruction of tradition*. London and New York: Routledge.

Cesarani, David, and Paul A. Levine, eds. 2002. *"Bystanders" to the Holocaust: A Reevaluation*. London: Frank Cass.

Clausewitz, Carl von. 1997 [1832]. *On War*. Trans. J. J. Graham, 1873. Ware, Hertfordshire: Wordsworth Classics of World Literature.

Connerton, Paul. 1989. *How Societies Remember*. Cambridge: Cambridge University Press.

Cooper, Joel. 2007. *Cognitive Dissonance: Fifty Years of a Classic Theory*. London: Sage.

Crapanzano, Vincent. 1986. "Hermes' Dilemma: The Masking of Subversion in Ethnographic Description." In *Writing Culture: The Poetics and Politics of Ethnography*, ed. J. Clifford and G. E. Marcus, 51–76. Berkeley: University of California Press.

Dagerman, Stig. 1996 [1947]. *Tysk Höst*. Stockholm: Norsteds.

Daniel, E. Valentine. 1996. *Charred Lullabies: Chapters in an Anthropography of Violence*. Princeton, N.J.: Princeton University Press.

Das, Veena, Arthur Kleinman, Mamphela Ramphele, and Pamela Reynolds, eds. 2000. *Violence and Subjectivity*. Berkeley: University of California Press.

Das, Veena, Arthur Kleinman, Margaret Lock, Mamphela Ramphele, and Pamela Reynolds, eds. 2001. *Remaking a World: Violence, Social Suffering, and Recovery*. Berkeley: University of California Press.

Des Pres, Terrence. 1976. *The Survivor: An Anatomy of Life in Death Camps*. New York: Oxford University Press.

Favret-Saada, Jeanne. 1980. *Deadly Words: Witchcraft in the Bocage*. Cambridge: Cambridge University Press.

Fein, Helen. 1993. *Genocide: A Sociological Perspective*. London: Sage.

Festinger, Leon. 1976 [1957]. *A Theory of Cognitive Dissonance*. Stanford, Calif.: Stanford University Press.

Filipović, Zlata. 1993. *Dnevnik Zlate Filipović*. Sarajevo: Medjunarodni centar za mir.

Finnström, Sverker. 2003. *Living with Bad Surroundings: War and Existential Uncertainty in Acholiland, Northern Uganda*. Uppsala Studies in Cultural Anthropology 35. Uppsala: Acta Universitatis Upsaliensis.

Gagnon, Valère P., Jr. 2006 *The Myth of Ethnic War: Serbia and Croatia in the 1990s*. Ithaca and London: Cornell University Press.

Gellner, Ernest. 1992 [1983]. *Nations and Nationalism*. Oxford: Blackwell.

Gjelten, Tom. 1995. *Sarajevo Daily: A City and Its Newspaper Under Siege*. New York: HarperCollins.

Glenny, Misha. 1992. *The Fall of Yugoslavia*. London: Penguin.

Green, Linda. 1994. "Fear as a Way of Life." *Cultural Anthropology* 9(2):227–56.

———. 1999. *Fear as a Way of Life: Mayan Widows in Rural Guatemala*. New York: Columbia University Press.

Greenberg, Robert D. 2004. *Language and Identity in the Balkans*. Oxford: Oxford University Press.

Gutman, Roy. 1993. *A Witness to Genocide: The First Inside Account of the Horrors of "Ethnic Cleansing" in Bosnia*. Shaftesbury, Dorset: Element.

Halilbegović, Nađa. 1994. *Sarajevsko djetinjstvo ratom ranjeno*. Sarajevo: Sany promex.

Halilović, Senahid. 1991. *Bosanski jezik*. Sarajevo: Biblioteka Ključanin.

———. 1995. *Bosanski jezik*. Sarajevo: Vijeće Kongresa bošnjačkih intelektualaca.

Hallie, Philip J. 1979. *Lest Innocent Blood Be Shed: The Story of the Village of Le Chambon and How Goodness Happened There*. London: Michael Joseph; New York: HarperCollins.

Harmon-Jones, Eddie, and Judson Mills, eds. 1997. *Cognitive Dissonance: Progress on a Pivotal Theory in Social Psychology*. Washington, D.C.: American Psychological Association.

Hedetoft, U. 1993. "National Identity and Mentalities of War in Three EC Countries." *Journal of Peace Research* 30(3):281–300.

Heidegger, Martin. 1996 [1927]. *Being and Time*. Albany: State University of New York Press.

Hettne, Björn. 1989. *Etniska konflikter och internationella relationer*. Rapport nr. 6 från DEIFO. Stockholm: DEIFO (Delegationen för invandrar forskning [The Delegation for Imigration Research]).

Hilberg, Raul. 1992. *Perpetrators, Victims, Bystanders: The Jewish Catastrophe, 1933–1945*. New York: HarperCollins.

Hinton, Alexander Laban. 1996. "Agents of Death: Explaining the Cambodian Genocide in Terms of Psychosocial Dissonance." *American Anthropologist* 98(4):818–31.

Hobsbawm, Eric. 1990. *Nations and Nationalism Since 1789: Programme, Myth, Reality*. Cambridge: Cambridge University Press.

Imamović, Enver, and Jozo Bošnjak. 1994. *Poznavanje društva 4. razred osnovne škole* [Knowing the Society: 4th Grade of Primary School]. Sarajevo: Ministarstvo obrazovanja, nauke, kulture i sporta.

Imamović, Mustafa, and Muhidin Pelešić. 1994. *Historija: 4. razred gimnazije* [History: 4th Grade of Gymnasium]. Sarajevo: Ministarstvo obrazovanja, nauke, kulture i sporta.

Isaković, Alija. 1992. *Rječnik karakteristične leksike u bosanskome jeziku*. Sarajevo: Svjetlost.

———. 1993. *Jezički podsjetnik iz bosanskoga jezika*. Sarajevo: Avicena.

———. 1994. *Antologija zla*. Sarajevo: Ljiljan.

Izetbegović, Alija. 1990 [1970]. *Islamska Deklaracija* [The Islamic Declaration]. Sarajevo: Bosna.

———. 1995. *Čudo bosanskog otpora: Odabrani govori, intervjui, izjave 1994; Alija Izetbegović*. Sarajevo: BIH Press.

———. 1996. *Govori, pisma, intervjui '95: Alija Izetbegović*. Sarajevo: TKP "Šahinpašić."

Jabri, Vivienne. 1996. *Discourses on Violence: Conflict Analysis Reconsidered*. Manchester: Manchester University Press.

Jahić, Dževad. 1991. *Jezik bosanskih Muslimana*. Sarajevo: Biblioteka Ključanin.

Jaspers, Karl. 1970 [1932]. *Philosophy*. Vol. 2. Chicago: University of Chicago Press.

Kapić, Suada. 1996. *Sarajevo Survival Map.* Text by Nihad Kreševljaković. Graphis design and illustrations by Ozren Pavlović. Sarajevo: FAMA.

Kaplan, Suzanne. 2002. "Children in the Holocaust: Dealing with Affects and Memory Images in Trauma and Generational Linking." Ph.D. diss., Stockholm University.

Karahasan, Dževad. 1993, Dnevnik selidbe. Zagreb: Durieux.

Karlaš, Radmila. 1998, "Vaga mojih emocija: Banjalučanka u Sarajevu." *Svijet* (Sarajevo), February 1.

Kebo, Ozren. 1996. *Sarajevo za početnike.* Sarajevo: Dani.

Kennan, George F. 1993. "The Balkan Crisis: 1913 and 1993." *New York Review of Books,* July 15, 3–7.

Kierkegaard, Sören. 1981 [1884]. *The Concept of Anxiety.* Princeton, N.J.: Princeton University Press.

Kleinman, Arthur, Veena Das, and Margaret Lock, eds. 1997. *Social Suffering.* Berkeley: University of California Press.

Kolind, Torsten. 2004. *Post-War Identifications: Counterdiscursive Practices in a Bosnian Town.* Aarhus: Institute of Anthropology, Archaeology, and Linguistics.

Kourouma, Ahmadou. 2000. *Allah n'est pas obligé.* Paris: Editions de Seuil.

———. 2006. *Allah Is Not Obliged.* Trans. Frank Wynne. London: William Heinemann.

Kubert, Joe. 1996. *Fax from Sarajevo: A Story of Survival.* Milwaukee, Wisc.: Dark Horse Books.

Kübler-Ross, Elisabeth. 2003 [1995]. *Döden är livsviktig.* Stockholm: Natur och Kultur. Originally published as *Death Is of Vital Importance: On Life, Death, and Life After Death* (Barrytown, N.Y.: Station Hill Press, 1995). Reissued as *The Tunnel and the Light* (New York: Avalon, 1999).

Lagumdžija, Razija. 1995. *Biljezi i ožiljci.* Sarajevo: OKO.

Levi, Primo. 1999 [1947]. *If This Is a Man* (Se questo é un uomo). Trans. Stuart Woolf. London: Abacus. Published in the United States as *Survival in Auschwitz* (New York: Touchstone, 1996).

———. 1989. *The Drowned and the Saved.* London: Abacus.

Levinas, Emmanuel. 1999 [1981]. *Alterity and Transcendence.* London: Athlone Press.

Levinger, Jasna. 1998. "Language and Identity in Bosnia-Herzegovina." In *Political Discourse in Transition in Europe 1989–1991,* ed. Paul A. Chilton, Mikhail V. Ilyin, and Jacob L. Mey, 251–64. Amsterdam: John Benjamins Publishing Company.

Löfving, Staffan. 2002. "An Unpredictable Past: Guerrillas, Mayas, and the Location of Oblivion in War-Torn Guatemala." Ph.D. diss., Uppsala University.

Löfving, Staffan, and Ivana Maček, eds. 2000. *On War—Revisited,* special issue of *Antropologiska studier* 66–67. (Stockholm University).

Lucić, Ivo. 1992, *Selo moje Ravno: Povijest stradanja Hrvata u Popovu.* Zagreb: Hrvatska hercegovačka zajednica "Herceg Stjepan."

Lukić, Darko. 1991. *Bašeskija, san o Sarajevu.* A play premiered in 1887 and given its hundredth performance in 2006.

Maček, Ivana. 2000. "Breaking the Silence." *On War—Revisited,* special issue of *Antropolgiska Studier* 66–67: 34–49.

———. 2001. "Predicament of War: Sarajevo experiences and ethics of war." In *An-*

thropology of Violence and Conflict, ed. Bettina F. Schmidt and Ingo W. Schroeder, 197–224. London and New York: Routledge.

———. 2005. "Sarajevan Soldier Story: Perceptions of War and Morality in Bosnia." In *No Peace No War: An Anthropology of Contemporary Armed Conflicts*, ed. Paul Richards, 57–76. Oxford: James Currey; Athens: Ohio University Press.

———. 2007. "'Imitation of Life': Negotiating Normality in Sarajevo under Siege." In *The New Bosnian Mosaic: Identities, Memories, and Moral Claims in a Post-War Society*, ed. Xavier Bougarel, Elissa Helms, and Ger Duijzings, 39–58. Aldershot, England and Burlington, USA: Ashgate.

Magner, Thomas, and Milena Marić. 2002. "Bosnian: The Crafting of a Language." *Geolinguistics* 28:55–65.

Magnusson, Kjell. 1993. *Den bosniska tragedian*. Stockholm: Utrikespolitiska institutet.

Malcolm, Noel. 1994. *Bosnia: A Short History*. London: Papermac.

Mazian, Florence. 1990. *Why Genocide? The Armenian and Jewish Experiences in Perspective*. Ames: Iowa State University Press.

McWilliams, Nancy. 1984. "The Psychology of the Altruist." *Psychoanalytic Psychology* 1:55–69.

———. 1994. *Psychoanalytic Diagnosis: Understanding Personality Structure in the Clinical Process*. New York: Guilford Press.

Miličević, Hrvoje. 1993. *Sarajevska ratna drama*. Sarajevo: s.n.

Morokvasić, Mirjana. 1998. "The Logics of Exclusion: Nationalism, Sexism, and the Yugoslav War." In *Gender, Ethnicity, and Political Ideologies*, ed. Nickie Charles and Helen M. Hintjens, 65–90. London: Routledge.

Nelson, Diane M. 1999. *A Finger in the Wound: Body Politics in Quincentennial Guatemala*. Berkeley: University of California Press.

Nordstrom, Carolyn. 1997. *A Different Kind of War Story*. Philadelphia: University of Pennsylvania Press.

———. 2004. *Shadows of War: Violence, Power, and International Profiteering in the Twenty-First Century*. Berkeley: University of California Press.

Nordstrom, Carolyn, and Jo-Ann Martin, eds. 1992a. "The Culture of Conflict: Field Reality and Theory." In *The Paths to Domination, Resistance, and Terror*, ed. Carolyn Nordstrom and Jo-Ann Martin, 3–17. Berkeley: University of California Press.

———. 1996. *The Paths to Domination, Resistance, and Terror*. Berkeley: University of California Press.

Nordstrom, Carolyn, and Antonius C. G. M. Robben, eds. 1995. *Fieldwork Under Fire: Contemporary Studies of Violence and Survival*. Berkeley: University of California Press.

Nutkiewicz, Michael. 2003. "Shame, Guilt, and Anguish in Holocaust Survivor Testimony." *Oral History Review* 30(1):1–22.

Owen, David. 1996 [1995]. *Balkan Odyssey*. London: Indigo.

Plan i program vjerskog odgoja i obrazovanja: Islamski, katolički, pravoslavni, jevrejski, adventistički. N.d. Zenica: Ministarstvo obrazovanja, nauke, kulture i sporta, Pedagoški zavod.

Port, Mattijs van de. 1998. *Gypsies, Wars, and Other Instances of the Wild: Civilisation and Its Discontents in a Serbian Town*. Amsterdam: Amsterdam University Press.

Porter, Jack Nusan. 1982. "What Is Genocide? Notes toward a Definition." In *Genocide and Human Rights: A Global Anthology*, ed. Jack Nusan Porter, 2–33. Washington, D.C.: University Press of America.

Powdermaker, Hortense. 1966. *Stranger and Friend: The Way of an Anthropologist*. New York: Norton.

Pratt, Mary Louise. 1986. "Fieldwork in Common Places." In *Writing Culture: The Poetics and Politics of Ethnography*, ed. J. Clifford and G. E. Marcus, 27–50. Berkeley: University of California Press.

Preporod. 1992, April 15. Sarajevo: Mešihat Islamske zajednice Bosne i Hercegovine.

Prstojević, Miroslav. 1994. *Sarajevo Survival Guide*. Photographs by Željko Puljić. Ed. Maja Razović and Alexandra Wagner. Sarajevo: FAMA; New York: Workman.

Ramet, Petra Sabrina. 1996. *Balkan Babel: The Disintegration of Yugoslavia from the Death of Tito to Ethnic War*. Boulder, Colo.: Westview Press.

Richards, Paul, ed. 2005. *No Peace, No War: An Anthropology of Contemporary Armed Conflicts*. Athens: Ohio University Press; Oxford: James Currey.

Rieff, David. 1996. *Slaughterhouse: Bosnia and the Failure of the West*. New York: Touchstone.

Robben, Antonius C. G. M., and Marcelo M. Suárez-Orozco, eds. 2000. *Cultures Under Siege: Collective Violence and Trauma*. Cambridge: Cambridge University Press.

Scarry, Elaine. 1985. *The Body in Pain: The Making and Unmaking of the World*. Oxford: Oxford University Press.

Schmidt, Bettina, and Ingo Schröder, eds. 2001. *Anthropology of Violence and Conflict*. London: Routledge.

Schmitt, Carl. 1976 [1928]. *The Concept of the Political*. New Brunswick, N.J.: Rutgers University Press.

Sekelj, Laslo. 1993. *Yugoslavia: The Process of Disintegration*. Boulder, Colo.: Social Sciences Monograph.

Sillitoe, Alan. 1959. *The Loneliness of the Long Distance Runner*. London: W. H. Allen/Virgin Books.

Sito-Sucic, Daria. 1996. "The Fragmentation of Serbo-Croatian into Three New Languages." *Transition* 2(24):10–13.

Škiljan, Dubravko. 2005. "Linguistic and Ethnic Communities." In *Balkan Currents: Essays in Honour of Kjell Magnusson*, ed. Tomislav Dulić, Roland Kostić, Ivana Maček, and Jasenka Trtak, 109–24. Uppsala Multiethnic Papers 49. Uppsala: Centre for Multiethnic Research, Uppsala University.

Sluka, Jeffrey A., ed. 2000. *Death Squad: The Anthropology of State Terror*. Philadelphia: University of Pennsylvania Press.

Službene novine Kantona Sarajevo [Official Newsletter of Sarajevan Canton] 19/1999.

Softić, Elma. 1994. *Sarajevski dani, sarajevske noći: Dnevnik i pisma 1992–94*. Zagreb: V. B. Z.

Sorabji, Cornelia. 1993. "Ethnic War in Bosnia?" *Radical Philosophy* 63:33–35.

———. 2006. "Managing Memories in Postwar Sarajevo: Individuals, Bad Memories, and New Wars." *Journal of the Royal Anthropological Institute*, n.s., 12:1–18.

Staub, Ervin. 1989. "The Evolution of Bystanders, German Psychoanalysts, and Lessons for Today." *Political Psychology* 10(1):39–52.

———. 1992. "Transforming the Bystanders: Altruism, Caring, and Social Responsibility." In *Genocide Watch*, ed. Helen Fein, 161–81. New Haven, Conn.: Yale University Press.

———. 2003. *The Psychology of Good and Evil: Why Children, Adults, and Groups Help and Harm Others*. Cambridge: Cambridge University Press.

Štraus, Ivan. 1995. *Arhitekti i barbari*. Sarajevo: Me_unarodni centar za mir.

Taussig, Michael. 1992. *The Nervous System*. London: Routledge.

Thomas, William I., and Florian Znaniecki. 1984. *The Polish Peasant in Europe and America*. Ed. Eli Zaretsky. Repr., Urbana: University of Illinois Press.

Trtak, Fahrija. 1996. "Kulturens roll i det belägrade Sarajevo." In *Krig, exil, återvändande*, ed. Kjell Magnusson, Midhat Medić, and Harald Runblom, 27–34. Uppsala: Centrum för multietnisk forskning, Uppsala University.

Trtak, Jasenka. 1999. "Språk och statsbildning: Språksplitringen i det forna Jugoslavien." *Multiethnica* 24–25:3–7.

UNHCR. 1994. *Information Notes on Former Yugoslavia*. No. 8/94. UNHCR Office of the Special Envoy for Former Yugoslavia.

Utas, Mats. 2003. *Sweet Battlefields: Youth and the Liberian Civil War*. Dissertations in Cultural Anthropology 1. Uppsala: Department of Cultural Anthropology and Ethnology, Uppsala University.

Veličković, Nenad. 1996. *Konačari*. Sarajevo: OKO.

Vonnegut, Kurt, Jr. 1974. *Wampeters, Foma, and Granfalloons*. New York: Delta Books.

Vucetic, Srdjan. 2004. "Identity Is a Joking Matter: Intergroup Humour in Bosnia." *Spaces of Identity: An Interdisciplinary Journal* 3(2):1–28.

Vuković, Željko. 1992. *Ubijanje Sarajeva*. Podgorica: Kron.

Vulliamy, Ed. 1994. *Seasons in Hell: Understanding Bosnia's War*. London: Simon and Schuster.

Woodward, S. L. 1995a. *Balkan Tragedy: Chaos and Dissolution after the Cold War*. Washington, D.C.: Brookings Institution Press.

———. 1995b. *Socialist Unemployment: The Political Economy of Yugoslavia, 1945–1990*. Princeton, N.J.: Princeton University Press.

Zimmermann, Warren. 1996. *Origins of a Catastrophe: Yugoslavia and Its Destroyers— America's Last Ambassador Tells What Happened and Why*. New York: Random House.

Zur, Judith N. 1998. *Violent Memories: Mayan War Widows in Guatemala*. Boulder, Colo.: Westview Press.

Index

Adra, 77
aggression, 96, 167, 170, 178, 186, 196, 204, 205
Akashi, Yasushi, 54
Andrić, Ivo, 23, 25, 155
Arabs, 69, 160
armed gangs, 96, 108–9
Army of Bosnia and Herzegovina (ABiH), 20, 27, 41, 109, 133, 140, 171, 204; Croats in, 164; hiding from, 44, 210; national division in, 164–64; and religion, 162–66; Serbs in, 164, 170; symbols of, 111; volunteers in, 174–75, 195, 210
Army of Republika Srpska. *See* Bosnian Serbs' Army

Bauman, Zygmunt, 34, 88
black market, 66–68, 79, 81–82, 84, 98
blue ways, 27, 66, 132, 227n2
Bosniac, 13–14, 125–26, 129, 204, 219, 232n13
Bosnian army. *See* Army of Bosnia and Herzegovina
Bosnian Croats' Army. *See* HVO
Bosnians, x, 111, 125–26, 173
Bosnian Serbs' Army, 27, 132, 198, 200–201, 229n2
Bringa, Tone, 107, 199
brotherhood and unity, 32, 60, 103, 125, 129, 141, 156, 169, 171, 189, 207

capitalism, 32, 84, 128, 132, 141, 218, 230n5
Caritas, 67, 157–60, 183
Catholics, 17, 177, 184–85; belief, 49; community, 16, 152, 156, 183; education, 154–55; family background, 125, 146; media, 138–39; in NGOs, 29; relations to others, 69, 101, 107, 131, 143; symbols of, 15, 111, 142. *See also* Caritas; church
cemetery: in central park, 141; Koševo, 140; Kovači, 41–42; for *šehidi*, 140–41

Cerić, Mustafa ef., 101
Chetniks, 101–3, 108, 169, 204
children, 62, 97–105, 107, 113, 195, 222; abroad, 98–100, 103, 221; care of, 37, 84, 102; education, 100, 154–56; and humanitarian aid, 157, 159; killed, 169, 204; leaving town, 30, 90, 99; from "mixed marriages," 30, 101–3, 156–57, 164, 176; orphans, 140, 159; protection of, 42, 44, 99, 178; and religion, 154–56, 160; return of, 100, 221
Christianization, 158
church, 25, 156; Catholic, 155, 160, 165–66, 183; going to, 152, 159–60, 162; Orthodox, 16, 23, 152, 178–79
Civilian Defense units, 210
civil war, 21, 186, 205
Clausewitz, Carl von, 205, 225n1
coffee, 17–18, 29, 73, 80, 106, 114, 117, 144, 149, 151, 171, 204
communication, 5, 11, 35, 69, 90, 95, 136, 217, 225n6
communism, 126, 131, 136, 141–42, 148, 152, 226n10, 230n5
Connerton, Paul, 232n10
creativity, 34–35, 38, 55–56, 62, 70, 75, 82
Croats, 13, 125–26, 219; discriminated against, 155, 164, 183; labels for, 169–70; relations to Muslims, 19, 167–68, 177, 183–86; relations to Serbs, 181, 184; religiosity, 177; Sarajevan, 14, 17, 183–84, 189; symbols of, 139, 145. *See also* Catholics; HVO; Ustashas
curfew, 78, 97, 151

Dagerman, Stig, 38
Dayton Peace Accords, 40, 65, 92, 164, 200–202, 218–19, 228n7, 229n1
displaced persons. *See* IDPs; refugees
Dobrotvor, 158

education, 58, 101, 112, 115, 130, 172–73, 188–89, 197, 204; abroad, 100; religious, 140, 154–56; schoolbooks, 155, 195, 204
employment, 19, 47, 56, 67, 69, 81–82, 84, 92–93, 97–100, 106, 116–17, 128, 159, 164, 179, 183, 199, 202–3, 208, 221–22
ethics, 168–69, 185–86, 189, 193–94, 205, 207–9, 212–13, 215
ethnic: affiliations, 156; background, 124, 126, 165; cleansing, 4, 90, 107–8, 162–63, 177, 181, 201, 204–5, 227n4, 230n1, 231n10; groups, 231n7; identity, 124; jokes, 51; pluralism, 105, 123, 174, 179–80, 182–84, 188; traditions, 124. *See also* identity; national
ethnonational. *See* identity; national
ethnonationalism. *See* nationalism
ethnoreligious. *See* ethnic; religion
European Union, 98, 196, 218–20; observers, 133

faith, 3, 88, 130, 132, 156, 161, 165, 171–73, 179, 230n4
families, 16, 32, 49, 86–87, 89, 95–105, 124; abroad, 77, 92, 98–99, 221; background, 125–26, 146–47, 161, 174–75, 183; protection of, 163, 209; security within, 86, 96; split, 90–92, 95–96, 98–100, 104; tensions, 85, 101; traditions, 124, 142, 148–49, 151–52, 188; war families, 22–23, 117–18
Favret-Saada, Jeanne, 12
fear, 8, 10, 31, 37, 44–46, 49–50, 65, 88, 93, 101–2, 104, 110, 117, 136, 148, 160, 162–63, 210, 213, 225n7, 228n10
Federation, Bosniac-Croat, 168, 170, 185, 218–19
fine arts, 36, 55, 57–58, 61
fourth nation, 187–88, 190
friends, 79, 86, 106, 111–19, 123, 126, 149, 151, 170, 185–86, 194; abroad, 22, 77, 92–94, 221; betrayal of, 179; lost, 114–16, 118–19, 189–90; loyalty, 179; mistrust, 107, 215; war friends, 11, 29–30, 116–17, 221

Gellner, Ernest, 171
genocide, xii, 136, 154, 185, 203, 205, 216, 228n10, 233n21

Glenny, Misha, 162, 196, 231n3
godparenthood, 87–88, 114, 227n2
Green, Linda, 225n7

Halilović, Senahid, 144
Hobsbawm, Eric, 212
household, 67, 95–98
humanitarian aid, 52, 63, 67–68, 70, 73, 82, 97, 157–58, 227n2. *See also* Caritas; Dobrotvor; IGASA; Merhamet; NGOs; Red Crescent; Red Cross; UNHCR
humiliation, 31, 46–47, 52, 60, 62, 66–70, 76–80, 84, 179, 185. *See also* shame
humor, 26, 31, 53, 62, 78–79, 119, 154, 177, 218, 223, 226n3. *See also* jokes
HVO, 20, 27, 107, 109, 118, 157, 164–65, 232n8

identity, 17, 34, 131–32, 142, 144, 147, 176, 191–92, 223; collective, 18, 208; ethnonational, 10, 123–25, 128, 132, 136, 146, 164–65, 167–68, 184–85, 225n8, 228n9; meanings of, 8, 167–69, 172, 197; national, 14, 32, 87, 101, 108, 123–24, 128, 132, 136–37, 146, 163, 168–71, 185–86, 189, 193–94, 209, 215; religious, 50, 123, 132, 148, 156, 158, 162, 167, 169, 194, 205, 208; Sarajevan, 87, 111, 180, 182, 186–90, 215; and war, 163, 208–9, 215. *See also* religion
IDPs, 18, 86, 111–12, 180, 184, 197, 226n11, 227n1, 227n3, 231n9
IGASA, 159, 171
international: contacts, 55, 59–60; economic involvement, 32, 84, 128, 219; and ethnic cleansing, 90; involvement in politics and war, ix, 64, 123, 131, 200–202, 205; media, vii–ix, 137, 200–201; not understanding, 13, 137; personnel, 28; politics, 4, 10, 64, 66, 131, 137, 200–201, 216, 218; recognition, 196. *See also* Dayton Peace Accords; humanitarian aid; UN; UNHCR
Isaković, Alija, 144–45, 203
Islam, 50; Bosnian, 172–73; in education, 154–55; foreign, 134–35; growing importance of, 69, 133–34, 139, 185; and political power, 129–30, 132; symbols of, 139–40, 144. *See also* humanitarian aid; Muslims; religion

Izetbegović, Alija, 101, 130, 139, 151, 172–74, 180, 182, 231n3

Jabri, Vivienne, 197, 208, 225n1
Jahić, Dževad, 144
Jews, 48, 149, 151–52, 226n10, 227n3
jokes, 15, 25, 42, 51–54, 57, 92, 104, 106, 111, 117, 147, 151, 157, 168, 222, 226n2, 226n13, 226n14. *See also* humor

Karadžić, Radovan, 102, 108, 171, 176
Karić, Enes, 130

language, 13, 136, 143–47, 155; of war experience, xi, 10–11, 31
limit situation, 10–11, 30, 35, 225n6

Magnusson, Kjell, 198
marriage, 100–105, 173; nationally mixed, 157, 174, 180, 183, 188, 228n9
media, 7, 46, 66, 136–39, 168, 196, 200–201, 214, 216; newspapers, 137–38; radio, 72, 136–39, 144–45, 176; television, 72, 136–39, 144, 152, 154, 168, 176, 195, 200. *See also* international
Merhamet, 67, 157, 171
Milošević, Slobodan, 102, 176
Mladić, Ratko, 108, 171, 176
mobilization: military, 96–97, 107, 164, 210; national and political, 32, 126, 148, 212
money, 23, 66, 69, 75, 77, 81, 85, 87, 156, 160, 168, 222; coupons, 68, 81–82, 222; deutsche marks, 45, 68–69, 75, 84, 87–88, 98, 159
morals, xi, 4–6, 8–10, 31–33, 35, 40, 47, 60, 63, 69, 78–81, 83–97, 112–13, 115, 129, 159–60, 172, 175, 177. *See also* ethics
mosque, 23, 134–35, 141, 204; going to, 130, 140, 149, 156, 160, 171, 173
mudahedini, 143
Muslims, 13, 125–26, 129, 155, 167–68, 171–78; in ABiH, 162–65, 208–12; cemeteries, 140–41; and Croats, 104–5, 177, 185–86; departure of, 90; between East and West, 132–35; fear and identity, 161–63, 204, 208–10, 214–15; humanitarian organizations, 157, 159,

172–73; humor, 25; indentifying differently, 87, 112, 114, 126, 142, 170, 186–90, 207, 209–12; media, 137–38; and neighbors, 107–8; in power, 128, 130, 179, 208; religious education, 154–55; religious holidays, 149–51; and Serbs, 100–102, 173–78, 180–83; symbols of identity, 15, 17, 49–50, 127, 139–46, 197, 205. *See also* Bosniac; IDPs

national: antagonism, 86, 167, 184, 208, 232n17; belonging, 9, 167–68, 179, 214; cross-national bonds, 101, 127, 155, 185, 229n1; differences, 100–101, 167, 186; division, 164–65, 167, 182, 184, 200, 203, 208; feelings, xi; heroes, 141–42, 159, 197, 229n3; heterogeneity, 170, 186–90, 218–19; identification, 171; labels, 125–26, 170–71, lenses, 14–16; minorities, 13, 145, 183; political parties, 130, 188, 219; protection, 163; sentiments, 18, 136; solidarity, 158; state, 129. *See also* identity; religious, traditions; mobilization
nationalism, 123, 126, 136, 141, 155, 189–90, 202–4, 212–15, 218–19; Croatian, x, 170, 183; ideology, xi, 32, 50, 192; and language, 142–47, 209; leaders and elites, x, 32, 129, 137, 162, 167, 172, 191–92, 196, 204, 213, 218–19, 221, 232n17; Muslim, 174, 176; non-nationalism, ix, 101, 104–5, 111–12, 127, 132, 151, 154, 156, 164, 171, 174, 181, 183, 186–90, 197, 206–7, 213; pressure of, 95, 101–4, 161; Serbian, 168, 170, 175, 233n18; signs and symbols of, 141–44, 203; and war, 167, 191–92, 208–9, 213, 215, 217, 232n17. *See also* Chetniks; SDA; SDS; Ustashas
NATO, 65, 118, 200–201, 219, 228n7, 230n5
neighbors, 32, 105–12; betrayal, 108, 110; change of relations, 7–8, 106–8, 123, 179, 185; gatherings, 80, 106, 149; help, 71, 79–80, 87, 101, 106, 180; leaving town, 92, 170, 181, 203–4, 210; mistrust, 104, 107–8, 181; protection, 86, 106, 108, 180, 215. *See also* IDPs
NGOs, 20–21, 28–29, 47, 67, 156, 159
Njegoš, 141
Nordstrom, Carolyn, 12, 34, 226n5
norms, viii, xi–xii, 5–10, 39, 79, 123, 130, 159, 161, 181, 188, 192–93, 216, 223; broken, 5–6, 8–9, 35–36, 46, 63–70, 129, 192, 199,

norms (*cont.*)
214; change of, 6–9, 31, 63–70, 82–85, 111, 143, 192; and feeling safe, 8; and meaning, 8, 46, 51, 83; new wartime norms, 9, 35–36, 45, 69, 186, 214; normlessness, 7, 82; and power, 8; preservation of, 62–63, 76, 82, 84, 129, 141; prewar, 9, 31, 55, 60, 62, 65, 88, 156, 203; questioned, 3. *See also* ethics; morals

OHR, 218–19, 221
Orthodox, 15, 104, 138, 142–43, 149, 152–54, 168, 185, 188; community, 16, 152, 179; family background, 125, 146, 179; labels for, 170. *See also* church
Oslobođenje, 137–38, 163
ostracism, 60, 95, 179, 183–84, 194, 230n1

papci, 90, 112, 127, 229n15
peace negotiations, ix, 117, 199–200
police, 81, 92, 97, 107, 139, 141, 219
Powdermaker, Hortense, 13
pravna država, 132
pride and dignity, 8, 31, 46–47, 60, 62, 67, 70, 76, 134, 154

raja, 51–52, 112–13, 116, 127, 169, 177, 222, 229n15
reconciliation, 95, 200
Red Crescent, 159
Red Cross, 93, 115
refugees, viii, 9, 22, 26, 30, 47, 77, 87–89, 108, 118, 154, 176, 198–99, 221, 226n5, 226n11, 227n1, 228n8; abroad, 100; Muslim, 131, 177, 180, 189; prospects of, 99, 166. *See also* IDPs
religion, 32, 113, 123, 128, 168; in the ABiH, 162–66; blended, 23, 87, 105, 114, 119, 126, 129, 154, 156, 181, 183, 188; communities, 15, 138, 157, 160, 162; congregations, 25; education, 154–56; ethnoreligious background, 17, 40, 50, 85, 124, 129, 146, 167, 171–72; and fear, 85, 148, 161, 165; foreign customs, 134–35, 139–40; greetings, 15, 142–43; holidays, 148–53; and humanitarian aid, 156–62; and nationalism, 50, 123,

148, 185; organizations, 31–32, 85, 148, 160; and politics, 123, 129–30, 132, 148, 172–73; as protection, 49, 165, 179; in public, 85, 130, 148, 150, 162; religiosity, 16–17, 49, 108, 112, 160–62, 170, 173, 177, 185; and survival, 63, 85, 162; traditions, 32, 124, 161. *See also* Catholics; church; ethnic; humanitarian aid; Muslims; national; Orthodox
resistance, 32, 51, 54, 76, 84, 111, 123, 126, 148, 167–68, 204, 207, 212

Šantić, Aleksa, 141–42
Scarry, Elaine, 208
SDA, 130, 139, 173, 219
SDS, 196, 203, 219
šehidi, 140–41, 159
Serbs, x, 13–14, 125–26, 141, 155, 167–68, 170, 173–74, 219; betrayal of, 95; guilt, 8, 102, 108, 129, 141, 162–63, 168, 170, 174–78, 181, 184, 200–201, 203–5, 209; harassed, 108–9, 144, 164, 178–80, 210; language, 144–46; leaders, 109, 125, 129, 132–33, 145, 176, 196; leaving, 93, 102, 115, 175–76, 180–81, 203–4, 210, 214; loyal, 101, 106, 123, 170, 174, 176, 208, 214–15; media, 134, 137, 168, 176; mistrusted, 101, 107–8, 214–15; protection of, 107, 178–79; in Sarajevo, 16, 18, 109, 112, 123, 129, 178, 180–82, 184, 196. *See also* Bosnian Serbs' Army; Chetniks; marriage; Orthodox; SDS
shame, 6, 8, 39, 62, 65–70, 90, 93–94, 110, 158, 176, 194–95, 225n4, 231n2. *See also* humiliation
shelling, xii, 7, 39, 41–46, 49–50, 65–66, 75, 94, 96–98, 106, 108, 110, 117, 153, 165, 171, 174, 176, 191, 198–201, 204, 206, 210, 214, 231n8, 232n7
Silajdžić, Haris, 130
silence, 10, 12, 108
snipers, ix, 9, 27, 31, 39, 41–42, 46, 50, 54, 76, 96–97, 127, 164, 168, 191, 196, 199, 202, 232n7
socialism, 14, 25, 84, 128, 131, 141, 218
soldier, viii–ix, xii, 45, 82, 90, 111, 140–41, 163, 191, 194–95, 206, 209–10, 212, 216–17; fallen, 160; as a perspective on war, 5, 33, 54, 160, 192–94, 197–200, 202–6,

208–9, 212, 214–17, 223; and religion,
165; trust among, 163–65, 214. *See also*
Chetniks; *mudahedini*; *šehidi*; UN;
Ustashas
survivor's guilt, 94, 227n5
survivor's pride, 154

Taussig, Michael, 3, 9, 11, 38
Tito, 152, 169, 218, 220, 223
truth, 10, 26, 113, 137–39, 155, 168, 205, 209;
contested, 7–8, 10–11
Tudjman, Franjo, 26, 145, 165, 181

UN, 20–21, 26–29, 41, 45, 54, 60, 66–69, 82, 90,
131, 133, 159, 196, 201, 218, 226n11,
226n14, 229n2, 231n9; employment
with, 98; identity card, 19–21, 28; soldiers, 28, 45, 54, 133, 152
UNHCR, 28, 111, 227n1; air bridge, 27, 29, 53;
humanitarian aid, 67–68, 76, 82, 227n2;
thermal foils, 70
Ustashas, 169

victims, ix, 21, 30, 40, 64, 126–27, 132–33, 137,
167, 177–78, 181, 185–86, 196–97, 204
Vonnegut, Kurt, 12

Yugonostalgists, 52, 171
Yugoslavia (former), 13, 68, 141, 145, 152, 175,
207, 227n3, 229n1; common ideas in,
17, 25, 57, 130, 159, 168–69, 228n11,
230n2, 230n4, 230n5, 231n7; the conflict and division of, x, 50, 123, 128–29,
136–37, 191; economic crisis in, 126;
national identities in, 124–25, 182;
young people of, viii. *See also* brotherhood and unity; communism; socialism; Tito; Yugoslavs
Yugoslav People's Army (former Yugoslavia),
vii, 90, 109, 140, 175, 204, 220
Yugoslavs (former), viii, x, 13, 104, 125–26, 171,
186, 188, 231n7

Acknowledgments

Writing this book was possible only because of the many people who at various stages helped me with my work. This experience has taught me that there is no such thing as single authorship, except that I alone bear the responsibility for any flaws that remain in this book.

First I wish to express my gratitude to all of the people whom I met in Sarajevo who, in the midst of their struggles to live decently under the most difficult conditions, found the warmth and friendliness to share their time, thoughts, and lives with me. Their names should appear in these acknowledgments, but I have chosen to protect their privacy, since some of the descriptions, interpretations, and arguments that I put forward might cause problems if individuals were identified as their source. Their words and wartime experiences fill this book, and I am sure they know who they are.

Second, I thank everyone in Zagreb—Bosnian, Croatian, and "internationals"—who worked at the Centre for Women Victims of War (Centar za žene žrtve rata) and Infoteka for generously sharing their knowledge and contacts, which were the starting point for my work in Sarajevo. As my own experiences with war began in Croatia, I thank my old friend and now my son's godfather, Adrian Ratkić, his cousin Tomislav Burzelić, and their family in Nova Gradiška for their Slavonian hospitality and guidance. Doing research about Bosnia was not popular in Zagreb during these years, so I thank my dear friends from school, Davorka Horvat and Biserka Drbohlav, for their help and warm friendship. I am grateful to my family in Zagreb, who tried the best they could to understand and support my "crazy calling." My thoughts go to my mother, who, in 1996, as a professor of the English language at Zagreb University, started to give courses in Sarajevo, where the Department of English had been reduced to only one person; to my father, who assisted some foreign NGOs in reaching Bosnia during the war and teaches part-time at the University of Bihać; and to my late grandmother—"the colonel's daughter," as she was called by the younger generations in the family, because her father was an Austro-Hungarian officer stationed in Sarajevo during the First World War. She lived through all four wars of the twentieth century that took place on the territories of the then-future and now-former Yugoslavia. Like many others of her generation, she lived in four different states: she was born in the Austro-Hungarian Empire, started work and family in the Kingdom of Yugoslavia, retired in the Socialist Federative Republic of Yugoslavia, and passed away in her ninety-eighth year in the contemporary Republic of Croatia.

My fieldwork in Croatia and Bosnia and Herzegovina would have been a lonely and impoverished venture without my good friends and travel companions, Karine Mannerfelt and Staffan Löfving. I am grateful for the friendship and the enriching anthropological discussions and journalistic experiences we shared during those years.

As a messenger between two worlds, the world of war-torn Sarajevo and the academic world in Sweden, I have been blessed with homes in both of them. In Sarajevo, words are insufficient to express the gratitude I feel toward my hosts who gave me a war home and a war family. At Uppsala University, my thanks go to the Department of Cultural Anthropology and Ethnology, its staff, and its students, who have from the very start provided an intellectually stimulating and supportive atmosphere. Most of all, thanks to those who became also my friends outside academia. Special thanks go to Bernhard Helander, who was always there for me when I needed to test my ideas, who read and commented on everything I wrote, and who gave me encouragement and understanding for the difficulties that come with fieldwork in war. His death is a great loss to all of us working in violent surroundings. At the Uppsala Programme for Holocaust and Genocide Studies, I am indebted to Kjell Magnusson for many exchanges over the years, as well as for bringing me to a challenging multidisciplinary milieu.

Outside my home institutions, I wish to thank Tone Bringa for her encouragement and invaluable collegiality from the very start of my work in Sarajevo, ranging from assistance with a UN identity card to helpful comments on several chapters of the manuscript. I have received important inspiration and support from Paul Richards, Peter Loizos, Michael Jackson, and most of all Carolyn Nordstrom, who has become a close colleague and a cherished friend. In Sweden, the community of scholars working on the former Yugoslavia is not large, which makes the exchanges I have had with Marita Eastmond and Maja Povrzanović Frykman especially valuable. Jasenka Trtak has been my main out-of-the-field informant, colleague, and dear friend. Her and her family's sharp observations and typically Sarajevan sense of humor have been a steady stream of light amid the overwhelming darkness of the war. Their knowledge and assistance have enriched this book immeasurably.

The tedious task of transcribing the tape-recorded interviews was accomplished with the expert and unselfish help of Vera Bjelanović, Gorana and Dragan Lukić, and Jasenka Trtak. Pamela Marston initially transformed my Croato-Swenglish into English. Grey Osterud, my American editor, improved the text with her language skills and cultural competence, but most of all, she found words for thoughts and feelings that I had not managed, or even dared, to acknowledge so clearly. To Grey I owe many of the scholarly and personal insights now articulated in these pages. But I am most grateful for all the warm and wise communication that unexpectedly made this editing process such fun. Special thanks go also to Peter Agree and Chris Hu at the University of Pennsylvania Press, as well as the anonymous readers of the original manuscript.

Writing about the siege of Sarajevo and studying genocide constitute a stressful venture, a sort of limit situation for what is professionally manageable within normal, peacetime work. I have been fortunate to receive both support and collegiality from psychologists and psychotherapists dealing with war trauma. Most of all, I am indebted to Maj-Britt Lindahl for being there and helping me find new ways of grappling with it whenever my world seemed to fall apart, as well as for commenting on several chapters. The insights, discussions, and human commitments that I learned and shared with my colleagues and supervisors at the Swedish Red Cross Centre for Victims of Torture in Uppsala and St. Lukas Psychotherapy Training Unit in Stockholm have been my lifeline throughout this work.

I wish to thank Åsa Vikström and her family and the Moksnes family for their care and support. My partner and colleague, Heidi Moksnes, and our son, Alvin, have not only been good sports while I was working on this book; most of all, they filled my life with meaning and joy whenever the meaninglessness threatened to become overwhelming. If life has taught me humility, sharing it with them has also filled me with awe and pride.

The research and writing of this book were supported financially mainly by a research grant from the Swedish Council for Planning and Coordination of Research (FRN) and also by the Department of Cultural Anthropology and Ethnology and the Programme for Holocaust and Genocide Studies, Uppsala University.

I wish to thank the publishers of the following works for permitting me to reproduce in this book text that has been published in Maček, Ivana, "Breaking the Silence." *On War—Revisited*, special issue of *Antropolgiska*

Studier 66–67(2000):34–49; Ivana Maček, "Predicament of War: Sarajevo Experiences and Ethics of War," in *Anthropology of Violence and Conflict*, ed. Bettina F. Schmidt and Indo W. Schroeder, 197–224 (London and New York: Routledge, 2001); Ivana Maček, "Sarajevan Soldier Story: Perceptions of War and Morality in Bosnia," in *No Peace No War: An Anthropology of Contemporary Armed Conflicts*, ed. Paul Richards, 57–76 (Oxford: James Currey; Athens: Ohio University Press, 2005); and Ivana Maček, "'Imitation of Life': Negotiating Normality in Sarajevo under Seige," in *The New Bosnian Mosaic: Identities, Memories, and Moral Claims in a Post-War Society*, ed. Xavier Bougarel, Elissa Helms, and Ger Duijzings, 39–58 (Aldershot, England and Burlington, USA: Ashgate, 2007).